The Business Student's Phrase Book

Palgrave Study Skills

Business Degree Success
Career Skills
Cite Them Right (10th edn)
e-Learning Skills (2nd edn)
Essentials of Essay Writing
Get Sorted
Great Ways to Learn Anatomy and Physiology (2nd edn)
How to Begin Studying English Literature (4th edn)
How to Study Foreign Languages
How to Study Linguistics (2nd edn)
How to Use Your Reading in Your Essays (2nd edn)
How to Write Better Essays (3rd edn)
How to Write Your Undergraduate Dissertation (2nd edn)
Improve Your Grammar (2nd edn)
Information Skills
The International Student Handbook
The Mature Student's Guide to Writing (3rd edn)
The Mature Student's Handbook
The Palgrave Student Planner
The Personal Tutor's Handbook
Practical Criticism
Presentation Skills for Students (3rd edn)
The Principles of Writing in Psychology
Professional Writing (3rd edn)
Researching Online
The Student Phrase Book
The Student's Guide to Writing (3rd edn)
Study Skills for International Postgraduates
Study Skills for Speakers of English as a Second Language
Studying History (4th edn)
Studying Law (4th edn)
Studying Modern Drama (2nd edn)
Studying Psychology (2nd edn)
Studying Physics
Success in Academic Writing
Smart Thinking
The Undergraduate Research Handbook
The Work-Based Learning Student Handbook (2nd edn)
Work Placements – A Survival Guide for Students
Write it Right (2nd edn)
Writing for Engineers (3rd edn)
Writing for Law
Writing for Nursing and Midwifery Students (2nd edn)
Writing History Essays (2nd edn)

Pocket Study Skills

14 Days to Exam Success
Analyzing a Case Study
Brilliant Writing Tips for Students
Completing Your PhD
Doing Research
Getting Critical (2nd edn)
Planning Your Dissertation
Planning Your Essay (2nd edn)
Planning Your PhD
Posters and Presentations
Reading and Making Notes (2nd edn)
Referencing and Understanding Plagiarism
Reflective Writing
Report Writing
Science Study Skills
Studying with Dyslexia
Success in Groupwork
Time Management
Where's Your Argument?
Writing for University (2nd edn)

Palgrave Research Skills

Authoring a PhD
The Foundations of Research (2nd edn)
Getting to Grips with Doctoral Research
Getting Published
The Good Supervisor (2nd edn)
PhD by Published Work
The PhD Viva
Planning Your Postgraduate Research
The PhD Writing Handbook
The Postgraduate Research Handbook (2nd edn)
The Professional Doctorate
Structuring Your Research Thesis

Palgrave Career Skills

Excel at Graduate Interviews
Graduate CVs and Covering Letters
Graduate Entrepreneurship
How to Succeed at Assessment Centres
Social Media for Your Student and Graduate Job Search
The Graduate Career Guidebook
Work Experience, Placements & Internships

For a complete listing of all our titles in this area please visit **he.palgrave.com/study-skills**

The Business Student's Phrase Book

Key Vocabulary for Effective Writing

Jeanne Godfrey

macmillan
education

palgrave

First published 2017 by
PALGRAVE

Palgrave in the UK is an imprint of Macmillan Publishers Limited, registered in England, company number 785998, of 4 Crinan Street, London, N1 9XW.

Palgrave® and Macmillan® are registered trademarks in the United States, the United Kingdom, Europe and other countries.

ISBN 978–1–137–58707–7 paperback

This book is printed on paper suitable for recycling and made from fully managed and sustained forest sources. Logging, pulping and manufacturing processes are expected to conform to the environmental regulations of the country of origin.

A catalogue record for this book is available from the British Library.

A catalog record for this book is available from the Library of Congress.

Printed in China

Other titles by the author:

Academic Writing
How to Use Your Reading in Your Essays
Reading and Making Notes
Reading and Note-making
The Student Phrase Book
Writing for University

Contents

Business strategy, models, methods and results   129

Analysing and identifying common themes   145

Evaluating ideas, evidence and impact   179

Concluding, applying ideas and making recommendations   206

Why and how to use this book

What *The Business Student's Phrase Book* gives you

The Business Student's Phrase Book gives you the words and phrases you need for assignments in business management, administration, HR, finance, systems analysis, project management, business law and corporate governance.

    The Business Student's Phrase Book **does not** present 'business vocabulary' – words such as *depreciation, econometric, fiscal* and *flotation*. You will learn the meaning of such words on your course and you can look them up in a business dictionary.

    The Business Student's Phrase Book **does** give you the general vocabulary (intermediate to advanced level) most commonly needed and used by business students for understanding texts and writing assignments – words such as those highlighted in bold below:

> The shareholders want the **recommendations** to be **implemented** immediately
> in order to **deter** further **accumulation** of debt.

Your business tutors will not explain this general vocabulary, yet it is vital for producing successful business writing and for communicating precisely and professionally. Using words in a 'nearly but not quite right' way is a common cause of low marks in assignments.

Why you might use a word incorrectly	How *The Business Student's Phrase Book* can help
• You don't know enough words.	• Presents around 1,500 words, with definitions and important word information given for nearly 1,000 of these. The words presented are appropriate for formal, clear and succinct business writing at university level.
• You can't learn new words using a dictionary because you don't know the words to look them up.	• Words are presented within 30 common business writing functions or contexts and are listed under these sections in the word table at the end of the book. **This means that you can start by looking up what you want to do and then find the words you need to do it.**

Why you might use a word incorrectly	How *The Business Student's Phrase Book* can help
• When trying to use your own words, you choose an incorrect 'synonym' from a thesaurus.	• Using a thesaurus often leads to word mistakes because words rarely have exact, appropriate synonyms. This book presents different word choices in the context of real example sentences, and part 2 of each section gives you clear, simple definitions and information on common mistakes and commonly confused words, such as:

collate	vs. *compile*	p. 131
method	vs. *methodology*	p. 132
similarly	vs. *correspondingly*	p. 163
subsequent vs. *consequent*		p. 110

• You partially understand a word when you read it but need full understanding to use it precisely in your writing. • You get the main word right but make a mistake with the words that come before or after.	• There is an alphabetical word index at the end of the book which you can use to find the definitions and other important information about words you come across in your reading. • Part 2 of each section tells you what other words and grammar structures are commonly used before and after the key word. For example: Stance: A **tough** // **firm** // **ethical** // **moral** stance **on** X.
• You don't spot your mistakes when checking your writing.	• Part 3 of each section gives you 10 incorrect sentences that have typical student errors, followed by the corrected sentences. You can use these to improve your proof-reading skills and avoid making similar mistakes yourself.

To sum up, you can use *The Business Student's Phrase Book* to:

- find and use new words while you are preparing and writing assignments
- check words you already partially know
- check words you come across in your reading
- develop your word knowledge and ability to use words correctly and precisely.

While helping you do the above, *The Business Student's Phrase Book* also gives you:

- important tips on key aspects of assignment writing
- examples of good academic writing style

- examples of how to incorporate and reference source material
- examples of real topics, issues and sources from a range of business fields.

How *The Business Student's Phrase Book* is structured

The book is divided into nine main themes and then further divided into 30 sections. Each section has three parts:

1 Words in action

This part of each section presents words within sentences from real and successful academic writing. The key words or phrases are underlined, with gaps in underlining to indicate different word groups.

- words with similar meanings are separated by /
- words that have different meanings are separated by //
- round brackets () indicate either a source reference or optional word.

Example sentences:

- Value capture is <u>an important // an essential / a crucial / a fundamental</u> <u>element</u> <u>in</u> business model design.
- <u>The growth of</u> the shale gas industry <u>is // has been</u> <u>(highly) contentious / controversial</u>.
- EU corporate governance legislation does not include explicit guidelines on ethical <u>issues</u> (Casson 2013).

2 Information to help you use these words correctly

This part of each section gives short, simple definitions, concentrating on the words and forms (noun, adjective, verb, adverb) most useful for academic writing and/or most often used incorrectly. Other useful information, such as common word combinations, the differences between commonly confused words and grammatical points, are also given.

Three symbols are used in part 2 of each section:

 Words that are always or often used with the key word

 Commonly confused words

❗ Other important points to note

3 Nearly but not quite right

This part of each section gives ten incorrect and corrected sentences from real student assignments. You can compare the two versions, or try to correct the sentences in the left-hand column before looking at the correct versions.

How *The Business Student's Phrase Book* references sources

Source material in *The Business Student's Phrase Book* is cited using the Harvard referencing system. Whenever a source used in an example sentence has more than two authors, *et al.* is used in order to save space. Note that in your own assignments you should list all the authors the first time you cite a source, and use only *et al.* for second and subsequent citations of the same source.

Aims and arguments

1 Introducing your topic and identifying the issues

Your essays should start by telling your reader why your topic is important and what the main issues are, and your reports should usually start by stating the aim and scope of your assignment (see section 2). Be careful not to start discussing the issues in detail in your introduction – leave that until the main body of your assignment.

1.1 Words in action

Establishing the importance of the topic and identifying the issues

▸ There is an <u>urgent / pressing</u> <u>need for</u> radical change in the US fast-food industry.

▸ Finding more predictive algorithms for financial forecasting <u>is paramount / of the utmost importance</u>.

▸ Value capture is <u>an important // an essential / a crucial / a critical / a fundamental</u> <u>element // theme</u> <u>in</u> business model design.

▸ The market landscape is the <u>first and most important</u> <u>aspect // factor</u> to consider when planning a start-up.

▸ The most important <u>function</u> of a manager is to lead.

▸ The study of naturalistic decision making <u>has acquired / has gained</u> <u>significance / importance</u> over the last few years.

▸ International migration <u>has emerged as // is emerging as</u> a major consequence of globalisation.

▸ <u>Recent</u> <u>developments / advances</u> in invisible fashion technology <u>have heightened interest</u> in this market.

▸ The <u>crux of the</u> <u>issue // problem // matter</u> is how to balance the interests of the different stakeholders.

▸ <u>Issues // questions</u> <u>around</u> intellectual property and open source software <u>are becoming increasingly important // visible</u>.

▸ <u>A main consideration in</u> government housing policy <u>is</u> neighbourhood dynamics.

▸ <u>Surprisingly</u>, EU corporate governance legislation does not include explicit guidelines on ethical <u>issues</u> (Casson 2013).

- A 2013 US Congressional Committee report found that non-performing real estate loans were <u>one of the leading causes of</u> // <u>the leading cause of</u> bank failures between 2008 and 2011.
- Business blogging <u>is a</u> recent <u>phenomenon</u>. / Business blogs <u>are</u> relatively recent and now <u>widely used phenomena</u>.

Emphasising the controversial nature of the topic

- Tourism is <u>arguably /debatably</u> the most important industry in Greece.
- <u>One of the most widely publicised</u> <u>debates</u> // <u>discussions</u> in UK Higher Education <u>is</u> the level of student fees.
- <u>There is widespread debate</u> <u>about / on</u> the failure of multinationals to manage and promote talent within their organisations.
- Chugh and Kern's 2016 model <u>raises the level of debate</u> <u>on / around</u> the role of 'self-threat' in organisational behaviour.
- <u>The question of whether to</u> legalise all drugs <u>is regularly debated in</u> the media.
- <u>The growth of</u> the shale gas industry <u>is</u> // <u>has been</u> <u>(highly) contentious / controversial</u>.
- <u>There is continued controversy over</u> how transnational organisations treat their labour force in poorer countries.
- <u>The question of whether</u> to introduce ID cards <u>is becoming increasingly complex</u> // <u>difficult / problematic</u>.
- Banks are finding it <u>increasingly difficult to justify</u> risk-taking practices to their European customers.
- There is evidence to demonstrate that succession is <u>a / an</u> <u>(highly / extremely) emotive issue</u> for family firms.

Highlighting a lack of research or discussion in relation to the topic

- <u>There has been</u> <u>little</u> // <u>inadequate</u> <u>research on</u> // <u>debate about / discussion about</u> // <u>attention given to</u> the implications of ending business entity tests.
- <u>There are insufficient studies on / There is insufficient research on</u> the efficacy of internships.
- <u>Previous research has</u> // <u>Previous studies have</u> <u>tended to focus on</u> the ethnicity <u>rather than</u> the age of offenders.
- <u>The fact that</u> cash flow <u>is a key factor in / plays a key role in</u> the success of a small business is often <u>overlooked</u>.

1.2 Information to help you use these words correctly

Words you probably already use correctly: *crucial, development, essential, function, fundamental, overlook.*
   Words defined in other sections: *justify* s30.

argue *v* **argument** *n* **arguably** *adv* **arguable** *adj*	*v* – (1) To use reasoning and evidence to support a statement. (2) To disagree, with or without supporting reasons or justification. *n* – (1) The process of using reasoning and sometimes also evidence to support a claim. (2) A quarrel or disagreement. *adv* – 'It can be argued'. Similar to *debatably*. Use *arguably* to show you are aware that others may disagree. *adj* – Open to argument or disagreement. Similar to *debatable*. 🤝 A **convincing / strong // cogent // coherent // reasonable / reasoned / rational / logical / valid** argument. A **weak // invalid / flawed / illogical / fallacious** argument.
aspect *n*	(1) A particular quality, part or feature of something. (2) Something's appearance. E.g. The premises have a rundown aspect. ☹ *Aspect* and *element* There is overlap, but *aspect* is usually used for qualities or viewpoints, while *element* is often used for concrete activities or parts of things. E.g. This report looks at the legal elements ✗ aspects ✓ of the case. We discuss the six key elements ✓ aspects ✗ needed to complete a project. 🤝 Lobbying is an important aspect **of** British politics.

consideration *n* **consider** *v*	*n* – (1) An issue, idea or action that needs thinking about. (2) Care and respect for others. E.g. The management team showed great consideration for junior colleagues. (3) In law or business, something of agreed financial value. E.g. At least 10% of the consideration should be paid within the first month. 🤝 To **take** X **into** / X **is under (careful)** consideration. ❗ *Considerable* (adj) means 'large' and *considerably* (adv) means 'much/a lot' (see section 13).
contentious *adj*	Causing disagreement
controversy *n* **controversial** *adj*	*n* – Public disagreement or debate. E.g. There is great controversy in the US over executive compensation. 🤝 X **causes** / **attracts** / **creates** controversy. Controversy **surrounding** / **concerning** / **over** X.
critical *adj* **critically** *adv* **criticism** *n* **criticise*** *v*	*adj* – (1) Containing an evaluation of both the negative and positive aspects of something, e.g. *critical evaluation*. (2) Essential, extremely important and/or a point of crisis. ❗ In project management the term *critical pathway* has a different, specialised meaning. *To criticise* means 'to find fault' and is not usually used in an academic context. E.g. I will criticise Khan's report. ✗ I will give a critical analysis of Khan's report. ✓ *-*ize* is also acceptable in British spelling and is always used in US spelling.
crux *n*	The most important or decisive point.

debate *n / v* **debatable** *adj* **debatably** *adv*	*n* – A public and/or formal event where people with different views try to persuade the majority or audience that theirs is the correct one. *adj* – Open to challenge and/or debate. Similar to *arguable*. *adv* – It can be argued. Similar to *arguably*. 🤝 *n* – There is debate **on / about / over** pension schemes. **Widespread / current / ongoing / public / political** debate on X. A **subject of (heated)** debate. *v* – X is **hotly** debated. ☹ *Debate* and *discuss* A discussion involves people who might hold similar or different positions, often with the aim of reaching a level of agreement rather than winning the argument.
element *n*	One part of something that has multiple parts.
emerge *v* **emergence** *n*	*v* – To gradually become apparent or to gradually develop.
emotive *adj*	Of a topic or issue, causing a strong emotional response. ☹ *Emotive* and *emotional* *Emotional* is a more general word describing personal feelings about life experiences.
factor *n / v*	*n* – One of several things that cause or influence something else. *v* – To include or exclude something as relevant when making a decision. 🤝 *n* – Customer satisfaction is an important factor **in** brand loyalty. A(n) **major / important // deciding / determining // causal //contributing** factor. *v* – We should factor migration **in to // out of** decisions over resources.

issue *n / v*	*n* – Something argued about that affects many people. Often used in political / social contexts.
	v – To give out or circulate.
paramount *adj*	More important than anything else.
	🤝 X **is** paramount. **It is** paramount **that** …
phenomenon *n*	Something that is interesting, unique or difficult to understand in nature, science or society.
	❗ The singular is *phenomenon* and the plural is *phenomena*.
	E.g. Social networking is a recent phenomenon.
pressing *adj*	Needing immediate action or attention. Similar to *urgent*.
role *n*	Something's function in a particular situation.
theme *n*	The main topic or idea.
widespread *adj*	Something that exists or happens (e.g. a belief, poverty, disease) over a large area.
	🤝 Widespread **use of // support for // acceptance of // criticism of // condemnation of // concern about // assumption that // belief that // rejection of // speculation // consultation // concern // ignorance // misunderstanding // corruption // disease / deprivation // suffering // poverty // unemployment.**
	A widespread **occurrence // phenomenon // assumption // belief // (mis) conception.**
	❗ *Widespread* can be used to describe a debate or problem but not a question or issue. E.g. It is a widespread question. **X**
	Wide spread and *spread wide* are both incorrect.

1.3 Nearly but not quite right

	Incorrect	Correct
1	I have examined the <u>factors</u> of legislation that apply to organisational grievance procedures.	I have examined the <u>aspects</u> of legislation that apply to organisational grievance procedures.
2	The question of whether to legalise drugs is <u>widespread</u> across EU member states.	The question of whether to legalise drugs is <u>a common one</u> across EU member states.
3	<u>Issues</u> have been raised <u>on</u> the reclassification of housing association borrowing as public debt.	<u>Questions</u> have been raised <u>over</u> the reclassification of housing association borrowing as public debt.
4	<u>A very small</u> consideration has been given to how noise levels affect staff in the workplace.	<u>Very little</u> consideration / attention has been given to how noise levels affect staff in the workplace.
5	Privatisation of prison security is a <u>controversy</u> in the UK.	Privatisation of prison security is a <u>controversial issue / topic</u> in the UK.
6	The aim of using little children in charity advertisements is to elicit an <u>emotive</u> response.	The aim of using little children in charity advertisements is to elicit an <u>emotional</u> response.
7	This type of software program is a recent <u>phenomena</u> in information technology.	This type of software program is a recent <u>phenomenon</u> in information technology.
8	Decriminalisation of cannabis in some US states is a <u>questionable issue</u>.	Decriminalisation of cannabis in some US states is a <u>controversial / contentious / debatable issue</u>.
9	In this essay I will <u>debate</u> that an autocratic leadership style is the most effective.	In this essay I will <u>argue</u> that an autocratic leadership style is the most effective.
10	The requirement to declare conviction history on job applications is an <u>emotional issue</u> in some US states.	The requirement to declare conviction history on job applications is an <u>emotive issue</u> in some US states.

2   Stating your aim and scope

In essays and reports you need to state your aim and scope (also referred to as *remit* and *terms of reference*).

When stating your aims be specific – are you going to analyse, examine, provide data, evaluate, discuss, make recommendations or do several of these things?

When stating your scope it is often useful to say what you are **not** going to cover as well as what you will discuss.

Note that the use of *I* is increasingly acceptable in academic writing, but check this with your tutor.

2.1   Words in action

Stating your aim

▸ The <u>purpose / objective / aim</u> of this report is to <u>identify</u> solutions to the company's personnel problems.

▸ Our <u>main objective is to</u> <u>identify</u> and <u>describe</u> what <u>measures / steps</u> need to be taken to <u>resolve</u> this issue.

▸ This essay <u>aims // attempts</u> <u>to</u> <u>establish</u> the most likely causes of low job satisfaction.

▸ I will <u>outline</u> the criticisms of Maslow's model and then <u>elaborate on / expand on</u> the claim that it is ethnocentric.

▸ In this review we will <u>enumerate</u> the different levels of FAS No. 157 <u>and assess</u> which levels have more value relevance.

▸ In this review we will enumerate and <u>appraise</u> the different levels of FAS No.157.

▸ This report gives an <u>overview of</u> problematic aspects of corporate governance, and then <u>examines //</u> <u>scrutinises</u> the ways in which differentiating the company board from other types of management can strengthen a company.

▸ I give a <u>(short) descriptive account of</u> the UK government's response to the EU Corporate Governance Framework in relation to shareholder co-operation <u>followed by</u> <u>an exploratory discussion</u> of the possible implications.

▸ I will <u>examine / investigate / look at / address</u> whether programming expertise increases systems analyst efficacy.

▸ We wish to <u>establish / ascertain</u> whether the new tax reforms will be detrimental to small businesses.

▸ This project <u>analyses the data</u> and <u>offers a (tentative) explanation for //</u> <u>attempts to determine the causes of</u> the currently low rate of youth unemployment.

▸ In my report I <u>speculate on</u> <u>the extent to which</u> a student's personality determines their final level of award.

▸ This essay <u>traces</u> the development of PPP frameworks, <u>critiques</u> legislation and <u>offers</u> some solutions to current problems.

Stating your scope

▸ This study <u>focuses on / centres on / is concerned with</u> the causes of relative poverty in the US.

▸ I will discuss training and development <u>within the wider context of</u> changing organisational culture.

▸ It is (not) <u>appropriate / relevant / pertinent to cover all</u> <u>areas of // aspects of</u> cost analysis in this essay.

▸ It is <u>not within / beyond / outside</u> <u>the scope / remit / terms of reference</u> of this report to discuss all elements of Fayol's management principles.

▸ I will <u>restrict / confine</u> the discussion <u>to the (narrow) context of</u> contract law.

▸ It is <u>not possible / not feasible</u> here to discuss <u>in depth</u> all the issues surrounding recruitment practices.

▸ I will examine here <u>only</u> <u>the (two) most relevant / salient aspects</u>, <u>namely</u>, ordinary and preference shares.

▸ This report examines <u>only</u> the problems <u>specifically</u> <u>attributed to // associated with // connected with</u> leadership.

2.2   Information to help you use these words correctly

Words you probably already use correctly: *aim, assess, associate, connect, context, descriptive, examine, identify, investigate, overview, purpose, steps.*

Words defined in other sections: *associated* s5, *attribute* s19, *claim* s24, *confine* s11, *measures* s30, *relevant* s22, *resolve* s12, *restrict* s11, *specific* s4.

analyse* *v* analysis *n*	*v* – To break something down into its basic elements in order to examine and reveal its important characteristics and/or meaning. ☹ *Analyse**, *analysis* and *analyses* *Analyse* is the verb, e.g. I will analyse the data. *Analysis* is the noun, e.g. The analysis is weak. *Analyses* is both the verb form for *he/she/it*, e.g. He analyses the results regularly, and the plural noun, e.g. I compared the two analyses. *The US spelling is *-yze*.
appraise *v* appraisal *n*	*v* – To examine and then give an estimation or opinion of something's state, value or effectiveness. Similar to *assess*.
ascertain *v*	To find out (formal). Similar to meaning (1) of *establish*.

critique *v / n*	*v* – To analyse and evaluate.
	n – A critical commentary or review, usually in art, literature, philosophy or political theory.
	😟 *Critique* and *critic*
	A *critic* is a person who writes reviews and/or is critical of something.
determine *v*	(1) To examine in order to find out.
	E.g. We will try to determine the cause of the crash.
	(2) To decide or control what happens.
	E.g. Bonuses are determined by productivity levels.
	🤝 To determine **what // how // why // when // whether // when // the reasons for // the causes of** X.
	❗ *To be determined* (adj) and *determination* (n) have different meanings (see section 6).
elaborate *v / adj*	*v* – To give more detailed information or to develop further.
	adj – Complicated and/or with many parts, e.g. An elaborate pattern.
enumerate *v*	*v* – To list, count out, name or give details of something one by one.
enumeration *n*	*n* – A list or count of something.
establish *v*	(1) To find out. Similar to *ascertain*.
	(2) To start an organisation or system.
	(3) To become accepted in a particular environment or role.
expand *v*	*v* – (1) To grow or make larger.
expansion *n*	(2) To give a fuller or more detailed explanation or discussion.
	😟 *Expand* and *expend*
	To expend means to spend or use money or resources.
	❗ *Expansive* means (1) large and/or extensive, (2) of a person, relaxed and communicative.

exploratory *adj*	Involving open-minded investigation. In academic study, an exploratory assignment is one that analyses and discusses evidence and different viewpoints on a topic or issue.
	😞 *Expl**ora**tory*, *expl**ana**tory* and *exp**osi**tory*
	Explanatory writing explains something else, e.g. Explanatory notes.
	Expository writing transmits information, such as directions, instructions and recipes.
feasible *adj*	Usually of specific tasks and projects, possible and capable of being done or dealt with.
	😞 *Feasible* and *likely*
	Likely is used to make predictions.
	E.g. It is feasible that life on other planets will be discovered. ✗
	It is likely / probable that life on other planets will be discovered. ✓
objective *n / adj*	*n* – An aim or goal.
	adj – Based only on facts and not influenced by feelings or beliefs (see section 23).
pertinent *adj*	Relevant or appropriate to a particular matter. Usually only used when talking about ideas, viewpoints or arguments.
	🤝 A pertinent **question** // **issue** // **fact** // **information** // **argument** // **idea**.
remit *n*	The tasks and area requested or required (the r<u>e</u>mit).
	❗ The verb *to r<u>e</u>mit* means to postpone or cancel a payment, or to give a payment as a gift. The noun for this meaning is *remittance*.
salient *adj*	The most relevant or important.
	🤝 Salient **points** // **features** // **issues** // **facts** // **properties**.

scope *n*	(1) The range of activity, ability, opportunity or possibility.
	(2) The opportunity or freedom to do something (see section 9).
	🤝 **Within // beyond** the scope **of** this essay.
	There is **unlimited // ample // limited / restricted** scope.
	To **broaden / widen / increase / expand / extend // narrow / restrict** the scope.
scrutinise* *v* **scrutiny** *n*	*v* – To examine carefully and thoroughly in order to check or find out specific information.
	🤝 *n* – To **be under / come under / be subject to / be subjected to / be the subject of** scrutiny.
	v – To **be** scrutinised **by** X **for (doing)** Y.
	*-ize is also acceptable in British spelling and is always used in US spelling.
trace *v / n*	*v* – (1) To find or describe the development / influence of something over time.
	(2) To follow the course of something.
	(3) To copy / mark the outline or pattern of something.
	❗ The noun (*a trace*) has several other, different meanings.

2.3 Nearly but not quite right

	Incorrect	Correct
1	The organisation is under scrutiny <u>to</u> the IRS.	The organisation is under / has come under scrutiny <u>by</u> the IRS.
2	Price to earnings ratio is one way to <u>analyse</u> the value of a company's shares.	Price to earnings ratio is one way to <u>appraise / assess / evaluate</u> the value of a company's shares.
3	The biotechnology industry is likely to <u>be expansive</u> over the next decade.	The biotechnology industry is likely <u>to expand</u> over the next decade.
4	The drawbacks of using a corporate report for financial information <u>are not in</u> the scope of this essay.	The drawbacks of using a corporate report for financial information <u>are not within / do not come within / are outside</u> the scope of this essay.
5	The building design is not <u>likely</u> due to the high cost of the specified materials.	The building design is not <u>feasible</u> due to the high cost of the specified materials.
6	This report will <u>analysis</u> the contingency approach to organisational structure.	This report will <u>analyse/ze</u> the contingency approach to organisational structure.
7	Baroness Hale ruled that the photographs were not pertinent <u>for</u> the newspaper's story.	Baroness Hale ruled that the photographs were not pertinent / relevant <u>to</u> the newspaper's story.
8	Footnotes can be used for <u>exploratory</u> purposes as well as to give references.	Footnotes can be used for <u>explanatory</u> purposes as well as to give references.
9	Coughlin became an extremely vocal <u>critique</u> of Roosevelt's banking system policy.	Coughlin became an extremely vocal <u>critic</u> of Roosevelt's banking system policy.
10	I have shown why both <u>analysis</u> are statistically significant.	I have shown why both <u>analyses</u> are statistically significant.

3   Stating and structuring your argument

For some assignments you will want to state or claim something (sometimes called *a proposition* or *thesis statement*) which you then explain, defend and develop to a conclusion. Section 3 gives you words and phrases for talking about propositions, assumptions and theory explicitly.

Note that just talking about a proposition or theory is **not** the same thing as actually making an argument, developing a theory or analysing assumptions. Actually doing these things involves a series of stages – analysing ideas, evaluating evidence and drawing conclusions – and so usually takes up the whole essay or report. You will need to use vocabulary from many sections of this book in order to complete these different steps, particularly sections 20–30.

3.1   Words in action

Making a proposition or claim

▸ I (will) show / demonstrate // argue // suggest / propose that an ethical approach is important for business success.

▸ This essay challenges the view // the idea that there is a causal link between number of siblings and earnings.

▸ I contest / refute Shell's claim that oil will remain in demand and in profit despite global agreements on climate change.

▸ We propose / assert / contend / maintain that there is a link between low self-esteem and externalising problems.

▸ My assertion / contention / proposition is that law firms must adapt their working practices if they are to meet the challenges of globalisation.

Talking about premise and assumption

▸ Corporate responsibility assumes / presupposes that ethics and the pursuit of profit are compatible.

▸ An (underlying) assumption / presupposition made by psychologists is that happier staff are more productive.

▸ VBM is based on / rests on / relies on / is built on / is founded on the idea // assumption // premise that value can be measured / of value being measurable.

▸ PPPs are predicated on management increasing efficiency / management's ability to increase efficiency.

Talking about thesis, hypothesis and theory

▸ The main <u>thesis</u> of Ritzer's book is that fast-food chains are the most influential example of business rationalisation.

▸ Wood's <u>hypothesis / conjecture</u> <u>is that</u> business and society are interdependent and so jointly responsible for how organisations behave.

▸ Fayolism was a <u>theory</u> of management devised at the turn of the 20th century.

Stating how you intend to order your points

▸ This essay will examine three ideas; <u>first, / firstly,</u> ... <u>second, / secondly,</u> ... <u>and finally,</u> ...

▸ An overview of the legislation <u>is followed by</u> a critical evaluation of the proposed amendments.

▸ <u>Following</u> an overview of the legislation <u>I will</u> critically evaluate the proposed amendments.

▸ <u>I will</u> examine the impact of the Employment Act 2008 <u>and in addition will</u> discuss possible amendments.

▸ <u>I will</u> discuss this issue <u>further when</u> I look at multinational corporations.

▸ <u>Further / Additional</u> analysis <u>is / will be given</u> in section two.

Linking points that support each other

▸ The employee might not understand their supervisor's intention. <u>In addition to this, / Additionally, / Furthermore, / Moreover,</u> ...

Linking points that contrast with each other

▸ Relief theory states that humour has developed in order to reduce tension. Superiority theory, <u>however, / on the other hand / by contrast</u>, suggests that humour is used chiefly to assert superiority.

Moving on to a new point

▸ <u>With regard to / Regarding / As regards / In respect of / Concerning / As for / Moving on to / Turning now to</u> ...

▸ <u>If we turn now to / If we look now at</u> the main cause of the financial crash in 2008, it is apparent that ...

Linking different sections of your assignment

▸ The business model outlined <u>above</u> is innovative because ...

▸ The table <u>below</u> shows the firm's income revenue over the last three years.

▸ The <u>previous / preceding</u> paragraph outlined the reasons for absenteeism given by employees.

▸ <u>Section one deals with</u> small businesses. <u>Subsequent sections look at</u> large businesses and ...

▸ <u>In the following</u> section I analyse the data collected and discuss some possible implications.

Linking points within a sentence

▶ It is important to distinguish between actual and relative poverty, and I will argue that <u>the former</u> concept is less relevant than <u>the latter</u>.

▶ Public–private partnerships and private finance initiatives are referred to here as PPPs and PFIs <u>respectively</u>.

▶ The <u>following</u> countries joined the European Union in 2004: the Czech Republic, Cyprus, …

3.2 Information to help you use these words correctly

Words you probably already use correctly: *above, additionally, based on, below, challenge, demonstrate, following, however, on the other hand, rest on, suggest.*
    Words defined in other sections*: preceding s15, subsequent s15.*

assertion *n* **assert** *v*	*n* – A statement of fact or belief. *v* – (1) To state a fact or belief. (2) To force others to recognise one's authority. ☹ *Assertion, contention* and *proposition* These are often used interchangeably; however, there are small differences in meaning. The main difference is that *proposition* is more formal and is often used in the context of logic and to give statements which are to be tested and proved or disproved.
assumption *n* **assume** *v*	*n* – A fact, idea or belief which is thought to be true but is not proven. An assumption can be explicitly stated but is more often used to refer to a hidden fact or idea within an argument. An assumption can therefore be similar to an unstated premise. *v* – (1) To take for granted. (2) To take on responsibility for or control of something. ☹ *Assumption / assume* and *presumption / presume*

Presumption / presume are used in real-life situations rather than academic contexts. They can also mean 'to act without authority or in an overconfident manner'.

E.g. People should be presumed innocent rather than guilty.

We presume she is dead.

They presumed to use my car without asking.

conjecture *n*	An opinion or explanation that has not yet been tested. Similar to *hypothesis*.
contention *n* **contend** *v*	*n* – A declaration of fact or belief to be argued. Similar to *assertion*. *v* – To state something to be argued, with or without evidence. Similar to *argue*.
former *adj*	(1) The first item mentioned in a list (usually of only two items). (2) Having existed in the past. E.g. The former director helped to develop new markets.
hypothesis *n* **hypothesise*** *v* **hypothetical** *adj*	*n* – A testable statement of how or why something happens, which has not yet been tested. *v* – To state a testable explanation / proposition. A **working** hypothesis. *Hypothesis, theory* and *thesis* Sometimes used interchangeably but do have different meanings – see *thesis* below. *-*ize* is also acceptable in British spelling and is always used in US spelling.
latter *adj*	(1) The second of two things mentioned. (2) The last stages of a process or time period. Similar to one meaning of *later*. E.g. In the latter / later stages of the design process, testing methods must be robust.

predicate *v / n*	*v* – To base a decision or action on the assumption that something else exists or will happen.
	E.g. Our approval is predicated on a linear model.
	❗ In logic and linguistics *a predicate / to predicate* have more specialised meanings.
premise *n*	A statement or principle used as the basis for an action or argument (the premises are said to 'imply' or 'entail' the conclusion).
	E.g. All her friends are tall. = major premise
	Joss is one of her friends. = minor premise
	Therefore, Joss is tall. = conclusion
	❗ The noun *premises* has the different meaning of an occupied building.
presuppose *v*	*v* – To assume or need to be true as a precondition.
presupposition *n*	*n* – A thing or statement assumed or needed to be true as a basis for something else.
	😟 *Presupposition / presuppose* and *assumption / assume*
	These can often be interchanged but there is a difference in meaning.
	A presupposition is something that needs to exist *before* something else can happen.
	An assumption can be made at any stage of a process or argument.
proposition *n*	*n* – (1) In an academic context, a statement that can be proved or disproved. The main proposition is sometimes called an *assertion* or *contention* (see above). Propositions on which an argument is based are premises, and the final proposition in an argument is the conclusion. If the proposition involves a testable explanation of something, it is also a hypothesis.
propose *v*	(2) In more general contexts, a proposition is an offer or suggestion.
	v – To suggest or put forward a plan or idea.

	🤝 To propose **a plan** // **a strategy** // **a solution** // **a measure** // **a policy** // **reforms** // **an amendment** // **legislation**.
	😞 *Proposition* and *proposal*
	A proposal is a suggestion or plan.
	E.g. There is a proposal for a new transport scheme.
refute *v* **refutation** *n*	*v* – To oppose a statement and try to prove that it is false. Similar to *contest* and *rebut*.
	🤝 To refute the **claim** // **suggestion** // **accusation** // **idea** // **theory** that …
respectively *adv*	Separately and in the same order as the items just mentioned.
	E.g. 'First in, first out' and 'last in, last out' are referred to as FIFO and LILO respectively.
	😞 *Respectively* and *respective*
	Respective is used to describe difference and separateness rather than order (see section 4).
speculate *v* **speculation** *n* **speculative** *adj*	*v* – (1) To form an idea or predict an event without evidence.
	E.g. We should base our growth model on past data rather than speculate on future sales.
	(2) To buy in order to take advantage in market value fluctuations.
	🤝 *v* – To speculate **that** + clause. To speculate **on** // **over** // **about** X.
	n – **Considerable** // **constant** // **intense** // **much** // **widespread** speculation.
	adj Speculative **applications** // **building** // **investments** // **trading**.
theory *n* **theorise*** *v* **theoretical** *adj*	*n* – A testable and often tested explanation of general principles of the natural world, accepted by experts as the best or one of the best explanations.
	😞 *Theory*, *thesis* and *hypothesis*
	These are sometimes used interchangeably, but there are some differences in meaning. See *hypothesis* above and *thesis* below.
	-ize is also acceptable in British spelling and is always used in US spelling.

thesis *n*	(1) A long written essay, article or book (usually at postgraduate level) which presents an argument or tests a hypothesis. Similar to *dissertation* or *treatise*. (2) A statement of something to be argued or yet to be tested. Similar to *proposition* or *theory*. *Thesis, theory* and *hypothesis* There is overlap and interchange between these. The main differences are that a thesis often refers to a written text, a theory usually refers to a widely recognised and established concept, and a hypothesis often refers to one person's ideas.
underlying *adj* **underlie** *n*	*adj* – Something hidden and/or existing below the surface. Often used to refer to the hidden causes of an action, event or belief. An underlying **assumption** // **belief** // **idea** // **concept** // **principle** // **cause**. *Underlie* and *underpin* These words are not usually interchangeable. Something that *underlies* something else can be positive or negative, major or minor. Something that *underpins* is an essential, supporting element. E.g. Strong government policy is needed to underpin the growth of Irish exports. For *undergo* see section 17. For *undermine* see section 27.

3.3   Nearly but not quite right

	Incorrect	Correct
1	This essay has shown that the model is based on limited and subjective data and is therefore merely a <u>theory</u> rather than established <u>hypothesis</u>.	This essay has shown that the model is based on limited and subjective data and is therefore merely a <u>hypothesis</u> rather than established <u>theory</u>.
2	I want to <u>put forward that</u> this advance in technology requires new legislation in order to develop.	I want to <u>argue / suggest / propose that</u> this advance … My <u>proposition is that</u> this advance …
3	A <u>presumption</u> of the monopolistic competition model is that firms can enter or exit the market freely.	An <u>assumption</u> of the monopolistic competition model is that firms can enter or exit the market freely.
4	My <u>proposal</u> is that using key performance indicators in schools is highly problematic.	My <u>proposition</u> is that using key performance indicators in schools is highly problematic.
5	We <u>hypothesis</u> that the positive correlation between sales and customer complaints is due to …	We <u>hypothesise/ze</u> that the positive correlation between sales and customer complaints is due to …
6	Arami (2016) suggests that successful leadership in the Kuwaiti oil and gas industry is <u>predicated with</u> good levels of visionary thinking.	Arami (2016) suggests that successful leadership in the Kuwaiti oil and gas industry is <u>predicated on</u> good levels of visionary thinking.
7	The project team <u>speculates on</u> winning the contract.	The project team <u>speculates that</u> they will win the contract.
8	Our <u>theory</u> is that male students will tend to give more positive answers than female students.	Our <u>hypothesis / proposition</u> is that male students will tend to give more positive answers than female students.
9	My analysis suggests that global central banks will <u>underlie</u> the country's currency in order to avoid financial collapse.	My analysis suggests that global central banks will <u>underpin</u> the country's currency in order to avoid financial collapse.
10	The main difference between role and person cultures is that the former uses bureaucratic hierarchy whereas <u>the later</u> revolves around individual personalities.	The main difference between role and person cultures is that the former uses bureaucratic hierarchy whereas <u>the latter</u> revolves around individual personalities.

Definitions, groupings and characteristics

4 Defining and classifying

Tutors often want you to define things in your own words. You may need to give just a brief definition, or a much longer (extended) definition which includes grouping or differentiating between similar terms, giving examples and discussing alternative definitions. Indeed, some assignments are composed entirely of developing and discussing a definition.

You will also find useful words and phrases in section 5.

4.1 Words in action

Defining

Key phrases

▸ X is <u>a type of</u> // <u>a branch of</u> // <u>a system of</u> // <u>a style of</u> // <u>a mode of</u> // <u>a model of</u> // <u>the study</u> of …

▸ X is <u>a process</u> // <u>a phenomenon</u> // <u>an organisation</u> // <u>a mechanism</u> // <u>a substance</u> // <u>a material</u> …

▸ X is <u>a framework</u> // <u>a hierarchy</u> // <u>an infrastructure</u> …

▸ X is <u>a paradigm</u> // <u>a construct</u> // <u>a concept</u> // <u>an approach</u> // <u>a perspective</u> // <u>a school of thought</u> // <u>an ideology</u> …

▸ In this report <u>I (will) define</u> economic growth as …

▸ A currency carry <u>is when</u> / <u>is defined as</u> / <u>can be defined as</u> / <u>can be termed as</u> / <u>refers to</u> …

▸ Total quality management <u>describes</u> // <u>is concerned with</u> / <u>deals with</u> …

▸ The term 'postmodernism' <u>has been applied to</u> / <u>is used to describe</u> // <u>has come to be used as</u> …

▸ Political anthropology <u>is primarily concerned with</u> …

▸ Neoliberalism <u>was originally associated with</u> / <u>originally meant</u> … but has now <u>acquired a (slightly // very) different meaning</u>.

▸ A <u>broad</u> // <u>narrow definition of</u> affirmative action is …

- Regenerative economics is <u>generally / widely // loosely understood to mean / to refer to</u> …
- A <u>generally / widely accepted definition of</u> arbitrage <u>is</u> …

Defining a term that does not have one clear definition
- <u>One definition of</u> corporate social responsibility is …
- There is <u>no universally agreed / generally accepted</u> definition of …
- There is <u>no // little consensus / agreement on / over what is meant by</u> interactivity.
- There are <u>several // various definitions of</u> quality.
- 'Freedom of speech' <u>has been interpreted in various ways</u>.
- 'Function' is <u>an ambiguous term</u> because it is used in so many different contexts.
- <u>What constitutes</u> a region <u>is (to some extent) subjective</u> because …

Referring to other people's definitions
- <u>In the literature</u> justice <u>is (usually // often) / tends to be defined as</u> …
- Kline (2009) <u>defines</u> progress <u>as</u> …
- Progress <u>has been defined as</u> … (Kline 2009).
- The theory of reasoned action is <u>(usually // often) attributed to</u> Fishbein and Ajzen (1975, 1980).

Categorising and classifying
Overarching categories
- 'Agrochemical' is <u>a generic / an umbrella term for</u> any chemical product used in agriculture.
- A mission statement should include the <u>overarching</u> objective of the business.
- 'Marketing' in the widest sense <u>encompasses</u> everything that relates to the customer.
- The top ten employability skills <u>include</u> verbal and written communication.
- The <u>meta</u>data should be able to describe all data subgroups.
- IVASS regulation no. 22 (2016) defines the concept of a <u>parent</u> company.

Grouping and categorising
- Matindale (2011) proposes a model for dealing with individuals <u>under</u> each <u>type / category of</u> leader.
- Subprimes are a <u>class // type / category of</u> mortgage with higher rates of interest.
- Economic models can be <u>classified / categorised according to / on the basis of</u> their function.
- The models are <u>classified / categorised as</u> discrete or continuous, <u>depending on</u> whether all variables are quantitative.
- John Lewis <u>comes under the category of</u> a private limited company.

- Any member of a LinkedIn discussion group can <u>create / form</u> <u>a subgroup within</u> the larger one.
- This report examines the use and misuse of <u>subsidiaries</u> in corporate tax avoidance schemes.
- LinkedIn groups can be <u>(further) subdivided into</u> various smaller ones to encourage more focused discussions.
- We have differentiated our advertising campaigns to reflect social <u>strata.</u>
- Zott et al. (2011) argue that our knowledge of business models is 'developing largely in <u>silos, according to</u> the interests of the <u>respective</u> researchers'.
- Education is an important <u>sphere of</u> economic activity in Western societies.
- WikiLeaks provides a way of bringing source material into the public <u>domain</u> anonymously.
- The retail gas industry <u>satisfies / fits / meets / fulfils</u> <u>the criterion</u> for an oligopoly.

Creating your own categories
- <u>I // We</u> <u>have based</u> <u>my // our</u> <u>classification on / categorisation on</u> three criteria: weight, cost and size.
- <u>I // We</u> <u>suggest // have adopted</u> <u>a classification / a categorisation based on</u> …
- <u>I // We</u> <u>suggest that</u> our model <u>should be classified as</u> quantitative because …
- <u>I // We</u> <u>classified / categorised</u> each product <u>according to</u> weight.

Classifying by emphasising difference
- Governance of harm or injury rather than responsibility <u>differentiates</u> tort from contract law.
- Cavitch (2014) <u>distinguishes / makes a distinction</u> <u>between</u> business trusts <u>and</u> other types of trust.
- Buchanan and Huczynski (2010) describe six <u>distinct / discrete</u> elements of organisational culture.
- Madsen et al. (2010) look at the <u>dichotomy / division between</u> innovation and imitation.

Classifying by composition
- Implement guidance <u>is composed of / comprises / consists of</u> …
- The United Kingdom and Ireland <u>constitute</u> the British Isles.
- High-quality advice <u>is</u> a (key) <u>element in</u> an effective legal aid system.

Classifying by singularity, units, uniqueness and exception
- John Lewis remains <u>the sole / only / single</u> UK example of a limited company with 100% employee shareholders.
- Our report will review the <u>unitary</u> development plans of five UK local authorities to look at …
- When it first opened, the Body Shop represented a <u>unique</u> management style.
- Derivative action is an important <u>exception to</u> the rule in *Foss* v *Harbottle*.

- The plastic has been developed <u>specifically</u> for use in space.
- The purpose of a social enterprise is not to make profit <u>per se</u> but to improve the social environment.

Organisational structures
- Government departments tend to be highly <u>bureaucratic // hierarchical</u>.
- The report examines how online communications can reduce the number of <u>tiers</u> and create a more <u>egalitarian // linear / flat</u> workplace.
- Since Chen and Tjosvola's 2006 research, effective <u>participative</u> leadership has increased.

Giving typical examples and naming the members of a group
- The US is <u>the archetype of a / the archetypal / the quintessential</u> free-market economy state.
- Lubna Olayan is <u>the embodiment / the epitome</u> of the powerful Arab business woman.
- Accounting software is <u>an excellent / a typical / a classic</u> <u>example of</u> how technology has revolutionised business.
- Construction accounting software <u>exemplifies / typifies / is an exemplar of</u> how technology has revolutionised business.
- There are two scope types within Porter's strategies, <u>namely</u> market segment and industry-wide.

4.2   Information to help you use these words correctly

Words and phrases you probably already use correctly: *broad, category, criterion, differentiate, flat, include, linear, loose, narrow, participative, school of thought, single, strata, subgroup, term, tier.*

   Words defined in other sections: *attribute* s19, *consensus* s12, *distinction* s21, *distinguish* s21, *ideology* s23, *paradigm* s18, *perspective* s23.

according to *adv*	(1) As stated by.
	(2) Corresponding to or in proportion to.
	E.g. Business should trade according to government regulations.
	! *According to* is only used to refer to others, not oneself.
	E.g. According to me, …✘
adopt *v* **adoption** *n*	*v* – (1) To choose to take or follow a particular idea, approach or course of action.
	(2) To become the legal parent of a child and raise it as your own.

The policy has been **widely** // **generally** adopted.

To adopt a **plan** // **policy** // **strategy** // **practice** // **principle** // **position** / **stance** / **approach** // **attitude** // **method**.

ambiguous *adj* **ambiguity** *n*	*adj* – Something that has more than one meaning and so may be interpreted differently in different contexts. *Ambiguous* and *vague* *Vague* means 'imprecise or unclear' rather than having more than one possible meaning. For the difference between *ambiguous* and *ambivalent* see section 23. ! *Ambiguity* has more specialised meanings in linguistics, maths and philosophy.
archetype *n* **archetypal** *adj*	*n* – A typical and excellent example of something that acts as a model and reference point for other things.
bureaucratic *adj* **bureaucracy** *n*	*adj* – Having a large number of officials and overly complicated procedures and rules.
class *n* **classify** *v* **classification** *n* **classified** *adj*	*n* – A group or category based on shared characteristics. *Class*, *category* and *type*. *Type* is the most general term. *Class* and *category* have the more specific meaning of things, goods or services that can be put in rank order. *Class* can also be used to name categories, e.g. Class A shares. ! The adjective *classified* has the additional meanings of (1) being officially secret, (2) relating to newspaper advertisements.
compose *v*	(1) 'Is made up of'. *Compose* can be used to describe something that has one or more elements, usually in the context of substances and materials. Similar to *consists of*. (2) To create a piece of music or poetry.

	! For meaning (1), *compose* is used with *to be* and *of*. E.g. Ice is composed of frozen water. Steel is composed of iron and carbon.
comprise *v*	'Is made up of'. Only used when more than one element makes up the whole. E.g. Ice comprises frozen water. ✗ Great Britain comprises England, Scotland and Wales. ✓ **!** *Comprise* does not use *to be* or *of* (although people do mistakenly use *comprise of*). E.g. Great Britain is comprised of England, Scotland and Wales. ✗ Great Britain comprises England, Scotland and Wales. ✓
consist *v*	'Is made of'. Similar to *is composed of* and *comprises*. **!** *Consist* only uses *of*. E.g. Great Britain is consists of England, Scotland and Wales. ✗ Great Britain consists of England, Scotland and Wales. ✓
constituent *n / adj*	*n* – (1) An element or component within a whole, e.g. A constituent company. (2) In politics, a member of a constituency. *adj* – Being one part of a whole.
constitute *v*	(1) 'Makes up'. The reverse relationship of *is composed of*, *comprises* and *consists of*. E.g. England, Scotland and Wales constitute Great Britain. (2) 'Is'. E.g. Racial abuse constitutes a criminal offence under UK law.
domain *n*	A specific area of activity. Similar to *sphere*. The / A **political** // **social** // **public** // **private** // **male** // **female** domain. *Domain* and *realm*

	Realm has a similar meaning to *domain* and *sphere* but is less common and usually used to talk about knowledge, experience or imagination. E.g. We feel that the CEO's wild plans are outside the realms of possibility.
egalitarian *adj*	Based on a system and/or belief that people should be treated equally.
encompass *v*	To include a large number or wide range of different things. E.g. Our study encompassed university students of all disciplines.
epitome *n* **epitomise*** *v*	*n* – An excellent and perfect example of a quality or type. Similar to *archetype* but usually used for qualities and types rather than things. E.g. *n* – He is the epitome of tolerance. *v* – He epitomises tolerance. *-*ize* is also acceptable in British spelling and is always used in US spelling.
exemplify *v* **exemplar** *n*	*v* – To be a typical and/or good example of.
hierarchical *adj*	Based on a system clearly divided into levels of rank and importance.
meta- *prefix*	(1) Of or about itself. (2) At a higher level of abstraction. E.g. Metadata is high-level data that describes all the other data within it. (3) Transformation, e.g. metamorphosis.
mode *n*	A specific way something is done, is expressed or happens, often when a choice of different methods or types exists. A mode **of production // communication // interaction // expression // thought // conduct // behaviour // transport**.
model *n / v*	*n* – (1) A way of doing something or a representation of how something works or behaves. E.g. The McLean's containerisation model revolutionised the shipping industry.

(2) A specific way of doing or behaving, usually seen as a good example or standard.

E.g. A model report.

v – To form, shape, base or use as an example.

A **basic** // **conventional** / **traditional** // **common** // **dominant** // **standard** // **excellent** // **positive** // **successful** // **business** model.

A model **of best practice** // **excellence** // **good behaviour**.

To **follow** / **adopt** / **use** / **apply** a model.

namely *adv*	'That is'. Similar to the abbreviation *i.e.* *Namely (i.e.)* and *for example (e.g.)* These abbreviations have different meanings. After *namely* you must list all the items in the group, not just some examples.
overarching *adj*	Covering or including all the others. All-encompassing.
per se *adv*	Considered by, of, or in itself. Similar in meaning to *intrinsic*. *Per se* is often used with an initial concession. E.g. I am not opposed to guns per se, but I am against private gun ownership.
quintessential *adj* **quintessentially** *adv*	*adj* – An excellent and perfect example of a quality or type. Similar to *archetypal*.
refer *v*	*Refer* has several meanings but when giving a definition it means 'is the word/term used for'. E.g. 'Grantor' refers to the person who gives out the grants. *Refers to* and *relates to* *Relates to* means 'is connected to'. The two phrases are sometimes used interchangeably but for giving a definition you should use *refers to*.

respective *adj*	Relating or belonging separately to the different categories or groups mentioned.
	😞 *Respective* and *respectively*
	These have different meaning. The adverb *respectively* means 'in the same order as just mentioned' (see section 3).
silo *n*	(1) A section or system within an organisation that operates in isolation.
	(2) A tower or chamber used for storage.
sole *adj*	The only one.
	🤝 The sole **exception** // **aim** // **objective** // **purpose** // **cause** // **intention** // **reason** // **justification** // **exception** // **means**.
	Sole **control** // **authority** // **charge**.
	A sole **proprietor** / **trader**.
specific *adj* **specifically** *adv*	*adj* – Clearly identified or defined.
	😞 *Specifically* and *specially*
	There is overlap but strictly speaking, *specially* and *special* mean 'unique' or 'only for this purpose'.
	E.g. The software is specially designed for small businesses.
	For e*specially* see section 28.
sphere *n*	(1) An area of activity, interest or influence. Similar to *domain*.
	(2) A round surface in three-dimensional space.
	🤝 The **private** // **public** // **political** // **social** // **economic** sphere.
	A sphere **of influence**.
strata *n*	Layers, levels or classes, particularly of social groups and organisations.
	❗ The singular form of the noun is *stratum*.

subjective *adj*	Based on feelings and beliefs rather than evidence or fact.
	Highly / extremely / largely // somewhat subjective.
	A subjective **opinion // viewpoint // response // assessment // approach // judgement**.
unique *adj*	The only one that exists. *Unique* emphasises that something is special and/or unusual.
	E.g. A unique **opportunity // viewpoint // collection // situation**.
unitary *adj* **unit** *n*	*adj* – (1) Acting as one (central) unit, e.g. A unitary government.
	(2) Being composed of units.
	In mathematics *unitary* has a more specialised meaning.

4.3 Nearly but not quite right

	Incorrect	Correct
1	It is not always helpful to <u>categorise</u> people <u>into</u> ethnic group<u>s</u>.	It is not always helpful to <u>categorise / classify</u> people <u>by / according to / in terms of</u> ethnic group.
2	One question is whether the Google search engine is <u>an archetype for</u> basic artificial intelligence.	One question is whether the Google search engine is <u>an example of</u> basic artificial intelligence.
3	There is one overriding <u>criteria</u> a defendant must meet before being granted an appeal.	There is one overriding <u>criterion</u> a defendant must meet before being granted an appeal.
4	'Poverty' is an <u>ambivalent</u> term. I will define it as …	'Poverty' is an <u>ambiguous</u> term. I will define it as …
5	A law firm <u>comprises of</u> a group of lawyers working together under a specific name.	A law firm <u>comprises / is composed of / consists of</u> a group of lawyers working together under a specific name.
6	'Fixed charge' <u>relates to</u> a cost that remains unchanged regardless of the amount of business conducted.	'Fixed charge' <u>refers to</u> a cost that remains unchanged regardless of the amount of business conducted.
7	There are many different types of assets, <u>namely</u> capital, tangible and underlying assets.	There are many different types of assets, <u>for example</u> capital, tangible and underlying assets.
8	A <u>wide</u> definition of competitive intelligence is the sharing of information about customers, products and competitors.	A <u>broad</u> definition of competitive intelligence is the sharing of information about customers, products and competitors.
9	<u>According to my argument</u>, project managers should take more account of Total Value Management.	<u>I argue that</u> project managers should take more account of Total Value Management.
10	BarkBuddy is <u>sole</u> because it uses the online dating language and format to help people find suitable pets to adopt.	BarkBuddy is <u>unique</u> because it uses the online dating language and format to help people find suitable pets to adopt.

5 Groupings, affiliations and being separate

5.1 Words in action

Belonging or being linked to a group

▸ This essay will look at the role of <u>peer</u> groups in value project management.

▸ Landsafe is <u>affiliated to</u> the Bank of America.

▸ As a subject, project management is closely <u>allied to</u> risk management and strategic planning.

▸ Despite the problems discussed, single-project <u>alliances</u> have advantages over long-term partnerships.

▸ An alternative to fully merged legal mega firms is the concept of <u>association,</u> in which co-operating firms present a <u>united</u> force externally but are separate legal and financial <u>entities</u>.

▸ We recommend that <u>a delegation of</u> industry leaders meets annually to discuss these issues.

▸ The Faroe Islands currently have <u>bilateral</u> trade agreements with Iceland, Norway and Switzerland.

Being incorporated into or joined together

▸ Numerous safety features have now been <u>incorporated into</u> this particular model.

▸ An economic union is a highly <u>integrated</u> system in which members' fiscal policies are harmonised.

▸ The previously separate provinces have recently been <u>absorbed into / assimilated into / subsumed under</u> the new national state.

▸ The report shows that in some smaller EU member states, banking <u>acquisitions // mergers // amalgamations / consolidation</u> happened more quickly than with some larger members.

▸ The regulations stipulate that <u>co-opted</u> members may not serve as president or vice-president.

▸ Anglesen (2001) overlooks an important aspect of state–local land <u>appropriation</u> conflicts.

▸ Although 'merger' and 'acquisition' are often seen together, we must be careful not to <u>conflate // confuse</u> the two terms.

Being separate, fragmented or broken up

▸ Small business entities should ensure that personal credit is <u>separate</u> from business credit.

▸ Our analysis shows that the CEO has a <u>unilateral</u> approach to decision making.

▸ Large, liquid stocks appear to benefit greatly from a <u>fragmented</u> market (O'Hara and Ye 2011).

▸ Our data, contrary to what Wedel and Kamakura argue, is that a marketing plan does not always need to be based on a <u>segmentation</u> analysis.

▸ We recommend that budget setting is <u>devolved to</u> regional managers rather than done centrally.

- The main issue is that the company directors are <u>detached / disengaged / disassociated</u> from other employees.
- The paper industry is an example of extreme <u>fragmentation</u>.
- Leyson showed how the onslaught of software formats has almost <u>dismantled</u> the music industry.
- The president can <u>dissolve</u> the lower house only with the sanction of the prime minister and council.

5.2   Information to help you use these words correctly

Words and phrases you probably already use correctly: *incorporate, integrate, separate, united.*
   Words defined in other sections: *constituent s4, respective s4.*

acquire *v* **acquisition** *n*	*v* – (1) To actively get or come to have. (2) To buy or take full or partial control of a company. 🤝 To acquire **skill / expertise / a reputation**.
affiliate *v / n* **affiliated** *adj*	*v* – To be officially connected to another (usually larger) organisation. *n* – A person or organisation connected to a larger one. 🤝 Affiliated **to / with** something.
alliance *n*	An agreement between people or organisations (called *allies*) to work with or help each other. 🤝 To **enter into / form / forge** an alliance with someone. An alliance **between** people. A **business / economic / global / international / trade** alliance. 😦 *Alliance* and *all**eg**iance* An *allegiance* is a personal, unofficial loyalty (see section 8).
allied *adj*	(1) Relating to members of a group (other allies). E.g. There are three allied member states being represented at the summit. (2) In combination or together with. E.g. Creativity can often be allied to depression. 🤝 Allied **to** X.

ally *n / v*	*n* – A person or organisation that cooperates, officially or unofficially, with another.
	v – To cooperate with another person or organisation for mutual benefit.
	n – A **close** // **faithful** / **loyal** // **reliable** // **key** // **powerful** // **valuable** // **potential** // **strategic** // **former** ally.
	To **be** // **become** // **prove to be** // **remain** an ally.
	v – To ally oneself **with** X.
amalgamate *v* **amalgamation** *n* **amalgamated** *adj*	*v* – To unite or combine to form one entity. Similar to *merge*.
	v – To amalgamate **with** X. To amalgamate X **with** / **into** Y.
	n – An amalgamation **of** X **and** Y.
appropriate *v* **appropriation** *n*	*v* – To take something that belongs to someone else without permission.
	Note that the above meaning of the verb is different from the adjective *appropriate* meaning 'suitable', as in 'A budget should be appropriate for the size of the project'.
assimilate *v* **assimilation** *n*	*v* – To integrate, absorb and/or understand something.
	E.g. It is important to assimilate new employees into the culture of the organisation.
associate *v / n / adj*	*v* – To connect things in your mind or to be connected with in some way.
	n – A business colleague or partner.
	adj – Someone who does a job but does not have all the rights or responsibilities of the role.
	v – To associate **oneself with** something/someone. To **be** associated **with** X.
	n – A **former** / **close** / **senior** associate.
	adj – An associate **lawyer** // **editor** // **director**.
associated *adj*	A group of companies officially linked in some way, or a company that was originally formed of different companies, e.g. The Associated Press.

bilateral *adj*	Involving two bodies, organisations or sides. Compare with *unilateral* below.
	🤝 A bilateral **agreement** / **decision** / **contract** / **action**.
conflate *v* **conflated** *adj* **conflation** *n*	*v* – To combine and/or confuse two or more things (usually concepts, terms or texts).
co-opt *v* **co-option** *n*	*v* – (1) To appoint someone (often temporarily) to a committee by invitation.
	(2) To assimilate a smaller / less powerful group (or some members of that group) in order to adopt some or all of their practices.
	❗ Note the difference between co-op**t** / co-op**ti**on and co-op / co-op**eration**.
delegate *n1* **delegation** *n2*	*n1* – A person who represents an organisation at a conference or committee.
	n2 – A group of people who represent others at a conference or committee.
	E.g. A delegation of trade leaders represented the UK at the business summit.
	🤝 A **high-level** // **top-level** // **government** // **business** // **trade** // **peace** // **union** delegation.
	To **lead** / **head** // **organise** // **welcome** a delegation.
	❗ See section 8 for a different meaning of *delegate* (*v*) and *delegation* (*n*).
detach *v* **detached** *adj*	*v* – To separate one thing from another. Similar to *disengage*.
	adj – Separate. Of people, someone who is emotionally separate or unconcerned (see section 6).
devolve *v* **devolution** *n*	*v* – To delegate power to a lower level, usually from a central power to more local units.
dismantle *v*	To take apart machinery, equipment, structures or organisations piece by piece.
dissolve *v*	(1) To turn a solid into a solution.
	E.g. To dissolve salt in hot water.
	(2) To end an official and/or legal arrangement.

entity *n*	(1) Something that exists separately from other things.
	(2) A business or other organisation that has its own legal and financial existence.
	🤝 A **separate** // **single** // **independent** // **commercial** // **corporate** // **public** // **private** entity.
fragmentation *n* **fragmented** *adj*	*n* – Where a market has several or many companies that are equally powerful.
	adj – Broken up into several or many pieces.
	❗ The noun *fragment* has the different meaning of a very small piece.
merge *v* **merger** *n*	*v* – To combine / mix one thing with another. Similar to *amalgamate*.
	n – The combining of two things / companies to form something new.
peer *n*	(1) Another person, group or company of similar type, level or status.
	(2) A member of the nobility in the UK or Ireland, e.g. A peer of the realm.
	❗ The verb *to peer* has the different meaning of looking hard to see something that is not easily visible.
	E.g. He peered into the darkness to see if anyone was there.
segment *v / n*	*v* – To divide the market into different parts based on customer profile or need.
	n – Part of a divided whole.
segmentation *n* **segmented** *adj*	*n* – The situation or strategy in which the market is divided into parts.
	adj – A situation in which the market is divided into different customer needs or groups.
subsume *v* **subsumed** *adj*	*v* – To include or absorb into something larger.
	E.g. All three firms will be subsumed under the group heading of 'leisure centres'.
	The projects have now been subsumed into the main management team workload.
unilateral *adj*	(1) Done or decided by one person or group.
	(2) One-sided or relating to or affecting only one side.

5.3 Nearly but not quite right

	Incorrect	Correct
1	The firm's spending on advertising is too <u>segmented</u> and needs strategising.	The firm's spending on advertising is too <u>fragmented</u> and needs strategising.
2	This report recommends that the board <u>co-op</u> members to help develop marketing and sales strategy.	This report recommends that the board <u>co-opt</u> members to help develop marketing and sales strategy.
3	It is not effective to assume that certain factors are always <u>associated to</u> good performance (Child 2007).	It is not effective to assume that certain factors are always <u>associated with</u> good performance (Child 2007).
4	Contracts should specify the rights and obligations of the other party's <u>allies</u>.	Contracts should specify the rights and obligations of the other party's <u>affiliates</u>.
5	The UK has relatively few business <u>entities</u> categories compared to Germany.	The UK has relatively few business <u>entity</u> categories compared to Germany.
6	If the proposed <u>merger</u> goes ahead, the employees of the target company are likely to see a drop in wages.	If the proposed <u>acquisition</u> goes ahead, the employees of the target company are likely to see a drop in wages.
7	As the goals of the two CEOs are incompatible, this report recommends that the partnership be <u>devolved</u>.	As the goals of the two CEOs are incompatible, this report recommends that the partnership be <u>dissolved</u>.
8	Bannister (2001) showed how vertical structures in the public sector can be <u>separated</u> to provide a more efficient service.	Bannister (2001) showed how vertical structures in the public sector can be <u>dismantled / taken apart</u> to provide a more efficient service.
9	Microsoft Office is currently the most successful <u>integral</u> software systems.	Microsoft Office is currently the most successful <u>integrated</u> software systems.
10	<u>Linking</u> the two departments will lead to greater efficiency, as a single unit needs only one project leader.	<u>Combining / amalgamating / merging</u> the two departments will lead to greater efficiency, as a single unit needs only one project leader.

6 Characteristics, qualities and skills

6.1 Words in action

Types of characteristics

‣ Strong leaders tend to have certain <u>intrinsic / innate</u> qualities in common.

‣ This report looks at the most effective ways the risks <u>inherent to</u> large construction projects can be managed.

‣ <u>Extrinsic</u> motivation comes from external sources such as a reward, coercion or fear of punishment.

‣ Charitable donations have <u>intangible</u> benefits such as good PR, and <u>tangible</u> advantages such as tax relief.

Positive characteristics

‣ The design <u>has</u> many <u>excellent // positive features / attributes / characteristics / traits / qualities</u>.

‣ Research suggests that programmers <u>endowed with // who have</u> social perceptiveness are</u> more successful.

‣ She <u>has</u> <u>acumen // integrity // charisma</u>. He <u>shows</u> <u>discretion.</u>

‣ She <u>is</u> <u>articulate // astute // capable // competent // conscientious // diplomatic // discreet // gregarious // ingenious // inspiring // personable // proactive // reputable // resilient // seasoned // shrewd // sociable // tactful // tolerant // versatile.</u>

Characteristics that can be either positive or negative depending on context or culture

‣ He <u>is</u> <u>amenable // malleable // austere // businesslike // cautious // determined // disinterested // dogmatic // driven // flexible // focused // intuitive // moral // reactive // relaxed // reserved // self-motivated.</u>

‣ He <u>is</u> <u>an introvert / an extrovert / a perfectionist.</u>

Negative characteristics

‣ She <u>has a tendency / has a propensity / is inclined to be</u> <u>complacent // evasive // disengaged // disingenuous // hesitant // incompetent // inept // manipulative // negative // offensive // patronising // pompous // opinionated // profligate // rapacious // rigid // tactless // volatile.</u>

‣ It <u>is</u> a <u>dysfunctional</u> workplace.

Skills

‣ The team is <u>skilled in</u> translation software. They <u>are a skilled</u> translation software team.

‣ The team <u>is</u> <u>adept at</u> using translation software.

‣ The post requires <u>an / the ability to</u> analyse data quickly.

‣ Interns are put on training programmes according to their <u>abilities / capabilities</u>.

‣ The new machines <u>are capable of</u> reducing assembly time by 12%.

‣ She has a <u>facility with</u> data and <u>for</u> quickly understanding new analysis software systems.

‣ He has the required <u>functional</u> <u>competence</u> for the job.

6.2 Information to help you use these words correctly

Words you probably already use correctly: *cautious, charisma, extrovert, flexible, focused, hesitant, innovative, inspiring, introvert, moral, proactive, reputable, reserved, self-motivated, sharp-witted, strict, tolerant, trait.*

ability *n*	(1) What you are able to do.
	(2) Skill or talent.
acumen *n*	The ability to make good decisions and judgements.
	🤝 She has **sound / good business / commercial / legal / financial** acumen.
adept *adj*	Skilled.
	🤝 He is adept **at** X.
amenable *adj*	(1) Willing to consider the suggestions and ideas of others (seen as a positive trait).
	(2) Easily persuaded or controlled by others (seen as a negative trait).
	🤝 Amenable **to change** // **to suggestions** // **to compromise** // **to offers**.
aptitude *n*	A natural ability or skill.
	🤝 To **have / show** a **natural** aptitude **for** X.

articulate *adj / v*	*adj* – Is able to speak fluently and intelligently.
	v – (1) To pronounce words clearly.
	(2) To bend, using a joint.
astute *adj*	Able to assess situations and people quickly and correctly. Similar to *shrewd* and *sharp-witted*.
attribute *n*	*n* – A characteristic, quality of feature.
attribute *v*	*v* – To think or state as being caused by (see section 19).
attributable *adj*	🤝 An **essential / a key // a positive // a negative** attribute.
	❗ Note the difference in both meaning and word stress between the noun and verb. The noun stress is <u>a</u>ttribute and the verb stress is at<u>tri</u>bute.
austere *adj*	*adj* – (1) Strict and serious.
austerity *n*	(2) Having a basic, uncomplicated appearance.
	n – When public spending is reduced and/or restricted.
	🤝 **Economic // fiscal / financial** austerity **measures // policy**.
capability *n*	*n* – The ability to do something.
capable *adj*	*adj* – Being able to do something well.
	🤝 *n* – To **have the** capability **to do** X **/ of doing** X.
	adj – She is capable **of** hav**ing** X. He **is** (a) capable (**person**).
	😟 *Capability* and *ability*
	Can sometimes be interchanged but there is a difference.
	Capability / capable are often used for possibility and things that might not actually happen.
	E.g. Zimbardo believes that we are all capable of committing evil acts.
	Ability / able are used in the context of skills and real-world action.

capacity *n*	(1) The maximum amount something can do, produce or hold.
	(2) Ability.
	🙁 *Cap**ac**ity* and *cap**ability***
	Has the capacity to do is interchangeable with *is capable of doing.* However, *capacity* is usually used for physical volumes as in (1). See also section 11.
competent *adj*	To have the skill to do something well.
	🤝 **Highly / fairly** competent.
complacent *adj*	Overly satisfied and confident and so not considering possible problems or dangers.
	🙁 *Compla**cent*** and *compla**isant***
	Complaisant means 'willing to please and consider the ideas of others'. Similar to the positive sense of *amenable* (1) above.
conscientious *adj*	Hard-working and wanting to do one's work well.
defensive *adj*	(1) Reacts strongly to criticism and is keen to justify one's own position.
	(2) Used or intended to defend, e.g. A defensive bunker.
detached *adj*	Emotionally separate and/or not interested in X. Similar to *disengaged.*
determined *adj*	Committed and firm about doing something.
diplomatic *adj*	(1) Acts so as not to hurt the other person's feelings. Similar to *tactful* but often used in a wider and/or political context.
	(2) Relating to relationships between countries.
discreet *adj* **discreetly** *adv* **discreetness** *n*	*adj* – Being tactful and/or not showing that you know something embarrassing or hurtful.
	E.g. The website arranges 'discreet relationships' for married people.
	❗ The noun *discreetness* is not often used. It is more common to use the noun *discretion* (only one *e*) – see below.
	🙁 *Discr**eet*** and *discr**ete***
	*Discr**ete*** means 'separate and distinct' (see section 21).

discretion *n* **discretionary** *adj*	*n* – (1) The quality of being discreet (see above). E.g. In the meeting he showed discretion. (2) The freedom to choose. E.g. Managers often have discretion over which training courses to attend. *adj* – Made or used by someone according to situation or preference (see section 9).
disengaged *adj*	Emotionally separate and/or not interested in X. Similar to *detached*.
dogmatic *adj*	Stubborn and opinionated, refusing to consider any other point of view, even in the face of contradictory evidence.
dysfunctional *adj*	Operating in an abnormal way, used to describe people or organisations, e.g. A dysfunctional business. *Dysfunctional*, *malfunction* and *non-functional* The verb and noun *malfunction* means 'not working properly' and is usually applied to machinery or bodily organs, e.g. Malfunctioning kidneys. *Non-functional* means not working at all.
endow *v* **endowment** *n*	*v* – (1) Of a quality or physical feature, given by nature. E.g. He is endowed with intelligence and wit. (2) To donate a (large) sum of money for public benefit.
evasive *adj* **evade** *v*	*adj* – Tending to avoid giving direct responses to (difficult) questions or issues.
extrinsic *adj*	An external element or coming from outside. An extrinsic **force / influence / value / motivation / reward**.
facility *n*	(1) A place or amenity used for a particular purpose. E.g. The office has good facilities. (2) A natural skill or ability. E.g. She has a facility for learning languages.

functional *adj* **function** *n*	*adj* – (1) Able to do what it is supposed to, or working in the expected way. (2) Relating to areas of skill or knowledge in an organisation. 🤝 **Fully / partially** functional. Functional **areas / expertise / departments**.
gregarious *adj*	Likes to be in social groups and gets on well with people. Similar to *sociable*.
incline *v* **inclination** *n*	*v* – (1) Is likely to do something or act in a particular way. Similar to *tend*. (2) To be willing or persuaded to do something. E.g. Hopefully the panel will be inclined to overlook my nervousness. *n* – (1) A natural tendency, interest or liking for. (2) A slope. 🤝 *v* – To **be** inclined **to** X. *n* – To **have** an inclination **towards / for** X**ing / to** X.
inept *adj*	Lacking the skills or knowledge to do the task. Similar to *incompetent*. ❗ *Inept* and *incompetent* are strongly negative and might cause offence.
ingenious *adj* **ingenuity** *n*	*adj* – Clever and inventive, particularly in finding ways to solve problems. ☹ *Ingenious* and *ingenuous* *Ingenuous* means 'innocent and trusting' (see *disingenuous* below).
inherent *adj*	Being an unremovable part or aspect of something. Similar to *intrinsic*. 🤝 An inherent **bias // ambiguity // contradiction // flaw // limitation // tension // weakness // uncertainty // danger // problem // difficulty // quality // tendency // ability // strength**.
innate *adj*	Natural, something you are born with. Used to describe the nature and characteristics of things. 🤝 Innate **talent // knowledge // behaviour // response // wisdom**. ☹ *Inherent*, *intrinsic* and *innate* There is overlap. However, *inherent* and *intrinsic* are closer synonyms, with *innate* being used to emphasise inborn, natural qualities.

intangible *adj*	Not existing in a physical sense or difficult to describe.
integrity *n*	Honesty and strong moral principles.
intrinsic *adj*	Being an unremovable part or aspect of something. Similar to *inherent*.
	🤝 Beauty is intrinsic **to** art.
	Intrinsic **value / worth // motivation // property // function**.
intuitive *adj* **intuition** *n*	*adj* – Having the ability to understand or know things through personal feelings rather than evidence.
manipulative *adj* **manipulate** *v* **manipulation** *n*	*adj* – Often trying to influence other people's behaviour or emotions without them knowing.
	v – To influence, alter or move people or things for a particular purpose.
	n – The influencing, altering or moving of people or things for a particular purpose.
	🤝 To manipulate **data // figures // statistics // people // the crowd // the public**.
mercenary *adj / n*	*adj* – Does things only to make money, regardless of ethics.
	n – A soldier who will fight for whoever will pay them.
offensive *adj / n* **offend** *v*	*adj* – (1) Tends to act in a rude or aggressive way that upsets the other person.
	(2) Attacking, aggressive or proactive.
	🤝 *adj* – To **be** offensive.
	n – To **be / go on** the offensive.
opinionated *adj*	Sticking to and expressing one's opinions, despite opposition.
patronising* *adj* **patronise*** *v*	*adj* – Tending to act in a seemingly kind or polite way but which makes the other person think that you see them as stupid or inferior.
	❗ The verb *to patronise* also has the positive meaning of supporting someone by being a client, customer or fund-giver.
	😦 *Patronising* and *condescending*
	These are sometimes interchanged but there is a difference in meaning.
	Condescending means explicitly showing that you think you are superior.

	*-*izing and -ize* are also acceptable in British spelling and are always used in US spelling.
perfectionist *n*	Someone who is not happy unless they feel their work (or that of others) is perfect.
personable *adj*	Looks and acts in a pleasant way and generally gets on well with others.
	! *Perso**nable**, perso**nal** and perso**nnel**.*
	Be careful to use the correct spelling for these three different words.
pompous *adj* **pomposity** *n*	*adj* – Acts in a self-important way.
profligate *adj*	Spends money and/or resources impulsively and without care.
propensity *n*	Is likely to act in a particular way. Similar to *tendency* and *inclination*.
rapacious *adj*	Aggressively greedy. Usually used in the context of money, land or markets.
reactive *adj*	Responds to problems or changes when they happen rather than actively trying to prevent them.
resilient *adj*	Able to recover quickly ('bounce back') after a negative experience. E.g. We need to ensure that the business will be resilient to price fluctuations.
rigid *adj*	Not flexible.
seasoned *adj*	Experienced.
shrewd *adj*	Able to assess situations and people quickly and correctly. Similar to *astute* and *sharp-witted*.
tactless *adj*	Acts in a way that shows a lack of sensitivity to the feelings of others.
tangible *adj*	Existing in a physical sense and/or is easy to see or touch.
versatile *adj*	Able to be used for or to do many different things.
volatile *adj*	Unstable, likely to change without warning.

6.3 Nearly but not quite right

	Incorrect	Correct
1	This essay examines attitudes of French citizens towards <u>high-skilled</u> immigrants.	This essay examines attitudes of French citizens towards <u>highly skilled</u> immigrants.
2	This data supports other studies (Maurer and Bartsch 2001, Dakhli and De Clercq 2004) showing that a culture of trust <u>gives</u> innovation.	This data supports other studies (Maurer and Bartsch 2001, Dakhli and De Clercq 2004) showing that a culture of trust <u>fosters / promotes / encourages</u> innovation.
3	Williamson and Zeng (2009) argue convincingly that Chinese MCs are <u>capable to succeed</u> in the long term in a variety of operational contexts.	Williamson and Zeng (2009) argue convincingly that Chinese MCs are <u>capable of</u> long-term <u>success</u> in a variety of operational contexts.
4	The committee did not go as far as to accuse the MP of lying but they did describe her answers as '<u>ingenious</u>'.	The committee did not go as far as to accuse the MP of lying but they did describe her answers as '<u>ingenuous</u>'.
5	Managers need to <u>be discretion</u> when dealing with sensitive staff issues.	Managers need to <u>be discreet</u> when … Managers need to <u>show / have discretion</u> when dealing with sensitive staff issues.
6	The report has found <u>that inherent flaws are with</u> the methodology.	The report has found <u>inherent flaws in</u> …
7	Before reaching the contract stage it is advisable to find out whether the other party is <u>amenable for</u> negotiation.	Before reaching the contract stage it is advisable to find out whether the other party is <u>amenable / open to</u> negotiation. <u>/ willing to</u> negotiate.
8	My analysis suggests that the building has the <u>ability</u> for up to 20 staff.	My analysis suggests that the building has the <u>capacity</u> for up to 20 staff.
9	My first recommendation is that the firms finds <u>a season</u> director with shrewd negotiating skills.	My first recommendation is that the firm finds <u>a seasoned / an experienced</u> director with shrewd negotiating skills.
10	The organisation is looking for accountants <u>who are at</u> a high level of financial acumen.	The organisation is looking for accountants <u>with / who have</u> a high level of financial acumen.

Events, situations and business contexts

7   Events, situations, advantages and disadvantages

See also sections 26 and 27 for other useful words and phrases

7.1   Words in action

Occurrence and events

▶ High-risk tourist destinations need crisis management plans to negate the impact of negative <u>occurrences</u> (Sonmez 1999).

▶ The 2015 Hiscox report looks <u>at the incidence of</u> employee theft in the US.

▶ The Pareto principle states that for most <u>events</u> the consequences arise from only a small number of causes.

▶ This report has analysed and evaluated the <u>phenomenon</u> of online personal entrepreneurialism.

▶ During the Great Depression <u>circumstances</u> were such that civil unrest became common.

▶ I argue that good HR management can only <u>manifest</u> itself if the company has a coherent business strategy.

Positive situations and possibility

▶ A business plan should not rely solely on a <u>favourable // advantageous // positive</u> market situation.

▶ The error was <u>fortunate / fortuitous / lucky</u> as it led to an improvement on the original design.

▶ One of the worst things a manager can do is to tell an employee that they are <u>fortunate / lucky</u> to have a job.

▶ The data shows that the management team is <u>harmonious</u> and has <u>an</u> excellent <u>rapport</u> with junior staff.

▶ The regional offices have an <u>energised</u> and cheerful <u>atmosphere / ambience</u>.

▶ Our report shows that the client received <u>equitable / fair</u> treatment.

▶ The organisation is currently operating at <u>optimal</u> levels of productivity.

- The company has <u>fared well</u> and has a <u>strong / robust / resilient</u> infrastructure. It is therefore likely to be <u>immune to</u> short-term competitive threats.
- The large contingency fund will <u>make</u> the business <u>immune to</u> market volatility.
- The large contingency fund will <u>protect / insulate</u> the business <u>from / against</u> market volatility.
- The strong economic forecast <u>bodes well for</u> both employees and customers.
- We have identified significant <u>latent / untapped</u> expertise on which managers are not capitalising.
- This report suggests that the company should focus on developing <u>emerging / nascent</u> markets.
- When crowdfunding first <u>gained purchase</u> in the UK, the financial regulator gave it what James (2016) calls 'hostile pronouncements'.

Advantages

- Cloud computing <u>can have advantages for / is advantageous to</u> smaller businesses (Truong 2010).
- This essay will demonstrate that there are three main <u>benefits / pros</u> to using anti-spyware software.
- The voting capacity of the US 'blue states' is <u>a boon to</u> democratic candidates.
- Cloud computing can be <u>a valuable asset to</u> small businesses in a crowded marketplace (Truong 2010).
- Charitable donations have <u>intangible benefits</u> such as positive PR, and <u>tangible advantages</u> such as tax relief.
- There <u>is</u> some <u>merit in</u> using a cognitive behavioural approach.
- I examine the different forms of <u>preferential</u> treatment sanctioned by Free Trade Agreements.

Negative situations and events

- The <u>adverse // hostile // disastrous / ruinous // dire</u> economic <u>conditions</u> contributed to the industry's <u>demise</u>.
- The company has had <u>many problems</u> / been <u>beset with problems</u> since it installed the new payroll software.
- Graafland et al. (2006) argue that most company <u>dilemmas</u> caused by religious belief involve the conflict between the person's moral standards and the practicalities of running a business.
- Hon (2009) examined the <u>predicaments</u> faced by the Chinese government in implementing a personnel system imported from the West.
- <u>Systemic</u> corruption in higher education clearly exists (Janashia 2015, Osipian 2009, Waite and Allen 2003).
- My survey indicates that the new foreign investment fees are <u>out of kilter with / misaligned with</u> the needs of the rural sector.

- Our data show that the HR team is <u>demotivated // demoralised</u>.
- Unemployed people can find certain aspects of the UK benefit system <u>perplexing</u>.
- The government has introduced an <u>austere</u> economic policy.
- Evidence shows that the number of <u>discrimination</u> claims continues to rise, despite attempts to make employees aware of <u>discriminatory</u> behaviour (Cates and Dorsey 2011).
- Adam's theory is based on the principle that <u>inequity</u> arises if employee input is not proportionate to output.
- We recommend this as the most effective CRM strategy for reactivating <u>dormant</u> customers.

Disadvantages

- I have shown that the <u>disadvantages</u> of using English globally do not outweigh the advantages.
- The new training scheme is <u>disadvantageous to</u> part-time staff.
- Customers are often not told about the <u>drawbacks / shortcomings / cons</u> of anti-spyware software.
- Using gross domestic product as an economic measure has severe <u>limitations</u>.
- There are significant <u>difficulties / problems</u> with using blanket pesticides.

7.2   Information to help you use these words correctly

Words you probably already use correctly: *benefit, con, demotivated, difficulty, drawback, event, favourable*, fortunate, occurrence, pro, problem*.

   **The US spelling is *favorable*.

   Words defined in other sections: *austere* s6, *intangible* s6, *phenomenon* s1, *resilient* s6, *tangible* s6.

advantage *n / v* **advantageous** *adj*	*n* – A benefit.
	The advantage **of** X **is** that / X **has an** advantage **over** Y.
	There is an advantage **in / to** look**ing** after your health.
	X **gives you** the advantage **of** hav**ing** Y.
	The advantages **outweigh // negate** the disadvantages.
	The adj *advantaged* has the different meaning of 'being wealthy and/or privileged'.
	E.g. He comes from an advantaged background.

adverse *adj*	Problematic and/or harmful.
	🤝 (An) adverse **impact** // **effect** // **change** // **conditions** // **consequences** // **circumstances**.
ambience *n* **ambient** *adj*	*n* – The atmosphere and character of the immediate environment.
asset *n*	(1) A useful or advantageous thing or person.
	(2) Something owned by an organisation or person.
	🤝 To **have / own / hold** // **acquire** // **buy** // **increase** // **release** // **unfreeze** assets.
	To **dispose of** // **freeze** // **sell** // **transfer** assets.
	Tangible // **intangible** // **valuable** // **important** assets.
bode *v*	To be a sign of a good or bad result.
	🤝 X bodes **well** // **ill**.
boon *n*	(1) A benefit.
	🤝 X **is a** boon **to** Y.
circumstance *n*	The condition or fact that affects a situation.
	🤝 The circumstances **surrounding** X. **Under** difficult circumstances.
	Exceptional // **special** // **normal** // **unusual** // **unforeseen** // **challenging** / **difficult** circumstances.
demise *n*	The end, collapse or failure of something.
	🤝 To **bring about / cause / lead to** // **accelerate / hasten the** demise **of** X.
demoralised* *adj* **demoralise*** *v*	*adj* – Lacking in motivation and/or hope of improvement.
	*-ized and *-ize* are also acceptable in British spelling and are always used in US spelling.
dilemma *n*	A situation in which you are not sure what to do, particularly which option to choose.

This **presents us with a difficult** // **common** dilemma.

X **creates a** dilemma **for** …

We are **faced with the** dilemma of X**ing** or Y**ing.**

dire *adj*	Very serious and/or urgent.

In dire **circumstances** / a dire **situation.**

In dire **need of help** // **improvement.**

disadvantage *n / v* **disadvantageous** *adj*	*n* – Something that is not beneficial. *v* – To put someone into an unbeneficial situation.

A **distinct** / **definite** // **significant** // **slight** // **economic** // **political** disadvantage.

To **feel** / **be at a** disadvantage.

The disadvantages **outweigh** // **negate** the advantages.

! The adjective *disadvantaged* has the different meaning of not having social and economic status. Similar to *deprived*.

E.g. Disadvantaged areas of the country need more economic support.

discriminatory *adj* **discriminate** *v* **discrimination** *n*	*adj* – Treated differently (either favourably or unfairly) due to prejudgement. E.g. The insurance policy is discriminatory in that it favours older drivers. The apartheid regime was extremely discriminatory.

! *Discriminate* and *discrimination* can also mean 'to differentiate' and 'recognition of difference' (see section 21).

dormant *adj*	Previously but not currently active.

To **lie** / **sit** / **remain** dormant. A dormant **account** // **company** // **assets.**

equitable *adj*	Fair and/or equal.
fare *v / n*	*v* – To do or perform in a particular way. *n* – (1) Money paid for travel. (2) Food.

To fare **well** // **badly**.

! *Fare* and *fair* have the same pronunciation but are different words.

fortuitous *adj*	Happening by chance and with a beneficial outcome.
immune *adj*	Protected against. X **is** immune **to** Y.
incidence *n*	The frequency or number of times something happens. A **high** // **low** // **reported** // **estimated** // **actual** incidence. To **increase** // **reduce the** incidence **of** X. A **fall** // **rise in the** incidence **of** X. *Incide**nce*** and *incide**nt*** An *incident* is an event, usually referring to something bad such as a car crash or fight. For *incidental* and *incidentally* see section 20.
inequity *n*	Lack of fairness, equality or justice.
insulate *v* **insulated** *adj*	Protect against heat loss, sound or negative events. Similar to *protect against* and *immune to*. Insulate X **against** Y.
latent *adj*	Potentially existing but not developed or activated. Latent **talent** // **skill** // **ability**.
manifest *adj / v*	*v* – To show or become obvious. E.g. Staff resentment can manifest itself in higher absenteeism. *adj* – Clear and obvious. E.g. The report highlights the research study's manifest flaws. X manifests **itself as** Y. X manifests **itself in the form of** Y.

merit *n / v*	*n* – The value, worth, positive features or excellence of something.
	v – To be worth doing or to deserve.
	🤝 *n* – The merit **of X is** that … There **is** merit **in** doing X. X **deserves** merit.
	To **discuss** // **judge** / **assess** // **question** / **investigate** // **consider** // **compare** // the merits **of** X.
	There is **little** // **considerable** / **great** merit **in** X.
	v – X merits **investigation** // **attention** // **consideration** // **discussion** // **examination**.
nascent *adj*	New, only just starting to develop.
perplexing *adj*	Unclear, confusing, worrying.
predicament *n*	A highly problematic situation.
preferential *adj*	More favourable than the others. Similar to *advantageous*.
	🤝 Preferential **treatment** // **rights** // **rates**.
purchase *n*	(1) Something bought.
	(2) A firm hold or grip.
	🤝 To **gain** purchase **on** / **in** X.
rapport *n*	A good relationship.
	🤝 To **have** // **build** / **create** // **develop** // **establish** // **maintain** rapport.
	❗ The 't' is silent.
regime *n*	A (strict) system of rules and processes that control an organisation, area or country.
rivalry *n*	A situation in which people or organisations compete fiercely.
	🤝 Rivalry **for** X. Rivalry **between** X **and** Y.
robust *adj*	Strong.
ruinous *adj* **ruin** *v / n*	*adj* – Causing (great) harm or destruction.

shortcoming *n*	A failure, deficiency or fault.
	😦 *Shortcoming* and *disadvantage*
	These two words have different meanings (see above for *disadvantage*).
systemic *adj*	Present in all parts of the organisation or system.
	🤝 Systemic **failure** // **corruption** // **racism** // **doping** // **change**.
	😦 *System**ic*** and *system**atic***
	Systematic is when something is done carefully and thoroughly (see section 18).

7.3 Nearly but not quite right

	Incorrect	Correct
1	Being an introvert can <u>give you</u> the merit of being more responsible.	Being an introvert <u>has the</u> merit of being more responsible.
2	Research has shown that students who come from more <u>advantage</u> backgrounds are more likely to pass.	Research has shown that students who come from more <u>privileged / advantaged / advantageous</u> backgrounds are more likely to pass.
3	Employers are often unwilling to state an employee's <u>disadvantages</u> in a reference.	Employers are often unwilling to state an employee's <u>shortcomings</u> in a reference.
4	One <u>advantage to have</u> a flat structure is a more trusting work environment.	One <u>advantage of having</u> a flat structure is a more trusting work environment.
5	Discrimination can <u>be through</u> various forms.	Discrimination can <u>occur in</u> various forms. Discrimination can <u>be manifested / be expressed in</u> various <u>ways</u>.
6	It can clearly be <u>manifested</u> from the chart that the results are similar to those of previous studies.	It can clearly be <u>seen</u> from the chart that the results are similar to those of previous studies.
7	The key recommendation is that the <u>systematic</u> distrust within the organisation is addressed immediately.	The key recommendation is that the <u>systemic</u> distrust within the organisation is addressed immediately.
8	Tung (1989) showed that cultural understanding increases <u>incidents</u> of successful negotiations.	Tung (1989) showed that cultural understanding increases <u>incidences</u> of successful negotiations.
9	Someone with a Type A personality can be both an <u>asset</u> and a liability <u>for</u> a team.	Someone with a Type A personality can be both an <u>asset</u> and a liability <u>to</u> a team.
10	Our survey suggests that <u>dormant</u> talent exists in the firm and that it needs to be explored and fostered.	Our survey suggests that <u>latent</u> talent exists in the firm and that it needs to be explored and fostered.

8   Ownership, responsibility and loyalty

8.1   Words in action

Ownership, roles and responsibility

‣ Advantages of <u>proprietary</u> software over open-source platforms include add-ons and bespoke features.

‣ Non-executives act in an advisory <u>capacity</u> and <u>are</u> not <u>responsible / accountable</u> / do not <u>have responsibility / accountability</u> <u>for</u> the running of the company.

‣ Abu-Rabia Quadar and Oplatka (2008) examine the experiences of Muslim women who have <u>supervisory</u> <u>roles</u> in education.

‣ <u>It is incumbent upon</u> managers to make sure their teams follow the organisation's ethical code.

‣ I will show that in this case the employer had a <u>duty</u> of care.

‣ When <u>designating</u> Power of Attorney you need to decide whether you want it to be 'durable' or 'springing'.

‣ The <u>remit</u> of the Cabinet Office Mystery Shopper scheme is to provide a route for suppliers to raise concerns about public procurement.

Delegating, allocating and assigning

‣ We recommend that in order to improve efficiency, management take action to improve their <u>delegation</u> skills.

‣ Makisimovic and Phillips' model does not always lead to large firms <u>allocating</u> resources more efficiently.

‣ This analysis looks at the most effective ways to <u>apportion</u> rental income between husband and wife.

‣ Our research proposes a new model for <u>assigning</u> the right tasks to the right people in an organisation.

‣ If you give someone general Power of Attorney you <u>entrust</u> all personal and business affairs to that agent.

Loyalty and interests

‣ A key driver for high product quality is to build customer <u>loyalty</u>.

‣ Employees should not be made to feel that they owe some type of <u>allegiance</u> to their line manager.

‣ Because John Lewis employees are also shareholders, they have <u>a vested interest in</u> company profitability.

8.2 Information to help you use these words correctly

Words you probably already use correctly: *duty*, *loyalty*, *supervisory*.
   Words defined in other sections: *capacity* s6, *deem* s26, *remit* s2.

accountable *adj*	To be responsible for a particular action, incident or thing.
	To **be** accountable.
	To **hold** // **make** someone accountable **for** something.
	To be **fully** // **directly** // **indirectly** // **publicly** // **personally** accountable.
allegiance *n*	Loyalty and commitment to a person, group or organisation. Often used in a military context.
	Allegiance and *alliance*
	An *alliance* is a formal agreement rather than unofficial loyalty (see section 5).
allocate *v* **allocation** *n*	*v* – To reserve or assign. Usually used in the context of resources and tasks.
apportion *v*	(1) To decide who is responsible for something.
	(2) To distribute something (usually money or assets) within a group or organisation. Similar to *share out*.
	To apportion **blame to** someone.
	To apportion the assets **among** // **between** X.
assign *v*	To give a particular task or responsibility to a person or group.
	Assign, *allocate* and *apportion*
	There is overlap between all three words.
	Apportion is slightly different because it means to actually share out, whereas *allocate* and *assign* can also mean to just decide what will go where.
delegate *v / n* **delegation** *n*	*v* – To give responsibility or authority to a person or group, usually a subordinate.
	E.g. As CEO it is important to be able to delegate.
	n – The giving of responsibility or authority to a person or group, usually a subordinate.

To delegate / the delegation of **authority** // **power** // **responsibility** // **control** // **decision making** // **a job** // **a task** to X.

! For a different meaning of *a delegate* (n) and *delegation* (n) see section 5.

designate *v*	To give a particular role, position or title to someone. E.g. She has been designated Sportswoman of the Year.
entrust *v*	To give someone the responsibility for keeping or taking care of something. To be entrusted **to do** X / **with** doing X. *Entrust* and *trust* If you entrust someone with something, you might also trust them (i.e. have confidence in them) but you might not.
incumbent *adj / n*	*adj* – (1) Holding the responsibility for doing something. (2) Currently holding an official position which has a time restriction. E.g. He is the incumbent director. *n* – A person or organisation that holds a particular official position. It is incumbent **upon** the board **to** X.
liability *n* **liable** *adj*	*n* – (1) A legal responsibility for something. (2) The amount of money an organisation/ person owes. *adj* – Is likely to (see section 30). *n* – To **admit** / **deny** liability. **Listed** liabilities. *v* – To **be (held)** liable **for** something.
proprietary *adj* **proprietor** *n*	*adj* – (1) Relating to ownership. (2) Having the name of the company on the product. A proprietary **brand** // **product** // **make** // **drug** // **medicine**.
vested interest *n*	A particular interest in something because you benefit from it.

8.3 Nearly but not quite right

	Incorrect	Correct
1	She is the <u>proprietary owner</u> of the retail outlet.	She is the <u>proprietor / owner</u> of the retail outlet.
2	The shop-floor assistants are <u>responsible for</u> their section managers.	The shop-floor assistants are <u>responsible to</u> their section managers.
3	I recommend that the manager <u>delegates</u> the job of answering client queries a suitable member of her team.	I recommend that the manager <u>delegates</u> the job of answering client queries <u>to</u> a suitable member of her team.
4	Brand <u>loyalties are</u> an established goal of advertising.	Brand <u>loyalty is</u> an established goal of advertising.
5	Property title deeds are usually <u>trusted</u> to the mortgage company or owners' solicitor.	Property title deeds are usually <u>entrusted</u> to the mortgage company or owners' solicitor.
6	A willingness to customise helps new customers <u>entrust</u> an online company (Koufaris and Hampton-Sosa 2004).	A willingness to customise helps new customers <u>trust</u> an online company (Koufaris and Hampton-Sosa 2004).
7	'Allocation of overheads' is the process of <u>portioning out</u> overheads to particular cost centres.	'Allocation of overheads' is the process of <u>apportioning / assigning</u> overheads to particular cost centres.
8	I support the argument that bank directors should <u>have personal liable</u> if they have not conducted rigorous checks for solvency risk.	I support the argument that bank directors should <u>be personally liable / have personal liability</u> if …
9	Section managers are <u>accountable to</u> their respective shop-floor assistants.	Section managers are <u>accountable for</u> their respective shop-floor assistants.
10	A supplier in a competitive market needs to build client <u>alliance</u>.	A supplier in a competitive market needs to build client <u>allegiance</u>.

9 Regulations, legalities and penalties

9.1 Words in action

Regulations and conditions

▸ It is important for a <u>regulator</u> to have a framework for the 'parameters of blame'; that is, its tolerance limits for failures by the firms it <u>regulates</u> (Black 2006).

▸ This report summarises <u>the legalities</u> of setting up as sole trader, and looks at how to avoid common pitfalls.

▸ The agreement of both houses of the Japanese parliament are required to <u>ratify / validate</u> a treaty.

▸ The <u>requisite / required</u> number of members is <u>prescribed / stipulated / set down / laid down</u> in its governing documents.

▸ UK contract law <u>stipulates</u> that if an asset used in a business belongs to an individual, personal <u>liability</u> exists as to that asset.

▸ When setting up a limited liability partnership, it is <u>mandatory</u> to have an LLP agreement with all members.

▸ In 2001 a Canadian appeals court upheld a city <u>edict</u> requiring owners of new hotels to keep current employees for at least three months.

▸ Entities dealing with personal data are <u>under an obligation</u> to <u>adhere to / abide by</u> data protection principles.

▸ Any organisation that deals with individual personal data is <u>bound by</u> the eight 'data protection principles'.

▸ A contract is <u>binding</u> once signed and dated by all relevant parties.

▸ Local producers are <u>constrained</u> by contract to deliver produce to the restaurant within 24 hours of harvesting.

▸ According to financial experts, the cost of banking <u>compliance</u> failure increased by over 300% in 2012.

▸ All electrical equipment manufacturers must <u>comply with</u> the 1994 Electrical Equipment (Safety) Regulations.

▸ Dutch tenancy contracts contain the <u>proviso</u> that tenants must adhere to waste recycling protocols.

▸ Measuring customer-perceived value should be a <u>prerequisite</u> of any marketing strategy (Ulaga and Chacour 2001, Eggert and Ulaga 2002, McDougall and Levesque 2000).

Allowed

▸ In the US, the government is <u>sanctioned / permitted / allowed / licensed</u> to take private land for public purposes under 'eminent domain' powers.

▸ T... ...it ... this case has given / granted permission to build on the land.

▸ T... ...missive agreements between states.

▸ ... up to £2,000 a year off their National Insurance

▸ ... corporation tax if they conduct no business in that

▸ ... income and expenditure.

▸ ...n / scope to challenge the board's proposals.

▸ ...retionary monetary policy tend to depend on

... not have permission / do not have license to share
...otection Act.

...y the Data Protection Act.

...ned from running / forbidden to run businesses.

...temic irregularities and misconduct / illicit behaviour.

...regulations if they do not keep themselves informed of

▸ The evidence ... isregarded / ignored health and safety regulations / rules.

▸ In Campbell vs DPD, the media's defence was based on infringement of freedom of speech legislation.

▸ I would not recommend using a different builder as this would invalidate the / break the / be a breach of contract.

▸ In the 1970s Ford was accused of negligence arising from deaths of passengers driving Ford Pintos.

Penalties

▸ Since 2015, US hospitals have incurred penalties // sanctions if they fail to meet the 'meaningful use' criteria.

▸ Since 2015, punitive measures have been in place for US hospitals that do not meet 'meaningful use' criteria.

- Employers who contravene the new regulations will be <u>sanctioned</u>.
- In the UK, convicted prisoners <u>forfeit</u> their right to vote, legislation that was upheld by the EU court in 2015.
- The UK government publishes details of current trade <u>sanctions</u> and <u>embargoes</u>.

Enforcement and external force

- I have argued that the <u>enforcement</u> of the Basel II regulations was one cause of the global banking crisis.
- This essay will discuss the <u>sanctions against</u> energy and other companies <u>imposed on</u> Russia by the EU.
- In weaker sectors, self-employment is in reality <u>forced upon / forced on / foisted upon</u> some people rather than being a choice.
- Over the last decade, European energy companies have <u>come under</u> increasing customer <u>pressure</u> to produce green energy (Wustenhagen and Bilharz 2006, Wiser et al. 2001, Wiser 1998).
- Our remit was to investigate managerial communication strategies to check for <u>coercive</u> behaviour.
- As Li (2015) suggests, perceived powerlessness and political exclusion have led to levels of <u>extortion</u> in southern transnational farmland deals.

9.2 Information to help you use these words correctly

Words you probably already use correctly: *allow, ban, embargo, freedom, ignore, legality, misconduct, permission, permit, pressure, regulate, regulation, rule.*

Words defined in other sections: *adhere* s23, *capacity* s6, *constrain* s11, *disregard* s25, *liability* s8, *mandate* s8, *parameter* s11, *protocol* s18, *restricted* s11, *scope* s2.

abide *v*	Act in accordance with.
	🤝 Abide **by the rules / regulations / the law**.
bind *v*	*v* – To impose a legal / contractual obligation.
binding *adj*	🤝 *v* – To **be** bound **by X. X is legally** binding.
	adj – A (legally) binding **agreement // contract // commitment**.
breach *v / n*	*v* – (1) To break or fail to follow a law or regulation.
	(2) To make a gap in, e.g. The bomb breached the wall.

	n – A breaking or failure to follow a law or regulation.
	v – To breach **copyright** // **a contract** // **a law** // **the regulations**.
	n – To **be in** breach **of** X.
	A breach **in trust** // **in confidence** // **in communication**.
coerce *v* **coercion** *n*	*v* – To get someone to do something using threats and/or force.
compliance *n* **comply** *v*	*n* – The obligation to obey regulations, legislation or a particular agreement.
	n – Compliance **procedures** // **standards** // **costs**.
	v – To comply **with** something.
contravene *v*	To go against or break a regulation, law or principle.
discretion *n* **discretionary** *adj*	*n* – (1) The freedom to decide.
	(2) Tactfulness (see section 6).
	adj – Available to be used or done if the user wishes.
	n – To **use your** discretion **in deciding** X.
	The decision was **left to our** discretion.
	The choice is **at your** discretion.
	adj – Discretionary **policy** // **power** // **funds** // **spending** / **expenditure** // **benefits** // **bonuses** // **payments**.
edict *n*	An order or ruling given by an official body.
eligible *adj* **eligibility** *n*	*adj* – Having permission to do or have something because you meet the required conditions.
	Eligible **for** X. Eligible **to** (do) Y.
enforce *v*	To make sure that a regulation, piece of legislation or restriction is obeyed.
	To **rigorously** // **strictly** // **fully** enforce.
	To enforce **(a) law** / **piece of legislation** // **standards** // **rule** // **ban** // **embargo** // **restriction** // **sanction**.

exempt *v* **exemption** *n*	*v* – To not have to do, pay or follow a regulation. 🤝 To be exempt **from** X.
extort *v*	To get something (usually money) from someone by threats, blackmail or force. 😕 *Extort* and *exhort* To *exhort* is to strongly encourage or persuade someone to do something.
flout *v*	To purposely and openly ignore or break a regulation or law.
foist *v*	To make someone accept something they don't want. 😕 *Foist* and *force* There is overlap but *foist* is used only when something is forced on someone. *Force* is a more general and common word used for both things and actions.
forbid *v*	To not allow or order not to do. 🤝 To forbid someone **to do** X. Y is forbidden **from** doing X.
forfeit *v / n*	*v* – To lose something (e.g. money, rights) as a penalty for breaking a regulation or law. ❗ In finance, *forfeiting* has a different, specialised meaning.
grant *v / n*	*v* – To officially give or allow. 🤝 To grant **a loan // mortgage // licence // patent // an extension // an injunction**.
illicit *adj*	Forbidden by law. Illegal.
impose *v*	To introduce a rule, regulation, restriction or law. 🤝 To impose **a ban // restriction // sanction // penalty // fine // punishment // tax / levy** on X. To impose **a deadline // condition // constraint // requirement**.
incur *v*	To have to pay or lose money as a result of doing something. 🤝 To incur **costs // a charge // a fine // a fee // a tax // a penalty**.

infringe *v* **infringement** *n*	*v* – (1) To break the law. (2) To weaken or damage things such as rights, freedoms, lands or borders.
invalidate *v* **invalid** *adj*	*v* – (1) To cause something to lose its legality or validity. (2) To disprove.
irregularity *n* **irregular** *adj*	*n* – (1) Where things are not being done in the correct or expected way. (2) Something that is not legal. (3) Something not regular in form.
latitude *n*	(1) Freedom or permission to do something. (2) The measurement of angular distance in relation to the equator.
leeway *n*	The available amount of freedom to move or act.
licence* *n* **license** *v* **licensed** *adj*	*n* – (1) An official document giving permission to do or own something. (2) The freedom to do something. *v* – To give someone permission to do, have, make or sell something. *The US spelling for both the noun and verb is -se.
mandate *n / v* **mandatory** *adj*	*n* – (1) An official order to do something. (2) Official permission to do something, usually by winning a vote. (3) The time period (term) of an elected person.
negligent *adj* **negligence** *n*	*adj* – Not giving enough care and attention to a legal responsibility.
obligation *n* **obligatory** *adj*	*n* – Something you are legally, morally or socially required to do.
permissive *adj*	Allowed but not obligatory. Often used in the context of laws, regulations and agreements.
prerequisite *n*	*n* – Something that must exist before something else is possible. An **essential** // **necessary** // **key** / **basic** / **fundamental** prerequisite.

prescribe *v*	To recommend or tell someone what to do or how to do something.
prohibit *v*	Not allowed by law.
	🤝 Prohibited **from** do**ing** X. X **is** prohibited (by Y).
proscribe *v*	To forbid by regulation or law.
	🙁 *Pro*scribe and *pre*scribe
	These words have almost opposite meanings. See *prescribe* above.
proviso *n*	A clause in a legal document that states what must be done.
	🤝 **With the** proviso **that** …
	🙁 *Proviso* and *caveat*
	A *caveat* is a warning (see section 27).
punitive *adj* **punitively** *adv*	*adj* – (1) Of costs or fines, so high that they are difficult to pay, e.g. A punitive tax.
	(2) Relating to a punishment.
	🤝 To **impose** punitive **costs** // **damages**.
	To **impose** / **make a** punitive **award against** someone.
	To **take** punitive **action** / **measures against** someone.
ratify *v* **ratification** *n*	*v* – To give formal agreement and make official.
	🤝 To ratify **a contract** // **an agreement** // **a treaty** // **a bill** / **a law** // **legislation**.
sanction *n* / *v*	*n* – An official order to limit or stop trade or communication with another state.
	v – (1) In law, to punish someone for doing something.
	(2) To officially give approval or permission.
	❗ Note the different and almost opposite meanings between the noun / verb (1) in which sanctions are a form of punishment, and verb (2) where 'to sanction' is to give approval or permission.

stipulate *v* **stipulation** *n*	*v* – To state exactly what is required. *n* – A statement of exactly what is required. 🤝 The **regulations** // **law** // **contract** // **instructions** // **standards** // **policy** stipulate(s) that …
valid *adj* **validate** *v*	*adj* – (1) Legal. (2) Logically justified or supported by evidence (see section 24).

9.3 Nearly but not quite right

	Incorrect	Correct
1	In the 1990s some aspects of the Danish social housing sector <u>had pressure</u>.	In the 1990s some aspects of the Danish social housing sector <u>were under pressure</u>.
2	Two members of staff were disciplined for <u>irregularity</u> towards a disabled colleague.	Two members of staff were disciplined for <u>misconduct</u> towards a disabled colleague.
3	The consultation paper recommends that accountants who help clients exploit tax avoidance schemes should <u>get</u> a <u>bigger</u> penalty than currently.	The consultation paper recommends that accountants who help clients exploit tax avoidance schemes should <u>incur / receive</u> a <u>stricter / harsher / higher</u> penalty than currently.
4	I have demonstrated that the loan <u>misconducts</u> were due to the new risk management software systems.	I have demonstrated that the loan <u>irregularities</u> were due to the new risk management software systems.
5	My data suggests that the organisation's new marketing strategy will indeed lead to increased sales, with the <u>proviso</u> that the data is provisional and still needs further analysis.	My data suggests that the organisation's new marketing strategy will indeed lead to increased sales, with the <u>caveat</u> that the data is provisional and still needs further analysis.
6	US antitrust laws <u>prescribe</u> 'unfair' practices such as price-fixing and large corporate mergers.	US antitrust laws <u>proscribe</u> 'unfair' practices such as price-fixing and large corporate mergers.
7	Lipman and Hall (2015) discuss whether CEOs should <u>have sanctions</u> for events or practices beyond their control.	Lipman and Hall (2015) discuss whether CEOs should <u>be sanctioned</u> for events or practices beyond their control.
8	This essay examines the implications of <u>exempting</u> multinationals' foreign profits <u>to</u> domestic taxation.	This essay examines the implications of <u>exempting</u> multinationals' foreign profits <u>from</u> domestic taxation.
9	The construction firm has <u>gained permission by</u> the local authority to build on the site.	The construction firm has <u>gained permission from / been granted permission by</u> the local authority to build on the site.
10	The tenant <u>breached</u> his rental agreement and was subsequently evicted.	The tenant <u>was in breach of / broke</u> his rental agreement and was subsequently evicted.

10 Encouragement, discouragement, avoidance, prevention, counteraction and elimination

10.1 Words in action

Encouraging

▸ RIBA educational boards <u>encourage / foster</u> innovation in how architecture is taught.

▸ Irwin (2015) examines the proposition that a growth in trade <u>is conducive to / promotes</u> social welfare.

▸ Better catering facilities and office environment will give staff a <u>boost</u> and increase job satisfaction.

▸ We recommend that the owners set up an '<u>incentives</u> and perks scheme' for employees.

▸ The 2016 Adante report suggests that importers would be <u>spurred on</u> if the currency was strengthened.

▸ The tax commissioner <u>urged</u> Ireland to drop its objections to multinationals filing a single European tax return.

▸ I argue that international charities <u>reinforce</u> negative stereotypes of African societies.

Discouraging and deterring

▸ We have demonstrated that hierarchical structures <u>discourage</u> innovation.

▸ According to Green (2015), the lack of available 4D film content is a <u>deterrent</u> to customers and has <u>hindered / impeded / hampered</u> sales.

▸ This essay will look at how austerity measures <u>deter / hinder / impede / inhibit</u> economic growth.

▸ The cost of making a house fully energy-efficient can be <u>prohibitive</u>.

Preventing

▸ <u>Preventing</u> or reducing workplace stress is crucial for both individual health and corporate productivity.

▸ In 2013 the EU competition commission <u>blocked / obstructed</u> Ryanair's bid to take over Aer Lingus.

▸ The protesters claimed they were <u>denied</u> access to legal representation.

▸ The method we used did <u>not enable // not permit / not allow</u> us to analyse each organisation separately.

▸ Employers are <u>forbidden to</u> charge employees for health or safety equipment.

Avoiding and the unavoidable

▸ A shell company allows the owner to move money through it and so <u>avoid (paying) / evade</u> taxes.

▸ Assunta (2004) looks at how tobacco companies <u>circumvented</u> Singapore's ban on cigarette advertising.

- Developing countries need to <u>avert / prevent</u> 'brain-drain' to places with efficient, skilled high production capability (Marchiori et al. 2013).
- Some business outgoings, such as sunk costs, are <u>unavoidable</u>.
- A funding decrease next year seems <u>inevitable</u>.

Cancelling out, counteracting and eliminating

- For any project the overall costs should not <u>cancel out / negate / nullify</u> benefits gained.
- We recommend that the company increases its advertising in order to <u>counteract</u> falling sales.
- A business can get tax relief by <u>offsetting</u> a trading loss against other gains in the same accounting period.
- According to the ILO, judging someone on ability rather than 'irrelevant characteristics' is key to <u>eliminating / eradicating</u> discrimination in the workplace.
- Translation technology may soon <u>obviate / eliminate</u> the business need for learning foreign languages.
- One aim of the government report is to <u>dispel</u> rumours of divisions within the party.

10.2   Information to help you use these words correctly

Words you probably already use correctly: *avoid, block, deny, discourage, enable, encourage, obstruct, prevent, promote*. Words defined in other sections: *forbid s9*.

avert *v*	To prevent something bad from happening.
	To (**narrowly**) avert (a) **catastrophe / disaster // conflict // crisis // strike // war**.
	! The noun *aversion* has the different meaning of a strong dislike.
	E.g. I have an aversion to fish.
boost *n / v*	*n* – An action or event that encourages, increases or improves something else.
	v – To increase or improve.
	v – X boosts Y.
	n – To **give // get // receive a** boost **from** X. X **gives** Y a boost.
circumvent *v*	To get round something and obtain your goal by a different means. Often used in the context of regulations and laws.

conducive *adj*	Making something easier / nicer to do or more likely to happen.
	🤝 X is conducive **to** Y.
counteract *v*	To do something in order to reduce the effects of something else.
deter *v*	*v* – To discourage, make something unlikely or prevent.
deterrent *n*	🤝 To deter X **from** doing Y.
dispel *v*	To make a rumour, belief, doubt or feeling cease to exist.
	😟 *Dispel*, *expel* and *disperse*
	To expel means to drive out by force.
	To disperse means to scatter or spread over a wide area (see section 14).
eliminate *v*	*v* – To completely remove something that is not needed or wanted.
elimination *n*	🤝 To eliminate **completely** // **systematically** // **effectively** // **permanently** // **successfully**.
	To eliminate **the need for** X. To eliminate **poverty** // **debt** // **war**.
eradicate *v*	To remove or destroy completely, particularly in the context of disease and animal populations. Similar to *eliminate*.
	🤝 To eradicate **disease** // **a virus** // **a pest**.
evade *v*	*v* – To purposely avoid something you don't want to talk about or do.
evasion *n*	🤝 To evade **the issue** // **the question** // **taxes** // **fees**.
foster *v*	To encourage, nurture or develop something.
	🤝 To foster **collaboration** // **cooperation** // **partnership** // **relations** // **growth** // **development** // **learning** // **creativity**.
hamper *v*	To delay or obstruct movement or progress. Similar to *disrupt*, *hinder*, *impede* and *obstruct*.
	🤝 To hamper **attempts** // **development** // **efforts** // **growth** // **progress** // **performance** // **movement** // **communication** // **understanding** // **recovery**.

hinder *v* **hindrance** *n*	*v* – To delay or obstruct movement or progress. Similar to *disrupt*, *impede* and *obstruct*. 🤝 As for *hamper* above.
impede *v*	To delay or obstruct movement or progress. Similar to *disrupt*, *hamper, hinder* and *obstruct*. 🤝 As for *hamper* above.
impetus *n*	Something which provides motivation for something else to happen more quickly. 🤝 X **provides** / **acts as** / **serves as an** impetus **for** Y. The **initial** / **original** impetus **for** X **was** // **came from** Y.
incentive *n* **incentivise*** *v*	*n* – Something that encourages someone to do something. 🤝 A **financial** incentive. An incentive **package** // **scheme**. To **offer** // **create** // **act as** an incentive. To **have no** // **little** incentive **to do** X. **-ize* is also acceptable in British spelling and is always used in US spelling.
inevitable *adj*	Certain to happen, usually relating to an unavoidable event or end result.
inhibit *v* **inhibitive/ory** *adj*	*v* – (1) To delay or obstruct. Similar to *disrupt*, *hamper, hinder* and *obstruct*. (2) To make someone self-conscious and unable to act. 🤝 As for *hamper* above.
negate *v* **negation** *n*	*v* – To cancel out. Similar to *nullify*.
nullify *v* **nullification** *n*	*v* – To cancel out. Similar to *negate*.
obviate *v*	(1) To remove the need for something. E.g. Mobile networks obviate the need for wired services. (2) To prevent or avoid. 🤝 To obviate **the need for** X.

offset *v*	To balance one effect with another so that the outcome does not greatly differ.
prohibitive *adj*	(1) Of a price, so high as to discourage or prevent something being bought or done.
	(2) Of legislation or regulations, forbidding or restricting something (see section 9).
spur *v / n*	*v* – To encourage.
	n – (1) An encouragement or incentive.
	(2) A small metal device on a rider's heel used to make a horse go faster.
	To spur someone **on** (to do X).
urge *v / n*	*v* – To strongly encourage or try to persuade.
	n – A strong desire to do something.

10.3   Nearly but not quite right

	Incorrect	Correct
1	Being a member of the House of Representatives _inhibits_ you from standing for Senate.	Being a member of the House of Representatives _excludes / prevents_ you from standing for Senate.
2	Philip Morris and other companies _avoided_ Singapore's advertising laws and promoted their products successfully.	Philip Morris and other companies _circumvented_ Singapore's advertising laws and promoted their products successfully.
3	The aim of the publicity campaign is to _disperse_ public fears about negative health effects of eating red meat.	The aim of the publicity campaign is to _dispel_ public fears about negative health effects of eating red meat.
4	The report claims that an 8–10% increase in energy efficiency will _obviate_ new power plants.	The report claims that an 8–10% increase in energy efficiency will _obviate the need for_ new power plants.
5	Private space travel companies assume it is _inexorable_ that industry will one day want to mine on other planets.	Private space travel companies assume it is _inevitable_ that industry will one day want to mine on other planets.
6	South Africa's new visa requirement are aimed at _counter acting_ child trafficking.	South Africa's new visa requirement are aimed at _counteracting_ child trafficking.
7	The new legislation will foster _employing_ immigrants.	The new legislation will foster _the employment of_ immigrants.
8	I discuss whether selling valuable assets is an effective way of _diverting_ bankruptcy.	I discuss whether selling valuable assets is an effective way of _averting / avoiding_ bankruptcy.
9	I suggest that the amount of investment needed for large-scale direct air capture is currently _deterring_.	I suggest that the amount of investment needed for large-scale direct air capture is currently _a deterrent / prohibitive_.
10	Communication and consultation can _be conductive to_ organisational change.	Communication and consultation can _be conducive to / facilitate_ organisational change.

11 Norms, limits, inclusion and exclusion

11.1 Words in action

Normality, norms, conformity and deviance

▸ It is <u>normal</u> business practice for a company to have external auditors.

▸ Webley (2014) addresses the need for universal <u>norms</u> of ethical behaviour in international business.

▸ We analyse examples of where <u>normative</u> business behaviour has become codified into law.

▸ Business writing <u>conventions</u> include a direct style which is not overly formal and avoidance of buzzwords.

▸ Studies suggest that top business leaders do not always <u>conform to</u> the image of the charismatic extrovert.

▸ <u>Abnormal</u> behaviour is defined as that which not only <u>deviates from</u> the norm but which is also undesirable.

Limits, limitations and restrictions

▸ An interest rate cap <u>puts a limit on / limits</u> the rate of interest for the agreed period.

▸ The main <u>limitation of</u> market research data is that it can never be accurate, as people tend to act artificially when asked questions.

▸ The accuracy of market research data <u>is limited</u>, as people tend to act artificially when asked questions.

▸ In 2016 the Australian government reduced immigration <u>quotas</u> for auditors and accountants by 50%.

▸ An important <u>parameter</u> for a contract management platform is the requirement profile of the organisation.

▸ Owing to time <u>constraints</u> we were only able to repeat the test once.

▸ The way in which small businesses distribute profit is <u>constrained by</u> legislation.

▸ Our report argues that austerity measures do not <u>restrict / curtail / curb</u> spending in the long term.

▸ An embargo is a form of government-induced <u>restriction</u> on international trade.

▸ Montgomery (2016) argues that 'macroeconomic policy should <u>confine</u> itself to maintaining stability'.

Boundaries

▸ The <u>boundary / demarcation</u> between what constitutes a small as opposed to a medium business varies somewhat between countries.

▸ This paper examines whether some tax revenue should be <u>ring-fenced</u> for public health care programmes.

- I recommend emphasising the USP of the product in order to limit market <u>encroachment</u> by competitors.
- This report examines how online advertising softens or even eliminates a clear customer interest <u>threshold</u>.

Including, excluding, marginalising and keeping separate

- In 2014, G20 member representatives endorsed a proposal to start developing a framework on <u>inclusive</u> private sector business practices.
- We found that openly homosexual employees were regularly <u>excluded from</u> senior management posts.
- <u>The exclusion of</u> women from the national team was questioned in Parliament.
- A mutually <u>exclusive</u> investment is when investing in one project necessitates the rejection of another.
- Being a member of the House of Representatives <u>precludes</u> them from standing for Senate.
- This case study looks at protective legislation for <u>marginalised</u> indigenous communities in Nepal.
- <u>Segregation</u> of duties reduces risk of fraud, as at least two people are responsible for the separate parts of any task.

11.2   Information to help you use these words correctly

Words you probably already use correctly: *boundary, normal, quota, ring-fence, separate.*

confine *v* **confined** *adj*	*v* – To keep something within certain limits. *adj* – Of a space, small or cramped. X confines **itself to** Y. To **be** confined **to** Y.
conform *v* **conformity** *n*	*v* – (1) To behave according to generally accepted social standards or other types of expectation. (2) To be similar to an already established type, form or idea. E.g. The restaurant conforms to people's idea of a family business.

constrain *v* **constraint** *n*	*v* – To force someone to do something in a particular way due to contractual or time restrictions. *n* – Something that controls, limits or restricts what you can do. *v* – X **is** constrained **by** Y. *n* – X **places** / **puts a** constraint **on** Y. To be **under (severe / strict) time** // **economic** // **budget** // **financial** // **time** constraints. To work **within financial** // **economic** // **legal** // **time** // **budgetary** constraints.
convention *n*	(1) The accepted way something is done. (2) An agreement between countries, usually less formal than a treaty. (3) In the US, a type of large conference.
curb *v / n*	*v* – To restrict or limit, often via the use of force or legislation. Similar to *curtail*. To curb one's **anger** // **temper** // **violence** // **freedom** // **growth** // **spending** // **inflation** // **crime**.
curtail *v* **curtailment** *n*	*v* – To restrict or limit, often via the use of force or legislation. Similar to *curb*. To curtail **freedom** // **growth** // **spending** // **inflation** // **crime**.
demarcation *n* **demarcate** *v*	*n* – The dividing line between things, ideas or concepts.
deviate *v* **deviation** *n*	*v* – To move away from common or accepted standards, values or behaviour.
encroach *v* **encroachment** *n*	*v* – To cross into someone else's territory or go beyond accepted social boundaries. To encroach **on** someone else's **territory** // **privacy**.

exclude *v* **exclusion** *n* **exclusive** *adj*	*v* – To keep or rule out. *adj* – (1) Keeping out other things. (2) Restricted to a particular person, group or area.
include *v* **inclusion** *n* **inclusive** *adj*	*v* – To contain or allow. *adj* – (1) Containing or allowing all elements of a group.
limit *n / v*	*n* – The furthest extent or boundary that is allowed or is possible. *v* – To restrict.
limitation *n*	(1) A rule, restriction or situation that restricts something. (2) A failing or deficiency. E.g. The proposal is generally good but it does have limitations.
limited *adj*	(1) Restricted in some way. (2) Of people, narrow-minded or lacking in ability.
marginalise* *v* **marginal** *adj* **marginally** *adv* **marginalisation*** *n*	*v* – To treat as unimportant or of low status or to exclude. Often used in the passive voice. E.g. The group was marginalised because of its religion. *adj* – (1) A very small amount or effect. (2) Not important, minor or excluded, e.g. A marginal political faction. (3) Unclear or disputed, e.g. A marginal territory. **!** *Marginal* has other specialised meanings in accounting and economics. *-*ize* and -*ization* are also acceptable in British spelling and are always used in US spelling.

norm *n* **normative** *adj*	*n* – The prescribed or generally accepted behaviour, standard or situation. *adj* – (1) Typical, prescribed or generally accepted. (2) A statement based on a value judgement rather than fact. 🤝 The **established** // **expected** // **prevailing** // **traditional** norm. A **cultural** // **social** // **religious** norm.
parameter *n*	(1) The specifications or facts that limit and shape what can be done. (2) A measurable quality or value. 🤝 To **set** // **define** // **establish** // **determine** the parameters. To **change** / **adjust** / **modify** // **vary** the parameters. To **fall** // **operate** / **work within the (specified)** parameters. **Broad** // **clear** // **general** // **financial** // **investment** parameters. **Certain** / **specific** // **specified** // **broad** // **strict** parameters. 😞 *Parameter* and *perimeter* A *perimeter* is the outer edge of a prison, field or other delineated area.
preclude *v*	To prevent and exclude the possibility of something else happening. *Preclude* describes a cause–effect relationship. 😞 *Preclude* and *exclude* These can sometimes be interchanged but *preclude* has a narrower meaning, as X must exist first in order to preclude Y.

restrict *v* **restriction** *n* **restricted** *adj1* **restrictive** *adj2*	*v* – To limit or prevent from increasing. *n* – An official, external limit or control. *adj1* – Limited or controlled, usually by external factors, e.g. A restricted market. *adj2* – Describing the thing that states and imposes restrictions, e.g. A restrictive clause in a contract. 🤝 *v* – To restrict **access to** X. To restrict **the sale // supply // use // number of** X. To restrict **yourself to** X. *n* – To **impose / place / put** restrictions **on** X. To **ease // lift // tighten** restrictions **on** X. *adj1* – Restricted **goods // services // supply // shares // stocks // securities**. *adj2* – Restrictive **laws // measures // policies // conditions // practices**.
segregation *n* **segregate** *v*	*n* – Forced separation from another / other groups. 🤝 *n* – **Racial // gender // ethnic // social // religious** segregation. To **resist // challenge // encourage // enforce // ensure // maintain // promote** segregation. *v* – To segregate X **from** Y.
threshold *n*	The level or point at which something starts to happen, change or move on to the next stage. 🤝 To **increase / raise // reach // lower** the threshold. To **be on the** threshold **of** becom**ing // doing // discover**ing X. An **income // insurance // salary // pain** threshold. A threshold **effect // price**.

11.3   Nearly but not quite right

	Incorrect	Correct
1	The regulations state that the term of office for trustees <u>has a limit of</u> three years.	The regulations state that the term of office for trustees is <u>limited to</u> three years.
2	I firstly summarise the impact of smoking <u>constraints</u> on the US restaurant business.	I firstly summarise the impact of smoking <u>restrictions</u> on the US restaurant business.
3	KPMG has introduced 'glide time' which allows staff to set some of their own work-home time <u>limits.</u>	KPMG has introduced 'glide time' which allows staff to set some of their own work-home time <u>parameters.</u>
4	Type B people are less <u>likely to deviation from</u> instructions yet can also be innovative.	Type B people are less likely <u>to deviate from</u> instructions yet can also be innovative.
5	A wealth of studies (Wang and Juslin 2009, Chen 2004, Chow 2004 and others) show that ancient <u>conventions</u> heavily influence current Asian management systems.	A wealth of studies (Wang and Juslin 2009, Chen 2004, Chow 2004 and others) show that ancient <u>traditions</u> heavily influence current Asian management systems.
6	To sustain <u>encroachment in the market,</u> a new product needs to have superior performance, features and perceived value for money.	To sustain market <u>encroachment,</u> a new product needs to have superior performance, features and perceived value for money.
7	Our strategy focuses on <u>segregating</u> consumers into groups according to their knowledge of the product.	Our strategy focuses on <u>separating / dividing</u> consumers into groups according to their knowledge of the product.
8	MUJI's <u>inclusion</u> development impact policy started with sourcing felt products from small suppliers in Kenya and Kyrgyzstan.	MUJI's <u>inclusive</u> development impact policy started with sourcing felt products from small suppliers in Kenya and Kyrgyzstan.
9	There are <u>limitations as to</u> how many staff we can train at any one time.	There are <u>limits as to</u> how many staff we can train at any one time.
10	I recommend that the retailer <u>confines</u> to opening only one new store in the area rather than three.	I recommend that the retailer <u>confines / limits itself to</u> opening only one new store in the area rather than three.

12 Risks, threats, disputes and resolution

12.1 Words in action

Risks and threats

▸ Managers who make important decisions without explanation <u>risk</u> alienat<u>ing</u> their employees.

▸ George, Ping and Donglin (2015) conclude that businesses with a 'high capital structure' are more <u>exposed to / vulnerable to / prone to (the risk of) / susceptible to / carry the risk of / at risk of</u> having future cash flow problems.

▸ A new competitor can <u>put at risk / put in jeopardy / jeopardise</u> the market share built up by other businesses.

▸ EU regulations and associated penalties for non-compliance can <u>be damaging to</u> US companies.

▸ Technological changes can <u>pose / be a threat to</u> small businesses that cannot afford new software platforms.

▸ This report examines how the 'deep web' economy might be <u>threatening</u> legitimate business sectors.

▸ When crowdfunding first arrived, the UK financial regulator gave what James (2016) calls an '<u>ominous</u>' warning about the dangers of this new phenomenon.

Disruption and disputes

▸ Dual role positions can <u>interfere with / disrupt</u> the smooth running of an organisation (Hyde et al. 2009).

▸ The strike by British Airways staff in 2011 caused severe <u>disruption</u> and cost over £150 million.

▸ Perceptions of unfair pay awards can <u>cause / create / sew</u> discord among staff.

▸ Inequity of pay between genders remains a <u>divisive</u> issue in many organisations.

▸ Plans for the filming of *The Hobbit* exacerbated an already <u>acrimonious / rancorous</u> dispute between the union for New Zealand actors and the film industry body.

▸ Winterson and Winterson (1989) examine the build-up to the <u>hostilities</u> of the 1984–85 UK miners' strike.

▸ When crowdfunding first gained purchase in the UK, the financial regulator gave it what James (2016 p. 2) calls '<u>hostile</u> pronouncements'.

▸ Our remit was to examine the reasons for the <u>adversarial</u> relationship between some regional branches.

▸ The government has become the <u>adversary</u> of some local councils over applications for shale gas wells.

- The US Psychological Society advises employees to 'discuss your concerns – not <u>confront</u> your boss' (2014 p. 2).
- I will look at case studies where in fact a <u>confrontational</u> approach has been productive.
- The government has stated clearly its intention to 'deliver shale' but local councils so far remain <u>intransigent</u>.
- The article criticises the government's <u>rigid / inflexible</u> <u>stance / position</u> / <u>intransigence</u> on strike action.
- A <u>deadlock</u> is when both sides remain <u>entrenched</u> in their positions.

Negotiation, agreement and resolution

- Preliminary findings show that most parties would welcome more support at both the start and end of <u>negotiations</u>.
- The union has asked to <u>negotiate</u> with the board to reach a <u>settlement</u> and <u>resolve</u> any remaining issues.
- I propose that the government's new planning guidelines are intended to give them <u>leverage</u> in deciding on large-scale planning applications.
- Strong's 2014 survey looks at <u>mediation</u> and <u>conciliation</u> in the international legal and business sectors.
- This essay has presented evidence to show that professional Chinese <u>intermediaries</u> play an important role in <u>settling disputes between</u> national companies and foreign investors. Such intermediaries are able to <u>intervene</u> and bring the dispute before the relevant official.
- The industrial <u>arbitration</u> process aims to <u>reconcile</u> the parties and obviate the need for court action.
- The parties are empowered to choose the <u>arbitrator / arbiter</u>, thereby feeling more in control of the process and more likely to <u>abide by</u> the decisions.
- The staff member <u>conceded</u> that he had lied about his reasons for taking compassionate leave.
- The Steve Jobs emails, released in 2013, demonstrate that he was not <u>amenable to / willing to / inclined to / disposed to</u> <u>make / open to making</u> <u>any concessions on</u> the pricing of ebooks.
- According to the industrial press (December 2014), discoveries of gas in the Eastern Mediterranean are helping to hasten a <u>rapprochement</u> between Greece and Turkey.
- In the strike process, majority rather than <u>unanimous</u> support is sufficient for initiating strike action.
- Management decided to hold a series of meetings in order <u>to reach</u> <u>an agreement / a consensus</u> on next steps.

12.2   Information to help you use these words correctly

Words you probably already use correctly: *agreement, damaging, harmful, inflexible, interfere, negotiate, risk, threat, unanimous.*

Words defined in other sections: *abide s9, amenable s6, rigid s6.*

acrimonious *adj* **acrimony** *n* **acrimoniously** *adv*	*adj* – Angry, bitter, with ill feeling. An acrimonious **dispute // debate // battle // exchange // takeover // split // departure**.
adversary *n* **adversarial** *adj*	*n* – An opponent. *adj* – (1) Of a process, system or activity, involving two opposing or conflicting sides. (2) The legal system in which both sides present evidence.
alienate *v* **alienation** *n*	*v* – To cause a person or group who were previously friendly to feel isolated, withdrawn or hostile. To alienate **employees // customers // colleagues**.
arbitration *n1* **arbitrator** *n2* **arbiter** *n3* **arbitrate** *v*	*n1* – The process whereby a group selects a third party to negotiate and reach a legally binding decision that ends a disagreement without the need to go to court. *n2* – The person appointed to lead the arbitration process. *n3* – A person who helps the negotiation process. *v* – To make a legally binding decision as the concluding part of the negotiation process. *Arbitrator* and *arbiter* Both words can have the same meaning but *arbiter* is less common and can also refer to someone who is not part of the official arbitration process.
concede *v* **concession** *n*	*v* – To (unwillingly) admit the truth or existence of something. E.g. The newspaper maintained that the facts in the article were true but conceded that the photographs did not add to the story. *n* – A bargain or compromise.

conciliation *n* **conciliate** *v* **conciliatory** *adj*	*n* – The process of helping groups in a disagreement hold discussions to try to end their dispute. *adj* – An action intended to calm and help end a disagreement.
confront *v* **confrontation** *n* **confrontational** *adj*	*v* – To meet or communicate directly and angrily with someone about a problem or issue.
consensus *n*	*n* – Majority or total agreement across a group or area. 🤝 **General** consensus. ❗ The adjective *consensual* has the slightly different meaning of involving permission or consent rather than agreement.
deadlock *n*	A situation in which sides cannot make any progress in resolving the disagreement. 🤝 There **is** a deadlock. To **reach** / **end in** / **break** a deadlock.
discord *n*	Lack of agreement / lack of harmony, or disagreement.
disposed *adj*	Tending or wanting to do something. Similar to *inclined*.
dispute *n / v*	*n* – An argument or disagreement. 🤝 *n* – A **legal** // **pay** // **industrial** // **bitter** // **long-running** dispute. A dispute **over** X. *v* – To dispute **the facts** // **findings** // **outcome** // **statement that** X.
disrupt *v* **disruptive** *adj*	*v* – To interrupt or prevent from continuing.
divisive *adj*	Causing disagreement.
entrenched *adj*	Established and/or held firmly, making change difficult.
expose *v* **exposed** *adj*	*v* – (1) To make visible or to reveal. (2) To cause something to be at risk.

hostile *adj* **hostility** *n*	*adj* – (1) Strongly against and/or aggressive. (2) In business, a situation in which one company wants to buy another against the owner's will. 🤝 A hostile **bid** // **takeover** // **acquisition** // **merger** // **deal** // **approach**.
inclined *adj*	Tending or wanting to do something. Similar to *disposed*.
jeopardise* *v* **jeopardy** *n*	*v* – To put at risk of harm, danger or loss. *-*ize* is also acceptable in British spelling and is always used in US spelling.
intermediary *n*	An organisation or person who communicates and/or makes arrangements between and on behalf of the parties involved.
intervene *v* **intervention** *n*	*v* – To become involved in something in order to try and help or change the situation.
intransigent *adj* **intransigence** *n*	*adj* – Inflexible, unwilling to change one's mind or position.
leverage *n*	Something that increases your chances of getting what you want. ❗ In finance, leverage has a more specialised meaning.
mediate *v* **mediation** *n* **mediator** *n*	*v* – To work to help bring a dispute or disagreement to an end. Similar to *conciliate*. 🤝 To mediate **a solution** // **settlement** // **compromise**. To mediate **an end to the dispute** // **crisis** // **strike**.
ominous *adj*	Giving the impression that something bad is going to happen.
prone *adj*	Is usually or often affected by or experiences something negative.
rancorous *adj* **rancour** *n*	*adj* – Angry, bitter, resentful.
rapprochement *n*	The improvement of relationships between previously hostile groups. Similar to *reconciliation*.

reconcile _v_ **reconciliation** _n_	_v_ – (1) To restore good relationships and/or to end a disagreement. (2) To make two previously conflicting things become compatible.
resolve _v_ **resolved** _adj_	_v_ – (1) To find a way to end or solve a problematic situation or issue. (2) To decide to do something, usually something difficult (see section 30). 😟 _Resolve_ and _solve_ There can be overlap but _resolve_ is usually used in the context of conflict, and _solve_ in the context of finding answers to puzzles and problems of maths, logic or logistics.
susceptible _adj_	At risk of, unprotected or easily damaged. Similar to _vulnerable_.
vulnerable _adj_	At risk of, unprotected or easily damaged. Similar to _susceptible_. 😟 _Vulnerable_, _susceptible_ and _prone_ _Prone_ has a slightly different meaning (see above) but they are sometimes interchangeable because being vulnerable / susceptible (unprotected) can mean that you are therefore also likely to experience (be prone to) something bad. Note also that you can say 'X is vulnerable/susceptible.' but you have to say 'X is prone **to** Y.'.

12.3   Nearly but not quite right

	Incorrect	Correct
1	When should a small company that is starting to operate globally use international <u>arbitrator</u> processes?	When should a small company that is starting to operate globally use international <u>arbitration</u> processes?
2	A key role of management is to be aware of the areas in the organisation most <u>vulnerable for</u> conflict.	A key role of management is to be aware of the areas in the organisation most <u>vulnerable /</u> <u>prone to</u> conflict.
3	The team needs to reach a <u>consensus</u> decision.	The team needs to reach <u>a consensus</u>. The team needs to reach <u>a generally agreed //</u> <u>unanimous</u> decision.
4	I suggest that the restructuring proposals put <u>into jeopardy</u> the current goodwill that exists within the team.	I suggest that the restructuring proposals put <u>in</u> <u>jeopardy</u> the current goodwill that exists within the team.
5	The evidence does not support the view that older employees are more <u>prone at</u> making mistakes.	The evidence does not support the view that older employees are more <u>prone to making /</u> <u>likely to make</u> mistakes.
6	Conflict avoidance can in fact mean that a group is more <u>at risk to have</u> long-term resentment.	Conflict avoidance can in fact mean that a group is more <u>at risk of having / vulnerable to</u> long-term resentment.
7	Researchers have applied Sun Tzu's principles to modern day business strategy, in particular the management of <u>confrontational</u> (McNeilly 1996, Lee and Sai On Ko 2000).	Researchers have applied Sun Tzu's principles to modern day business strategy, in particular the management of <u>confrontation</u> (McNeilly 1996, Lee and Sai On Ko 2000).
8	The deadlock is a result of <u>intransigence</u> positions of both parties.	The deadlock is a result of <u>intransigent</u> positions of both parties.
9	Using an outside intermediary usually makes parties more <u>exposed</u> to making concessions.	Using an outside intermediary usually makes parties more <u>disposed</u> to making concessions.
10	The second way to inadvertently <u>distant</u> a client is to talk negatively about your competitors.	The second way to inadvertently <u>distance /</u> <u>alienate</u> a client is to talk negatively about your competitors.

Size, amount and distribution

13   Size, proportion, degree, level and extent

This section contains words and phrases for approximate amounts (e.g. *a large number of*), but of course you will also need to use precise numerical values when discussing your data.

Note also that most adjectives to describe size (e.g. *small*) can also be used to describe amount (see section 14).

13.1   Words in action

Size, number and measurement

▸ The pay increase has had a <u>minimal / negligible</u> // <u>small / marginal</u> // <u>appreciable / discernible / noticeable</u> // <u>considerable / marked / major / significant / substantial / pronounced</u> effect on productivity.

▸ There are still relatively <u>few</u> studies on the economics of happiness.

▸ There were <u>a number of / several</u> options the government could have taken.

▸ <u>A large number of</u> // <u>A small number of</u> students returned the questionnaire.

▸ According to a report in 2015, <u>numerous</u> SMEs in the region still do not have their own website.

▸ <u>A total of</u> 305 questionnaires were completed.

▸ The <u>enormity / magnitude</u> of the task may be off-putting to smaller organisations.

▸ The experiment was designed <u>to quantify / measure</u> the relative levels of male and female participation.

▸ The <u>scale / extent</u> of the corruption in the organisation is being investigated.

Proportion, in proportion, fraction and ratio

▸ Average propensity to save (APS) is the <u>proportion of</u> income saved rather than spent.

▸ Adam's theory is based on the principle that inequity arises if employee input is not <u>proportionate</u> to output.

- A <u>disproportionate</u> number of jobs come from new businesses, according to the NBER (2016).
- The emerging industrial economy in the smaller Gulf states is based <u>predominantly</u> on oil (Niblock 2015).
- The government's strategy has been only <u>partially</u> successful.
- The <u>(vast) majority of</u> private sector businesses are SMEs, according to 2015 UK government statistics.
- Class A drug users represent only <u>a (small) minority of</u> people who take drugs.
- Of the 85 employees, <u>just</u> <u>under</u> // <u>over</u> <u>a third</u> // <u>a half</u> // <u>a quarter</u> said they felt underpaid.
- <u>The top</u> 10 per cent scored 20 <u>or above</u> and <u>the bottom</u> 10 <u>per cent</u> scored 5 <u>or below</u>.
- The <u>percentage</u> increase in UK air fares from November to December 2015 was the highest since 2002.
- <u>The ratio of</u> women <u>to</u> men <u>is</u> roughly 1:9. / There is <u>a ratio of</u> 1 male <u>to</u> every female.

Level, capacity and dimension

- Harmonised <u>minimum</u> safety <u>levels</u> / <u>minimum levels of</u> safety are essential for transport networks.
- Our remit was to look at ways of ensuring <u>a high</u> <u>level of</u> / <u>degree of</u> accuracy in accounting procedures.
- Scores above 110 indicate a <u>higher than average</u> / <u>an above-average</u> IQ and scores under 90 indicate <u>a lower than average</u> / <u>a below-average</u> level of intelligence.
- The data show that the <u>mean</u> / <u>average</u> number of hours worked in Canada was 36.6 in 2014.
- The CEO was quoted as saying that the company needs to 'raise its game by several <u>orders of magnitude</u>'.
- This cartridge has <u>a maximum capacity of</u> 800 GB. / <u>The maximum capacity of</u> this cartridge <u>is</u> 800 GB.
- The diagram gives the <u>(approximate) dimensions of</u> the fan (i.e. to the nearest centimetre).

13.2 Information to help you use these words correctly

Words you probably already use correctly: *considerable, enormity, extent, level, major, maximum, minimal, minimum, noticeable, number, ratio, significant.*
   Words defined in other sections: *marginal* s11, *profound* s26.

appreciable *adj*	A noticeable or significant amount or degree. Similar to *substantial* and *considerable*.
approximate *adj* **approximately** *adv*	*adj* – Fairly accurate but not precise. 😟 *Approximately*, *roughly* and *generally* *Approximately* and *roughly* have similar meanings but *roughly* is more informal. *Generally* means 'most of the time' or 'in most cases' and should not be used to refer to numerical values or amounts.
average *n / v*	*n* – (1) The result of adding different amounts and then dividing by the number of amounts. Similar to *arithmetic mean*. (2) The usual, normal or typical amount.
capacity *n*	The maximum amount something can contain or produce (see section 6). 😟 *Capacity*, *capability* and *ability*. See section 6.
degree *n*	(1) A unit of measurement for temperature and angle. (2) The extent, size or level of things connected to quality, feelings or impact. E.g. The components were produced to a high degree of accuracy. To a large degree / extent, people are not interested in political action. (3) An educational award. 🤝 To a **high** // **large** // **considerable** // **remarkable** // **surprising** // **small** // **limited** degree.
dimension *n*	(1) The scope or physical measurements of something. (2) An aspect or part of something. E.g. The debate had an educational dimension. 🤝 An **added** / **additional** // **different** // **extra** // **further** // **new** dimension. A **political** // **social** // **educational** dimension.

discernible *adj* **discern** *v*	*adj* – Noticeable, able to be seen. *v* – To see or notice, often something small or hard to see. 🤝 A discernible **difference** // **impact** // **effect** // **change** // **influence** // **improvement** // **shift** // **pattern** // **theme** // **trend** // **link** // **benefit**.
disproportionate *adj*	Not in the appropriate or corresponding amount, size or ration to something else.
enormity *n*	Great / large size or extent.
exceptional *adj* **exception** *n* **except** *v*	*adj* – (1) Excellent, unusually good and impressive. E.g. She is an exceptional manager. (2) Very unusual. E.g. We will give a refund only under exceptional circumstances. *n / v* – Related to something that is not included. E.g. An exception to the rule.
magnitude *n*	Size or extent. ❗ In mathematics, an order of magnitude is a tenfold (x 10) increase. Used more generally, the phrase 'several orders of magnitude' means 'a very large extent / amount'.
marked *adj*	Very noticeable. 🤝 A marked **difference** // **contrast** // **discrepancy** // **increase** // **decrease** // **impact**.
mean *n*	The result of adding different amounts and then dividing by the number of amounts. Also called the *arithmetic mean*.
negligible *adj*	Very small and/or unimportant.

partially *adv* **partial** *adj*	*adv* – Not completely or only to some extent. *adj* – (1) Incomplete or only in parts. (2) Biased. (3) 'Having a liking for'. **!** Notice the three very different meanings of *partial*. 😦 *Partially* and *partly* Some overlap but there is some difference in meaning. *Partially* emphasises that something has not happened to completion. E.g. The advertising campaign was partially successful. *Partly* emphasises the idea of different parts or elements. E.g. The house is built partly of concrete and partly of wood. For *impartial* see section 23.
predominantly *adv* **predominant** *adj* **predominance** *n* **predominate** *v*	*adv* – Mainly. *adj* – (1) The main, largest or most common. E.g. The predominant colour in the room was red. (2) The most common and therefore most powerful (for *dominant* see section 26). E.g. The predominant opinion was that the treaty should be signed.
proportion *n1* **proportional** *adj1* **proportionate** *adj*	*n1* – A share, number or ratio in relation to the whole. *adj1* – Corresponding in amount, size or ratio to something else. Similar to *proportionate* and *in proportion*. E.g. The team size should be proportional / in proportion / proportionate to the amount of work involved. 🤝 X is **in** // **out of** proportion **to** Y. We need to keep **a sense of** proportion. **!** In maths, *proportional* and *proportionality* have the more precise meaning of two things that have equal ratios and always increase and/or decrease by a constant ratio.

13.3 Nearly but not quite right

	Incorrect	Correct
1	There was no <u>discerning</u> difference between the two products.	There was no <u>discernible / appreciable / noticeable</u> difference between the two products.
2	The report claims that the CEO has missed <u>several</u> acquisition opportunities – at least nine in the last two years alone.	The report claims that the CEO has missed <u>numerous</u> acquisition opportunities – at least five in the last two years alone.
3	The growth rate of the Latin US mobile sector depends, to a <u>high degree</u>, on how robust licence renewal processes become.	The growth rate of the Latin US mobile sector depends, to a <u>large degree / extent</u>, on how robust licence renewal processes become.
4	The UK population is <u>generally</u> 61 million.	The UK population is <u>approximately</u> 61 million.
5	There is a <u>large possibility</u> that the experiment was flawed.	There is a <u>strong possibility</u> that the experiment was flawed.
6	The population is rising by <u>three percentage</u> a year.	The population is rising by <u>three per cent / 3%</u> a year.
7	This debate can be interpreted <u>in</u> two different levels.	This debate can be interpreted <u>on</u> two different levels.
8	The company's wireless security needs to be set to the <u>strongest</u> level.	The company's wireless security needs to be set to the <u>highest</u> level.
9	The <u>extent of</u> job satisfaction has an impact on general happiness.	The <u>degree of / level of</u> job satisfaction has an impact on general happiness.
10	A business's fraud prevention procedure should be <u>in proportional to</u> the risks faced.	A business's fraud prevention procedure should be <u>proportional / in proportion / proportionate to</u> the risks faced.

14 Amount, distribution and supply

14.1 Words in action

Presence and absence

▸ I argue that the <u>presence</u> of a large business premises in the area should, on balance, be welcomed.

▸ A neglected area of investigation is the relative <u>absence</u> of competition in the financial sector.

Too much

▸ The survey results support the idea that, as Leggat (2008) observed, <u>too much</u> specialisation in management roles contributes to a disconnect between managers and clinicians.

▸ Businesses in the region pay <u>excessively</u> high tax, as rates are calculated on turnover rather than profit.

▸ The contract stipulates that the interim estimate value should not <u>exceed</u> that of the final proposal.

▸ The <u>excess / surplus / surfeit / glut / oversupply</u> of sugar is driving down market prices.

▸ I recommend that a root and branch review is carried out to identify <u>superfluous</u> areas of expenditure.

▸ People with an <u>over</u>developed sense of competitiveness have a higher incidence of chest pain.

Plenty of

▸ There is <u>an abundance of / ample</u> evidence to show that job satisfaction is linked to well-being.

▸ Due to the warm weather there has been a <u>prolific</u> supply of UK apples, which has driven down the price.

The right amount and enough

▸ The data indicate that the business does not currently have <u>the right / appropriate</u> level of funding.

▸ There are many websites giving advice on how to predict <u>ideal</u> numbers of staff needed.

▸ The right to have <u>adequate</u> housing is enshrined in the International Covenant on ESC Rights.

▸ We now have <u>sufficient / enough</u> data and will publish our preliminary findings shortly.

Very little and not enough

▸ The charity charges only <u>nominal</u> rents to tenants.

▸ We will examine the relationship between <u>a lack / dearth / scarcity of</u> resources and business innovation.

▸ This report reviews the literature on current skills <u>shortages</u> in the UK.

- A revenue <u>shortfall / deficit</u> can be defined as a negative gap between predicted and actual revenue.
- The team do <u>not have sufficient / have insufficient</u> funding to continue their research.

Common and rare

- Computer-aided design (CAD) is now <u>common / ubiquitous</u> across many industries.
- The Global Barter Network in Argentina flourished in the wake of <u>widespread / pervasive</u> redundancies.
- We question the statement that absenteeism has <u>pervaded</u> the Australian teaching profession.
- The food industry has argued that the <u>prevalence</u> of obesity is due mainly to lifestyle choices.
- The case studies presented support Morris and Frei's position, that a customer-at-core business is a <u>rarity</u>.

Distribution and supply

- Retail outlets tend to <u>cluster / be grouped / are (often) concentrated in</u> particular areas rather than being spread <u>uniformly / in a uniform way</u>.
- Australia has a <u>sparse</u> population overall but relatively <u>dense</u> pockets of urban habitation.
- Virtual conferencing is a boon to geographically <u>dispersed</u> organisations.
- Hook and Tang (2013) point out that current climate change models are based on incorrect assumptions about future fossil fuel <u>supply</u> and <u>depletion</u>.
- I demonstrate that in a <u>saturated</u> market, gaining a bigger market share is the quickest way to achieve growth.

14.2   Information to help you use these words correctly

Words you probably use correctly already: *absence, adequate, amount, appropriate, common, depletion, ideal, lack, over-, presence, shortage, surplus, under-, uneven, uniform.*
   Words defined in other sections: *widespread* s1.

abundance *n* **abundant** *adj*	*n* – More than enough. Similar to *plentifulness*.
ample *adj*	More than enough. 🤝 Ample **evidence of // proof of // research on // justification for // scope for // supply of // quantity of // space for // capacity.**
dearth *n*	A severe or total lack of.

deficiency *n* **deficient** *adj*	*n* – (1) A fault or inadequate standard. (2) A lack of something in the body, e.g. A vitamin deficiency. E.g. The report highlighted the company's deficiencies. 🤝 X **is** deficient **in** Y.
dense *adj*	Crowded or closely compacted.
disperse *v* **dispersal** *n*	*v* – To spread out or break up. 🤝 The sales team are **geographically** // **widely** dispersed. To disperse **rioters** // **crowds** // **groups** // **demonstrators**.
exceed *v* **excess** *n / adj* **excessive** *adj*	*n* – Of amounts, more than is needed. 🤝 *n* – **An** excess **of** Y. **The** // **any** excess **is** Y. To **pay the** excess **on** X. *adj* – Excess **amounts** // **cash** // **capacity** // **cost** // **demand** // **fare** // **supply**. *adj* – Excessive **amounts of** // **fees** // **prices**.
glut *n*	Too much. Usually used in the context of food and other market commodities. Similar to *excess, surplus* and *surfeit*.
insufficient *adj*	Not enough. 😟 *Insufficient* and *inadequate* These can be interchanged but *inadequate* usually means 'not good enough' rather than 'not enough'.
nominal *adj*	(1) A very small amount and/or much less than expected. (2) A given title or role that is 'in name only'. 🤝 A nominal **amount** // **fee** // **price** // **cost** // **salary** // **value** // **rent**. ❗ *Nominal account* // *capital* // *damages* // *interest rate* // *ledger* all have different, specialised meanings.
permeate *v*	To spread or occur (often slowly) throughout something. Similar to *pervade*.

pervade *v* **pervasive** *adj*	*v* – To spread or occur throughout something. Similar to *permeate*. *adj* – Widespread and dominant. 🤝 A pervasive **influence** // **attitude** // **presence** // **problem** // **belief**.
prevalent *adj* **prevalence** *n*	*adj* – Common and/or dominant, often within a small area or at a particular point in time. 🤝 The prevalence **of** X.
prolific *adj*	Very productive and/or plentiful.
rare *adj* **rarity** *n*	*adj* – Not happening or found often. 🤝 **Increasingly** // **surprisingly** // **extremely** rare. A rare **commodity** // **chance** / **opportunity** // **skill** // **talent** // **event** // **occasion** // **example** // **exception**.
scarce *adj* **scarcity** *n*	*adj* – Not easy to get and/or existing in only small amounts. 🤝 *adj* – A scarce **resource**. *n* – A scarcity **of resources** // **food** // **land** // **money** // **water** // **material** // **skilled labour**. 😟 *Rare* and *scarce* There is overlap but as indicated above, *rare* is a 'positive' word, while *scarce* has the negative meaning of 'not enough'.
shortfall *n*	Not as much as was predicted or expected. Similar to *deficit*.
sparse *adj*	Not much of something and thinly spread over an area. 🤝 A sparse **population**.
sufficient *adj*	Enough. 😟 *Sufficient* and *adequate* These can be interchanged but *adequate* usually means 'good enough' rather than 'enough'.
superfluous *adj*	Not needed, often because there is already more than enough.

surfeit *n*	Too much of something, usually used in the context of food and other market commodities. Similar to *excess, surplus* and *glut*.
	There is **a** surfeit **of** X.
ubiquitous *adj*	Very common and/or occurring everywhere.

14.3 Nearly but not quite right

	Incorrect	Correct
1	Inspectors found that the hotel had <u>insufficient</u> hygiene standards and so rescinded its licence.	Inspectors found that the hotel had <u>inadequate</u> hygiene standards and so rescinded its licence.
2	There is a <u>prevalent</u> of student housing in the area.	There is a <u>prevalence</u> of student housing in the area.
3	The labour <u>shortfall</u> in Canada is particularly acute in the following occupations: ...	The labour <u>shortage</u> in Canada is particularly acute in the following occupations: ...
4	Older firms tend to have more <u>under valued</u> assets.	Older firms tend to have more <u>undervalued</u> assets.
5	I have shown that concerns about globalisation and new competitors are <u>a commonality</u> in German SMEs.	I have shown that concerns about globalisation and new competitors are <u>common</u> in German SMEs.
6	Staff at Ujjivan have no job titles – such a cooperative environment is <u>scarce</u> in the financial services sector.	Staff at Ujjivan have no job titles – such a cooperative environment is <u>rare</u> in the financial services sector.
7	There <u>is a large amount of</u> data files.	There <u>are a large number of</u> data files.
8	The vendor rating system is not well suited to large organisations because it <u>lacks in</u> uniformity.	The vendor rating system is not well suited to large organisations because it <u>lacks / is lacking in</u> uniformity.
9	My analysis has uncovered <u>abundant</u> errors in the accounts.	My analysis has uncovered <u>many / numerous</u> errors in the accounts.
10	I suggest that four appraisals a year is <u>excess</u>.	I suggest that four appraisals a year is <u>excessive</u>.

Time, trends and change

15 Time, sequence, duration and frequency

15.1 Words in action

Past to present

▸ This report will firstly give an overview of <u>past / previous</u> studies on job satisfaction and well-being.

▸ Mumbai was <u>formerly / previously</u> known as Bombay. / The <u>former</u> name of Mumbai was Bombay.

▸ <u>With hindsight / In retrospect</u> it would have been better to use a larger sample for our study.

▸ <u>As yet / So far / Up to now</u> there has been little narrowing of the gender pay gap in the hotel industry.

▸ The largest construction project ever conducted in Europe <u>is underway / has started / has begun.</u>

Present

▸ The <u>current</u> proportion of non-finance businesses engaged in international trade is 16.8% (ONS 2016).

▸ The <u>Contemporary</u> Business Issues (CBI) exam covers current global issues relevant to accountancy.

▸ Liaison between the WHO and companies who have a presence in South America is <u>ongoing</u>.

First occurrence and future

▸ <u>The advent of / The arrival of</u> cellular technology enabled widespread use of mobile phones.

▸ The company's strategy has been a failure from the <u>outset</u>.

▸ As Barrett (2014) discusses, the rate of technological development in solar geoengineering is <u>unprecedented</u>.

▸ Several prominent economists are suggesting that another global financial crisis is <u>imminent / impending</u>.

▸ We recommend that any <u>future</u> high-level promotions are more carefully costed.

Before, after and sequence

▸ The <u>chronology</u> of Amazon's acquisitions and investments is well documented.

▸ The Coca-Cola company <u>preceded / predates / antedates</u> Pepsi.

▸ A white paper usually states policy intention <u>prior to</u> a new piece of legislation.

▸ Turing's machine was a <u>forerunner of / precursor to</u> the modern personal computer.

▸ The integrated company benefits from being able to control both <u>upstream</u> and <u>downstream</u> activities.

▸ Micro enterprises in India have been invaluable to those left behind by the credit policies of <u>successive</u> governments (Karmakar 2000 and Nasir 2013).

▸ Hangen et al. (2012) look at the effect of stock price volatility on <u>subsequent</u> return expectations.

▸ The <u>previous</u> report gave an <u>interim</u> analysis and the <u>final</u> report will be published next month.

▸ The BMM conference is <u>biannual</u>, whereas the International Conference on Services Marketing is <u>biennial</u>.

▸ For this study staff were asked to <u>alternate</u> between standing and sitting at their computers every 30 minutes.

▸ The <u>penultimate</u> step in the redundancy collective consultation process is to issue termination notices.

▸ We recommend that the (time) <u>lag</u> between employee appraisal and written feedback is shortened.

Occurring at (almost) the same time

▸ This report looks at the impact of the <u>instantaneous</u> marketing now possible via real-time communication.

▸ It is useful to run two browsers <u>concurrently / simultaneously</u> in order to access all websites.

▸ A fall in price <u>is</u> often <u>accompanied by / contemporaneous with</u> increase in demand.

▸ A fall in price often <u>coincides with</u> increase in demand.

▸ A balance sheet is usually produced <u>to coincide / to accompany</u> the end of a reporting period.

▸ Our analysis suggests that monetary and fiscal policies need to work <u>in tandem</u> rather than separately.

Duration

▸ The <u>duration</u> of a fixed-term contract depends on what has been agreed between employer and employee.

▸ We report on the <u>short and medium-term</u> effects of the organisation's restructuring.

- According to the report, high-end hotels have a relatively large number of <u>transient / temporary</u> employees.
- From April 2007, applicants for <u>permanent</u> residence in the UK have had to take a 'Life in the UK' test.
- A business visa does not grant you permission to stay <u>for an indefinite period / indefinitely</u>.
- The debate over the status of social work has been running <u>throughout</u> this century.
- The myth <u>persists</u> that Western firms do business in China mainly because of cheap labour (Jiang 2012).
- We decided to <u>extend / prolong</u> the interviews with the younger participants.

Frequency

- The company has had <u>constant / continuous / continual // frequent / repeated / regular // recurrent // intermittent // periodic // infrequent // occasional</u> problems with internet connectivity.
- The internet provider claims that the connection problem was an <u>isolated</u> incident.

Breaks

- Negotiations were <u>suspended</u> during the local elections.
- There was a <u>hiatus</u> in the negotiations during the local elections.
- '<u>Lapse</u> risk' is risk of mistakes due to inactivity, for example a customer failing to keep up insurance premiums.

The right time

- The Monopolies Commission investigation on the Google algorithm is <u>timely</u>, as several new search engines have recently come on to the market.

15.2   Information to help you use these words correctly

Words you probably already use correctly: *chronology, continue, currently, extend, forerunner, indefinite, instantaneous, isolated, past, permanent, previous/ly, recurrent, simultaneous, short/medium/long term, suspend, tandem.*

alternate *v / adj*	*v* – To move back and forth between two things or conditions. *adj* – Every other of two things. E.g. He worked alternate weeks. 😟 *Alternate* and *alternative* An *alternative* is a noun meaning 'another option or possibility'. E.g. If this strategy fails, there are alternative approaches we can take.
biannual *adj*	Occurring two times each year. *Bi* = two + *annual* = each year.
biennial *adj*	Occurring once every two years. *Bi* = two + *ennial* = the period of years.
concurrently *adv* **concurrent** *adj*	*adv* – At the same time. Similar to *simultaneously*. Often used in scientific and operational contexts. E.g. The new software allows more business processes to run concurrently.
constant *adj*	(1) Happening or existing over time without interruption. Similar to *continuous*. (2) Remaining unchanged over time.
contemporaneous *adj*	Existing or happening at the same time. 😟 *Contemporary* (adj) and *contemporaneous* There is overlap – see adj (2) below. *Contemporary* is the more common word.
contemporary *adj* / *n*	*adj* – (1) Modern or current. E.g. Many contemporary artists have websites. (2) Existing or done together at the same time. E.g. Leonard's newspaper reports provide a contemporary / contemporaneous record of the 1929 Wall Street crash. *n* – Living at the same time. E.g. Shelley and Byron were contemporaries. ❗ Note the two different meanings of the adjective *contemporary* which can cause confusion.

continual *adj* **continually** *adv*	*adj* – Happening frequently, with or without interruptions. Often used for negative things and to emphasise stopping and starting. Similar to *constant* and *continuous*. E.g. We had continual problems with the data analysis software.
continuity *n*	A situation in which something continues smoothly without break or interruption.
continuous *adj*	Happening or existing over time, often without interruption. Similar to *constant* and *continual*.
downstream *adj*	Relating to the later or last stages in a process.
former *adj*	(1) Having existed in the past. (2) The first item mentioned in a list (see section 3).
formerly *adv*	Of or happening in the past. 😟 *Former/ly* and *previous/ly* *Former/ly* is usually only used to talk about names, titles and positions. E.g. Mumbai was formerly / previously called Bombay. *Previous/ly* is the more general word and is used to describe sequence. E.g. This report is similar to one I've read previously. ❗ With both *former* and *previous* there is a difference in meaning between *the* and *a*. E.g. She is the former / previous boss = the boss immediately before the current one. She is a former / previous boss = one of any of the previous bosses.
hiatus *n*	A gap or pause. Usually used in the context of official procedures and processes.
hindsight *n*	An understanding or realisation of something only after it has happened. 🤝 **With** hindsight.

imminent *adj*	About to or likely to happen very soon. Used for both positive and negative things.
	☹ *Imminent* and *eminent*
	Eminent means someone who is an expert and/or admired and respected.
impending *adj*	About to or likely to happen very soon. Similar to *imminent* but used only for negative things and before the noun.
	E.g. Impending success. ✘ Disaster is impending. ✘ Impending disaster. ✓
interim *n / adj*	*n* – The time between two events. Often used to describe a temporary position while a more permanent one is arranged.
intermittent *adj*	Happening at irregular intervals.
lag *n / v*	*n* – A delay or time gap between two things.
	v – To make slower progress than others or than expected.
	🤝 To lag **behind** X.
lapse *v / n*	*n* – (1) A (brief) failure or gap.
	E.g. A lapse in mortgage payments.
	(2) A weakness or mistake caused by lack of attention or inaction.
	E.g. A lapse in hygiene standards.
latter *adj*	(1) The second of two things mentioned (see section 3).
	(2) The last stages of a process or time period. Similar to one meaning of *later*.
	E.g. The latter / later stages of the process are the most expensive.
outset *n*	The beginning or start.
penultimate *adj*	The one before the last in a series.
periodic *adj*	Happening at intervals (regular or irregular).
persist *v* **persistence** *adj*	*v* – To continue, even in the face of obstacles and resistance.

precede *v* **preceding** *adj*	*v* – To happen or go before in time, order or position. 😔 *Proceed* and *precede* To *proceed* is to go forward or to keep doing something.
precursor *n*	Something that comes before something else of a similar type and influences it in an important way.
predate *v*	(1) To happen or exist before something else, often with the meaning of 'to be older than'. Similar to *antedate*. (2) To mark with a date earlier than the actual one. E.g. To predate a cheque.
prior *adj*	Existing or coming before in time, order or importance. 😔 *Prior* and *previous* There is overlap but *prior* is more formal and can be used as a preposition. E.g. I contacted the solicitors prior to / before meeting. ✓ I contacted the solicitors previous to meeting. ✗
prolong *v*	To extend the amount of time. 🤝 To prolong **life // survival // suffering // conflict // an interview // a meeting**.
retrospect *n*	A review of something after it has happened. Similar to *hindsight*. 🤝 **In** retrospect.

subsequent *adj*	Coming or happening afterwards.
	☹ *Subsequent* and *consequent*
	Subsequent is the wider term. *Consequent* also means 'coming or happening afterwards' but only as a result of a previous event (see section 19).
	E.g. Lack of leadership in the company and consequent ✗ / subsequent ✓ market shrinkage caused it to go bankrupt last year.
	Lack of leadership in the company and a consequent ✓ / subsequent ✓ drop in its productivity caused it to go bankrupt last year.
successive *adj*	Existing or happening one after another (in a series).
timely *adj*	Happening or done at an appropriate and/or useful time.
transient *adj*	Lasting for a (very) short time.
underway *adj*	Having recently started. Usually used in the context of planned, large and difficult projects and activities.
unprecedented *adj*	Never happened before. Often used to refer to something unusual or remarkable.
upstream *adj / adv*	*adj* – Relating to the early / earlier stages in a process.

15.3　Nearly but not quite right

	Incorrect	Correct
1	<u>In hindsight</u> we could have worked more as a team.	<u>With hindsight</u> we could have worked more as a team.
2	An economic upturn is <u>impending</u>.	An economic upturn is <u>imminent</u>.
3	The firm is expecting its third <u>subsequent</u> annual award.	The firm is expecting its third <u>successive</u> annual award.
4	This essay will discuss hyperinflation and <u>following</u> political instability.	This essay will discuss hyperinflation and <u>subsequent / consequent</u> political instability.
5	This report recommends <u>biennial</u> meetings – one in March and one in September.	This report recommends <u>biannual</u> meetings – one in March and one in September.
6	<u>Previous</u> to becoming CEO she worked as Head of Legal at Rawlings.	<u>Prior</u> to becoming CEO she worked as Head of Legal at Rawlings.
7	I outline an <u>alternate</u> pricing mechanism for ebook sales.	I outline an <u>alternative</u> pricing mechanism for ebook sales.
8	The Spring 2017 OECD report suggests that a turnaround is <u>eminent</u> for the Indonesian economy.	The Spring 2017 OECD report suggests that a turnaround is <u>imminent</u> for the Indonesian economy.
9	Fayol's principles and Taylor's <u>consequent</u> scientific model developed separately but have both been influential.	Fayol's principles and Taylor's <u>subsequent</u> scientific model developed separately but have both been influential.
10	A new assistant director will not be in post until next month and <u>for the interim</u> the chief executive will deal with any urgent issues.	A new assistant director will not be in post until next month and <u>in the interim</u> the chief executive will deal with any urgent issues.

16 Increase, decrease, trends, cycles and speed

See also section 17 for other useful words and phrases. Example sentences starting with * indicate that the nouns or adjectives describing size of increase or decrease are in order of smallest to largest.

16.1 Words in action

Increase

▸ Global GDP from seaborne trade has increased / risen to about 60 trillion US dollars (OECD 2017).

▸ The government increased / raised taxes on alcohol last year in an attempt to deter heavy drinking.

▸ * This report predicts an uptick // uptrend // upswing // upsurge // a surge / a boom in market activity.

▸ Prices have escalated since the last quarter.

▸ We suggest that the upgrading of São Paulo's urban transport has been a major factor in the city's success.

Decrease

▸ India's GDP decreased / fell in the first quarter of the year.

▸ The company's reputation has diminished / lessened in recent months.

▸ The European car market shrank / contracted by 4% from April to June.

▸ According to Letwin (2016), there has been a reduction in the number of companies outsourcing IT activities.

▸ Two newspapers recently ceased paper production as a result of a downtrend dating back to the 1940s.

▸ The economic downturn / downswing has contributed to the increased gap between rich and poor.

▸ In 2016 Exxon Mobile's credit rating was downgraded by two points.

Highest, lowest and recovery

▸ Sales have reached a peak / hit a high / spiked // slumped // hit bottom / a low // bottomed out / troughed.

▸ * After poor figures last month, sales have picked up // recovered // revived // bounced back to last year's levels.

Amount of increase or decrease

▸ The graph shows a minimal / negligible / small / slight / subtle rise / increase in share value.

▸ * The graph shows a noticeable // marked / significant / pronounced / substantial fluctuation // decline / decrease / fall / drop / dip in share value.

▸ Prices rose // fell slightly // noticeably // markedly / significantly.

Speed or rate of increase or decrease

‣ The graph shows a gradual // steady rise / increase in share value.
‣ The graph shows a dramatic / sharp / sudden / galloping decline / decrease / fall / drop in share value.
‣ The graph shows that there was a dramatic / sharp / sudden fluctuation / dip in share value.
‣ Sales dipped // plummeted / plunged in the last quarter.
‣ * Prices rose // fell gradually // steadily // sharply // suddenly // dramatically last quarter.
‣ The new policy has been shown to accelerate // decelerate the rate of economic growth.
‣ Client demand for clearer terms and conditions has been gathering speed // momentum / impetus / force.
‣ Research shows that the rate of tax avoidance schemes has increased exponentially over the last decade.
‣ The changes to the German taxation system over the last decade have been incremental.
‣ The rate of change over the month was greater // less than expected.

Stability, balance and lack of movement

‣ Sales have retained / kept their level of the previous month. / Sales have stayed level over the previous month.
‣ Our results suggest that student numbers are likely to level off / level out / reach a plateau next year.
‣ Customer complaints have stabilised / become stable since the redesign of the website.
‣ The point at which supply balances with / aligns with demand is termed 'market equilibrium'.
‣ Sales figures have remained static / fixed / stationary over the last twelve months.
‣ I argue that innovative leadership can enable growth, even in a tepid / sluggish // stagnant market.
‣ The case studies show how cognitive inertia in senior management can lead to the collapse of a business.

Instability

‣ The Turkish retail sector is in (a state of) flux due to partial economic recovery and major market changes.
‣ Mutual funds cause short-term volatility / instability in credit markets.
‣ Customer traffic in regional branches has been variable.

Trends and cycles

▸ I look at whether economic recession perpetuates (vicious) <u>cycles</u> of poverty within a family or community.

16.2 Information to help you use these words correctly

Words you probably already use correctly: *accelerate, balance, boom, bounce back, decelerate, decrease, equilibrium, fixed, increase, lessen, peak, pick up, plateau, rate, recover, reduce, shrink, stable, stationary, trend, up/downtrend, up/downturn, downgrade, upgrade.*

Words defined in other sections: *volatile s6.*

bottom *v / n*	*v* – To reach the lowest level before starting to rise again. (Informal.)
	v – To bottom **out**.
	n – To **reach / hit rock** bottom.
consistent *adj*	Unchanging.
contract *v / n* **contraction** *n*	*v* – (1) To become smaller. Similar to *shrink*.
	(2) To form an agreement (a contract) with someone.
	n – The state of becoming smaller or less.
	v – The economy contracted **by** 5%.
	n – A contraction **in** the sector.
cycle *n* **cyclical** *adj*	*n* – An event or group of events that happens in repeated patterns.
	A **boom-and-bust** // **annual / yearly** // **budget** // **planning** // **life** // **development** // **reporting** cycle.
	A cycle **of growth** // **debt** // **poverty**.
	A **vicious** // **virtuous** cycle.

diminish *v*	(1) To become or cause to become less.
	(2) To take away from something's or someone's power, authority or reputation.
	🤝 To diminish **in strength** // **size** // **power** // **authority** // **importance** / **significance** // **popularity** // **credibility**.
	The **capacity** // **resource** // **supply** // **number** // **impact** // **risk** // **threat** // **likelihood** // **chance of** Y diminishes // has diminished // will diminish.
downtick *n*	Of sales, prices, production and stocks, a small decrease.
downturn *n*	Of sales, prices, production and stocks, a decrease.
escalate *v* **escalation** *n*	*v* – To increase quickly.
	🤝 The **problems** // **issues** // **conflict** // **dispute** // **protests** has / have escalated.
exponential *adj* **exponentially** *adv*	*adj* – Increasingly rapid.
	🤝 Exponential **growth** // **rate**.
	adv – At an increasingly rapid rate.
	❗ *Exponent, exponential* and *exponentially* have more specialised meanings in mathematics.
fluctuate *v* **fluctuating** *adj* **fluctuation** *n*	*v* – To go up and down in an unstable manner.
flux *n*	In a state of change.
	❗ In science, *flux* is the rate at which energy or matter flows.
galloping *adj*	Increasing very quickly.
	🤝 Galloping **inflation** // **growth** // **prices** // **sales**.
impetus *n*	Building up / increasing in speed, size or force. Similar to *momentum*.
	🤝 To **gather** / **gain** impetus.
incremental *adj*	Having a series of small, regular changes.

inertia *n*	A state in which there is little or no energy, interest, activity or change.
	🤝 **Managerial // government // team // department // market** inertia.
momentum *n*	Building up / increasing in speed, size or force. Similar to *impetus*.
plummet *v / n*	*v* – To fall or drop very suddenly. Similar to *plunge*.
plunge *v / n*	*v* – To fall or drop very suddenly. Similar to *plummet*.
raise *v / n*	*v* – (1) To purposely increase or lift to a higher or better level or position.
	(2) To cause to be heard or considered.
	E.g. At the meeting he raised the possibility of a merger.
	(3) To collect or gather.
	E.g. To raise funds.
	(4) To bring up a child or animal.
	n – A purposeful and planned increase or lift to a higher or better level or position.
	❗ *To raise* uses a direct object or agent in a sentence.
	E.g. The government will raise in an attempt to deter heavy drinking. ✗
	The government will raise tax on alcohol to deter heavy drinking. ✓
	Taxes will raise. ✗
	Taxes will be raised (by the government). ✓
	🤝 To raise **the level // the limit // the bar // the rate // standards // interest rates // the money // our sights // our game**.
revive *v* **revival** *n*	*v* – To come back or be restored to a previous (better) position or level.

rise *v / n*	*v* – To go or come up.
	E.g. Prices rose last year. Prices have risen since last year.
	n – An increase.
	! To rise does not use a direct object and cannot be used in the passive voice.
	E.g. The government will rise tax on alcohol in an attempt to deter heavy drinking. ✗
	Taxes will be rised by the government. ✗
	Taxes will rise as part of a government initiative to deter heavy drinking. ✓
	Taxes will rise. ✓
	Rise, raise and *arise*
	Rise and *raise* have slightly different meanings and different grammatical structures (see above).
	To arise means 'to come into existence / originate' and is usually used when a problem, issue or situation first develops.
	E.g. The issue arose at the meeting.
	An older meaning of *arise* is 'to get up' (similar to *rise*) but is no longer commonly used.
	! The phrase *to give rise to* means 'cause' (see section 19).
sluggish *adj*	Of markets or people, operating or moving slowly.
	A sluggish **market // industry // sector // economy**.
slump *v / n*	*v* – To suddenly decrease or reduce.
stagnant *adj* **stagnation** *n* **stagnate** *v*	*adj* – (1) Lacking any movement, activity or growth, often for long periods of time. Similar to *static* but used in an even more negative sense.
	(2) Of water or atmosphere, having little or no oxygen or flow.
	Economic // price // salary // market stagnation.

static *adj*	Lacking any movement, activity or growth. Sometimes used in the negative sense of being unable to move or change.
	😞 *Static* and *stable*
	Stable is when the lack of movement is a positive thing.
subtle *adj*	Very small, often such that it is difficult to notice or find.
surge *n / v*	*n* – A sudden large increase.
	v – To suddenly increase.
tepid *adj*	(1) Not very strong, fast or high.
	(2) Not very hot. Similar to *lukewarm*.
trough *n*	The lowest level before increasing again.
	🤝 **Peaks and** troughs **in** X.
upsurge *n*	Of sales, prices, production and stocks, a sudden large increase.
	🤝 An upsurge **in** X.
upswing *n*	Of sales, prices, production and stocks, an increase.
uptick *n*	Of sales, prices, production and stocks, a small increase.
variable *adj*	Changing often, not fixed or able to change often.

16.3   Nearly but not quite right

	Incorrect	Correct
1	Productivity has <u>risen highly</u>.	Productivity has <u>risen sharply / steeply / dramatically</u>.
2	The report states that the US stock market <u>shrink</u> is the largest since 1984.	The report states that the US stock market <u>shrinkage</u> is the largest since 1984.
3	The upward movement on the demand curve indicates that demand has <u>lowered</u>.	The upward movement on the demand curve indicates that demand has <u>contracted / shrunk / decreased</u>.
4	Data show that the cost of raw materials <u>raised</u> last quarter.	Data show that the cost of raw materials <u>rose</u> last quarter.
5	Hirsch et al. (2001) asserted that universities were <u>at a state of flux</u>.	Hirsch et al. (2001) asserted that universities were <u>in a state of flux</u>.
6	The current round of redundancies is likely to <u>slump</u> capacity for further growth.	The current round of redundancies is likely to <u>reduce / diminish / decrease / lessen</u> capacity for further growth.
7	<u>Static</u> sales over the last year have given us enough revenue to complete the refurbishment.	<u>Stable</u> sales over the last year have given us enough revenue to complete the refurbishment.
8	This essay uses the new model developed by Jorda et al. (2016) to examine the <u>cycle</u> nature of real estate lending and financial instability.	This essay uses the new model developed by Jorda et al. (2016) to examine the <u>cyclical</u> nature of real estate lending and financial instability.
9	The problem <u>rose</u> out of the lack of honest communication in the team.	The problem <u>arose</u> out of the lack of honest communication in the team.
10	Demand has <u>kept level during</u> the last year.	Demand has <u>remained / stayed level over</u> the last year.

17 Change, development, growth and progress

See also section 16 for other useful words and phrases.

17.1 Words in action

Moving and moving away

‣ B2B organisations are <u>moving / shifting</u> more <u>towards</u> a focus on added customer value rather than just price.

‣ Many B2B companies are <u>diverting</u> resources <u>/ moving / shifting away</u> <u>from</u> competitive pricing <u>to</u> customer service and added value.

‣ The company's decision to team up with a pharmaceutical giant is a <u>departure from</u> its usual approach.

‣ The data show that China is <u>undergoing</u> <u>a shift away from</u> manufacturing <u>towards</u> the services sector.

Change and transition

‣ The data strongly suggest that <u>the main change in</u> US environment is the growth in small businesses.

‣ The announcement represents <u>a radical change in</u> tax policy / <u>a radical departure from</u> previous policy.

‣ The political boundaries of the region are extremely <u>changeable / mutable</u>.

‣ The computer software is <u>flexible / versatile / adaptable</u> enough to cope with all gaming platforms.

‣ The team <u>modified / adapted / adjusted / altered</u> its procedures to give more time for sample analysis.

‣ The 2014 South African Equity Act <u>amendments / reforms</u> have helped reduce work discrimination.

‣ <u>A revised / A revision of</u> the pay structure would help to make up for the minimum wage increase.

‣ This report shows that average pay has been <u>revised</u> upwards in the US civil engineering sector.

‣ Management should <u>revise / amend</u> its strategic plan in the light of the results of the above SWOT analysis.

‣ The 2014 IMF report on the <u>restructuring / reorganising</u> of the Spanish banking sector stated that the changes have 'substantially reduced' the possibility of banks destabilising the economy.

‣ I disagree with Casadesus-Masanell and Ricart (2009) and will show how Catalan companies have <u>reconfigured</u> their models in order to adapt to the modern business environment.

‣ I suggest that there are significant issues with <u>converting</u> commercial buildings <u>into</u> residential properties.

- An effective management team should be able to provide a smooth <u>transition</u> from outgoing to incoming CEO.
- The invention of the printing press <u>transformed</u> European society.
- In the retail sector EDI has largely <u>superseded</u> paper-based invoicing.

Growth, development and progress

- The <u>proliferation of / expansion of / (vigorous) growth of / increase in</u> mutual funds adds to market instability.
- There has been a <u>resurgence</u> in demand for vinyl records, with UK annual sales now over one million (BPI 2014).
- Over the last few years Russia has been continuing to <u>accumulate / amass</u> gold reserves.
- The <u>cumulative</u> effect of non-management can, over time, cause serious staff role and remit issues.
- <u>Accrued</u> income is that which has been earned but not yet received.
- A business model that is <u>scalable</u> is important for a start-up if it wants to grow quickly and profitably.
- <u>Developments in // The evolution of</u> bio-engineering techniques <u>have / has</u> had a profound effect on pharmaceuticals.
- The outlined strategy should enable the firm to make <u>great strides / great progress in</u> the digital market.
- Our survey shows that staff feel the training programme is <u>progressing well // slowly is making good // little / poor progress</u>.

Stopping

- This report looks at why many companies have <u>ceased / stopped</u> outsourcing their IT activities.
- If a business wishes to <u>cease</u> trading, the first step is to create a resolution to <u>dissolve</u>.

17.2   Information to help you use these words correctly

Words you probably already use correctly: *develop, downgrade, progress, reorganise*, upgrade.*
   *-ize is also acceptable in British spelling and is always used in US spelling.
   Words defined in other sections: *expand* s2, *exponentially* s16, *versatile* s6.

accrue *v* **accrual** *n*	*v* – Of money or benefits, to increase over a period of time. 🤝 Accrued **benefits** // **depreciation** // **income** // **interest**.
accumulate *v* **accumulation** *n* **accumulative** *adj*	*v* – To build up or increase over time. 🤝 To accumulate **assets** // **capital** // **profit** // **interest** // **wealth** // **debt** // **evidence** // **knowledge** // **skill**. 😦 ***Ac**cumulate* and *cumulate* To *cumulate* means 'to gather and combine'. E.g. To cumulate the sales figures. The nouns and adjectives of the two words have similar meanings, but *accumulation* is the more common noun, and *cumulative* is the more common adjective. E.g. Accumulation of debt is what most worries students today. The return on the investment is cumulative.
adapt *v* **adaptable** *adj*	*v* – (1) To make changes to something so that it can be used for a different purpose. Similar in meaning to *modify*. (2) To get used to a new situation. 🤝 To **easily / readily / quickly // successfully** adapt. To **find it** difficult **to** adapt. To adapt **well to** X. To adapt X **to** Y. To adapt to **change** // **the environment** // **circumstances** // **a way of life** // **a situation** // **surroundings**.
adjust *v* **adjustable** *adj* **adjustment** *n*	*v* – (1) To make small changes to something so that it is more suitable. 🤝 *v* – To adjust **the temperature** // **your position** // **your screen** // **your chair** // **sales figures**. An adjusted **share price**. *adj* – An adjustable **system** // **rate** // **mortgage**. *n* – To **make an** adjustment **to** X. An adjustment **account** // **factor**.

alter *v* **alteration** *n*	*v* – To make small or large changes to something for a particular purpose. *Alter* is a general term and so can be used instead of *amend*, *adapt*, *adjust* or *modify*, except for meaning (2) of *adapt*. 🤝 To **make** alterations **to** X.
amass *v*	To build up, gather or increase over time. Similar to *accumulate*.
amend *v* **amendment** *n*	*v* – To make particular changes (often corrections) to a text, document, agreement or legislation. ❗ *Emend* is a formal and much less common word meaning 'to make changes to a text'.
cease *v* **cessation** *n*	*v* – (1) To stop doing something. (2) To come or bring to an end. 🤝 To cease **trading** // **operations** // **manufacturing** // **production** // **work** // **fighting** // **hostilities**.
changeable *adj*	(1) Capable of change or of being changed. (2) Of people, having the characteristic of often changing opinion or attitude in an unpredictable way.
convert *v* / *n* **conversion** *n*	*v* – To change from one type of system, thing or belief into another. ❗ A <u>convert</u> is someone who has changed from agreeing with one idea or religious belief to another.
departure *n*	(1) The action of leaving. (2) A change in usual behaviour, action or direction.
dissolve *v* **dissolution** *n*	*v* – (1) To end an official organisation, group or agreement. E.g. To dissolve the company. (2) To break up a solid into a liquid to form a solution. *n* – The ending of an official organisation, group or agreement.

divert *v* **diversion** *n*	*v* – (1) To cause to change direction or purpose. (2) To take attention away from something else. Similar to *distract* (see section 25). 🤝 To divert **money** // **funds** // **resources from** X **to** Y. ❗ *Divert* has specialised meanings in commerce, transport and communications.
evolve *v* **evolution** *n*	*v* – To develop gradually. Often used to describe development from something simple to something more complex. 🤝 To evolve (**from** X) **into** Y.
modify *v* **modification** *n*	*v* – (1) To make small changes to something specific, such as a particular process, plan, method, document or law. Similar in meaning to *amend*. (2) To make changes so that it can be used for a different purpose. Similar to meaning (1) of *adapt*. E.g. To modify a machine, building or software.
mutable *adj*	Capable of change or of being changed. Similar to meaning (1) of *changeable*.
proliferation *n* **proliferate** *v*	*n* – A rapid, often large increase.
radical *adj / n* **radically** *adv*	*adj* – (1) Fundamental and/or large. (2) Extreme, very different from the norm. (3) Promoting fundamental political and social change. 🤝 (A) radical **shift** // **transformation** // **change** // **improvement** // **restructuring** // **reform**.
reconfigure *v* **reconfiguration** *n*	*v* – To change the arrangement or structure of something. Usually used in technical and mechanical contexts. (For *configuration* see section 18.) 🤝 To reconfigure **hardware** // **software** // **a system** // **a plan** // **a project** // **a budget**.
reform *v / n*	*v* – To make improvements to an organisation, system, sector or law.

resurgence *n*	The (often rapid) return of something that had previously declined or disappeared.
revise *v* **revised** *adj* **revisable** *adj*	*v* – (1) To correct or change, sometimes in order to improve and/or make more accurate. Similar to *amend*. (2) To relearn knowledge in preparation for an exam. To revise **plans** // **an estimate** // **an amount** // **a forecast** // **an offer** // **a bid** // **a target** // **proposals** // **guidelines** // **a deal** // **a contract** / **an agreement** // **legislation** // **tax** // **earnings**.
scalable *adj*	Able to be made larger or applied to a larger quantity or area.
shift *v* / *n*	*v* – To move physical position or attitude. *n* – A shift **in attitude** // **focus** // **attention** // **position** // **stance** // **perspective**. *v* – To shift **the blame** // **the burden** // **responsibility** // **allegiance** // **loyalty**. To shift X **away from** Y. To shift **towards** X.
stride *n* / *v*	*n* – A large step. *v* – To walk with long, decisive steps.
transform *v* **transformation** *n* **transformational** *adj*	*v* – To change fundamentally and/or completely. *n* – A fundamental and/or complete change.
transition *n* **transitional** *adj*	*n* – The process of changing from one situation or position to another. To **make a** transition. To **undergo a** transition. A **seamless** / **smooth** / **easy** // **successful** // **painful** // **difficult** // **gradual** // **sudden** transition.

undergo *v*	To experience something (often bad or unpleasant) or to go through a process of change.
	To undergo **transformation** // **revision** / **modification** // **repair** // **restructuring**.
	To undergo **surgery** // **treatment** // **testing** // **pain** // **hardship** // **suffering**.
vigorous *adj* **vigour*** *n*	Strong and energetic.
	*The US spelling is *vigor*. Note that the adjective is spelt the same way in UK and US spelling.

17.3 Nearly but not quite right

	Incorrect	Correct
1	Over the last two decades China has <u>taken</u> great strides in road infrastructure.	Over the last two decades China has <u>made</u> great strides in road infrastructure.
2	The <u>transformation</u> from private to public company can be difficult.	The <u>transition</u> from private to public company can be difficult.
3	This report recommends <u>substantial modifications</u> to the budget.	This report recommends <u>substantial changes / alterations</u> to the budget.
4	When a business <u>is ceased</u>, the person responsible for the business must notify the registrar within thirty days.	When a business <u>closes / stops trading</u>, the person responsible for the business must notify … The <u>cessation of a business requires notification</u> to the registrar within thirty days.
5	Over the last two decades China has <u>done</u> great progress in road infrastructure.	Over the last two decades China has <u>made</u> great progress in road infrastructure.
6	Researchers are <u>undergoing</u> studies <u>about</u> the possible effects of the drug.	Researchers are <u>conducting</u> studies <u>on</u> the possible effects of the drug.
7	The quarterly report documents still need further <u>adjustments</u>.	The quarterly report documents still need further <u>revision/s</u>.
8	We plan to <u>alter</u> our budget plans every three months in order to limit unnecessary spending.	We plan to <u>revise</u> our budget plans every three months in order to limit unnecessary spending.
9	An employer must <u>accrue</u> properly documented evidence before firing an employee.	An employer must <u>accumulate</u> properly documented evidence before firing an employee.
10	This report predicts <u>vigoros</u> growth over the next decade.	This report predicts <u>vigorous</u> growth over the next decade.

Business strategy, models, methods and results

18 Strategy, models, methodology and method

18.1 Words in action

Discussing business strategies and models

▸ This report looks at the benefits of using private funding as part of a new venture's investment <u>strategy</u>.

▸ I propose a <u>model</u> for <u>tailoring</u> operational <u>strategy</u> according to the director's leadership style.

▸ Some large cybercrime groups now <u>model</u> themselves on legitimate businesses.

▸ I have used IBM's component <u>business modelling</u> to help see how we might operate in real market scenarios.

▸ We <u>devised / constructed / formulated</u> a model that takes into account recent changes in consumer behaviour.

▸ McLean's <u>business model</u> was new because it integrated road transport and shipping <u>logistics</u>.

▸ Our <u>rationale</u> for promoting an <u>ethical strategy</u> is that businesses need to be trusted in order to remain profitable in the long term (Fritzsche 2005, Svensson and Wood 2008).

▸ The move towards using a cold-calling company is, I suggest, a <u>tactical</u> error.

Describing your methodology and assumptions

▸ My <u>methodology</u> was to first use <u>quantitative</u> methods (analysing the empirical data) and then <u>qualitative</u> methods (interviews) to gain additional information about individual employees.

▸ Working with a large amount of data allowed me to do detailed <u>statistical analysis</u>.

▸ The study is <u>descriptive</u> and aims to find out what consumers think of companies that do not have websites.

▸ I decided that an <u>exploratory approach</u> was needed initially, to assess <u>the scope of survey</u> needed.

▸ I conducted the study using the scientific <u>paradigm</u>.

▸ We <u>adopted</u> customer profiling as we felt this was <u>the best method</u> for deciding marketing strategy.

- I chose to use a variety of relevant <u>case studies</u> to <u>address</u> the <u>research question</u>.
- We used <u>anonymous</u> <u>questionnaires</u> so as not to cause offence if the feedback was negative.
- Our analysis was based on <u>primary data</u>, i.e. the company's annual report accounts for the last three years.
- I also used <u>literature</u> on issues and problems surrounding pension schemes as important <u>secondary sources</u>.
- The evidence base arises from a <u>systematic</u> <u>review</u> of relevant studies.
- One important <u>assumption</u> was that the product would remain 'innovative' for at least three years.

Describing your method

- I first <u>framed</u> our research question and then <u>conducted</u> an <u>initial / preliminary review</u> of relevant studies.
- I then <u>refined</u> the question and conducted a more <u>in-depth systematic</u> <u>analysis</u> using the <u>predetermined / prescribed</u> <u>protocols</u> and forms of analysis given below.
- We <u>configured</u> the software so that it meets the specific payroll requirements of the company.
- The participants were <u>allocated / assigned</u> randomly to one of five groups.
- Each product model was <u>subjected to / underwent</u> a series of four tests.
- The test had <u>rigorous / thorough</u> <u>safeguards against</u> bias, namely having the results <u>reviewed</u> by two external experts.
- I <u>took</u> <u>steps / measures</u> to guard against bias by having the results <u>verified</u> by two external experts.
- The experiment was repeated by other teams to see whether our results could be <u>replicated / reproduced.</u>
- The sets of figures were <u>collated</u> at the end of each week.
- A database was then <u>compiled</u> and used to look for significant <u>correlations</u>.
- We <u>collaborated</u> with a team of researchers from Glasgow.

Sequence of stages in your method

- <u>Prior to / Before</u> the consultation, participants were sent an email outlining the <u>rationale</u> for the meetings.
- <u>Once we had</u> received the questionnaires we went in-store as 'secret shoppers'.
- <u>The first // next // penultimate // final step</u> in the <u>process</u> was to …
- <u>At // During</u> the initial // intermediate // final stage / phase I …

Parameters, limits and limitations of your method

▸ We followed closely the instructions <u>stipulated / specified</u> in the written protocol.

▸ I ensured that all values were <u>within</u> <u>the specific / the specified parameters</u>.

▸ Owing to time <u>constraints</u> the test was only repeated once.

▸ We were <u>limited as to</u> how much we could achieve in the time given.

▸ The employer put <u>limitations</u> on where the interviews could be conducted.

18.2 Information to help you use these words correctly

Words you probably already use correctly: *address, anonymous, collaborate, conduct, formulate, in-depth, initial, safeguard, source, thorough, verify.*

Words defined in other sections: *allocate* s8, *analyse* s2, *assign* s8, *constraint* s11, *construct* s20, *correlation* s22, *diversify* s21, *evaluate* s2, *integrate* s20, *limitation* s11, *measures* s30, *parameter* s11, *penultimate* s15, *prior* s15, *specific* s4, *stipulate* s9, *undergo* s17.

adopt *v* **adoption** *n*	*v* – To start using a particular method, idea or plan. 🤝 X is / has been **widely / generally // universally** adopted. To adopt **an approach // a policy // a method // a plan // an idea // a principle // a strategy // a position // a viewpoint / a stance.**
collate *v* **collation** *n*	*v* – To gather and put information in order so that you can compare and analyse it.
compile *v* **compilation** *n*	*v* – To produce something you didn't have before by bringing information together. 😟 *Collate* and *compile* There is overlap but the two things are done for different purposes – *collate* for analysis and *compile* for production. Sometimes the first stage is to *collate* and then to *compile* something from this analysis. E.g. I collated the data and compiled a list of the companies that are based in the northeast and have more than 200 employees.

configure *v* **configuration** *n*	*v* – To arrange or structure something so that it can function for a particular purpose. 🤝 To configure (a) **system** // **program** // **hardware** // **software** // **data**.
descriptive *adj*	In research, to state (describe) what has been found rather than to investigate causes or suggest solutions.
devise *v*	To create or invent a way of doing something. 🤝 To devise **a plan** // **method** // **model** // **strategy** // **policy** // **scheme** // **technique** // **way of doing** X. 😟 *Devise* and *invent* There is overlap but *invent* is usually used in the context of physical objects or processes.
frame *v / n*	*v* – To design a way of doing or communicating something. Similar to *formulate*, *devise* and *construct* (construct also means to build a physical structure) but usually used in the context of questions, ideas, thoughts and theories.
logistics *n* **logistical** *adj*	*n* – The planning of where resources or goods need to be at particular times in order to run a process or business.
methodology *n* **methodological** *adj*	*n* – The overall research approach and 'way of thinking' behind the research. A methodology section usually includes an explanation and discussion of the research approach and method/s used. 😟 *Methodology* and *method* The method(s) is/are the specific procedures used to conduct the research. ❗ The two words are sometimes used interchangeably in business and management. 😟 *Methodological* and *methodical* *Methodological* is the adjective related to *methodology*. E.g. This essay will examine the methodological foundations of market research. The adjective *methodical* means 'thorough and organised'. E.g. The job requires someone who can work in a methodical manner.

model *n / v*	*n* – In business, the assumptions and plan of how a business can attract customers and create revenue. Compare with *strategy*.
	v – To imitate or base practices or behaviour on something else.
paradigm *n*	(1) A framework, set of ideas or worldview that underpins and directs an area of research. The research is usually discussed in the methodology section of a report.
	(2) A typical and/or excellent example of something.
	🤝 A paradigm **shift**.
preliminary *adj*	Done or coming before a more important or fuller part of something.
	🤝 (A) preliminary **study** // **investigation** // **results** // **conclusions** // **data** // **evidence** // **survey** // **trial** // **test**.
prescriptive *adj*	Following a given or established procedure or set of rules.
	❗ *Proscriptive* means 'not allowed' (see section 9).
primary *adj*	(1) The original, first-hand information or data.
	(2) The most important.
protocol *n*	An established set of rules, procedures or formal situations.
qualitative *adj*	Any research method that collects information (e.g. attitudes, feelings or beliefs) which cannot be expressed in, or reduced to, numerical values. Examples of qualitative methods are participant observation and interviews.
quantitative *adj*	Any research method that collects empirical (observable), numerical or statistical data. A quantitative approach is part of what is referred to as the 'scientific method'.
rationale *n*	The reason/s for a particular plan, decision or action.
	🙁 *Rationale* and *rational*
	Rational (adj) means 'logical and sensible'.
	E.g. They made a rational decision.
	❗ The verb to *rationalise* has a different meaning (see section 30).

refine *v*	(1) To make improvements to a plan, idea, process or system.
	(2) To remove impurities from products such as oil, sugar, wheat and rice.
replicate *v*	To copy or reproduce exactly. In the scientific method, results are verified by others performing the same experiment and being able to get similar results.
review *n / v*	*v* – (1) To examine studies and other literature to look for information that might be useful in addressing your research question.
	(2) To examine someone else's research in order to give advice and critical comments for improvement before publication.
	(3) To give a personal opinion of a book, journal article or film.
secondary *adj*	(1) In research, data taken from a source which did not create that data.
	(2) Not the most important.
strategy *n* **strategic** *adj* **strategise*** *v*	*n* – The plan of action(s) taken in order to move towards a goal. One business might have many strategies which address different areas and levels within the organisation.
	☹ *Strategy* and *plan*
	There is overlap, but *plan* is a much more general term.
	For *vision*, *mission* and *goal* see section 30.
	*-ize is also acceptable in British spelling and is always used in US spelling.
subject *v / adj*	*v* – To force or cause someone to experience something unpleasant (to undergo something). Often used in the passive voice and with *to*.
	E.g. The business will be subjected to several legal investigations.
	adj – Conditional upon.
	E.g. The bank will grant the loan, subject to them being satisfied with the credit check.
	☹ *Subjected* to and *subject* to
	As shown above, the verb and adjective carry different meanings.

systematic *adj*	According to a particular system, method or plan.
	🤝 A systematic **approach** // **classification** // **course**.
	😟 *Systematic* and *systemic*
	Systemic means spread throughout a whole system (see section 7).
tactic *n* **tactical** *adj*	*n* – The detailed action(s) taken in order to fulfil the business strategy/ies. Tactics can be planned or unplanned, reacting to day-to-day changes. Often used in the context of a competitive situation.
	E.g. Google has been accused of using unfair tactics against other search engines.
tailor *v*	To alter or arrange something so that it fits its purpose.

18.3 Nearly but not quite right

	Incorrect	Correct
1	Their report uses only <u>other people's information</u> and therefore is not reliable.	Their report uses only <u>secondary sources</u> and therefore is not reliable.
2	The first section of this report <u>writes a review of</u> relevant studies.	The first section of this report <u>reviews</u> relevant studies.
3	A <u>systemic</u> approach to staff appraisal is needed.	A <u>systematic</u> approach to staff appraisal is needed.
4	We <u>compiled</u> the answers from this year's questionnaires in order to compare them with last year's.	We <u>collated</u> the answers from this year's questionnaires in order to compare them with last year's.
5	In my view, the government's <u>rational</u> for raising business rates is not clear.	In my view, the government's <u>rationale</u> for raising business rates is not clear.
6	I recommend <u>doing</u> stronger measures to minimise damage to the goods in transit.	I recommend <u>taking</u> stronger measures to minimise damage to the goods in transit.
7	This essay will look at how to <u>safeguard</u> a business <u>for</u> disruption caused by staff absence.	This essay will look at how to <u>safeguard</u> a business <u>against</u> disruption caused by staff absence.
8	I support Dahl et al. (2016) in that <u>strategy</u> thinking should be something organisations do as integrated practice.	I support Dahl et al. (2016) in that <u>strategic</u> thinking should be something organisations do as integrated practice.
9	The <u>methods</u> section of this paper describes which two statistical formulas I used and why this combined approach was the most appropriate.	The <u>methodology</u> section of this paper describes which two statistical formulas I used and why this combined approach was the most appropriate.
10	The number of senior lectureship promotions in any year is not <u>subjected to</u> a quota.	The number of senior lectureship promotions in any year is not <u>subject to</u> a quota.

19 Cause, effect, results and findings

See also sections 18 and 22 for useful words and phrases.

19.1 Words in action

Note that the first two groups of words in this section are divided into 'cause to effect' and 'effect to cause' for presentation purposes only; many of them can be used (with appropriate grammatical changes) to describe both cause to effect and effect to cause.

For example:

Cause to effect	Effect to cause
An increase in the cost of raw materials <u>results in</u> prices ris<u>ing</u>.	Price rises <u>are a result of</u> an increase in raw materials.
An interaction of various market forces <u>determine</u> currency exchange rates.	Currency exchange rates are <u>determined by</u> an interaction of various market forces.

Cause to effect

▸ There is (often) <u>a causal link</u> <u>between</u> an increase in the cost of raw materials and inflation.

▸ An increase in the cost of raw materials <u>causes</u> prices <u>to</u> rise / <u>results in</u> prices ris<u>ing</u>.

▸ High or full employment <u>is a key factor in</u> / <u>is instrumental in</u> // <u>contributes to</u> (caus<u>ing</u>) demand-pull inflation.

▸ Debates on independence can <u>provoke / elicit / engender / create / cause</u> strong emotions among voters.

▸ The external review <u>prompted</u> us to invest in better safety equipment.

▸ An increase in the cost of raw materials can <u>trigger / give rise to</u> inflation.

▸ A complex interaction of various market forces <u>determine</u> currency exchange rates.

▸ An excess of aggregate demand in an economy is <u>a determinant of</u> demand-pull inflation.

▸ One <u>outcome of</u> an increase in raw material prices <u>is that</u> the cost is passed onto the consumer.

▸ An increase in the cost of raw materials <u>affects</u> high street prices, <u>causing</u> the cost of living <u>to</u> rise.

▸ An increase in the cost of raw materials <u>has the effect of</u> rais<u>ing</u> the general price level.

▸ This essay analyses the factors that <u>impinge on</u> productivity in a small business.

▸ The complexity and length of the questionnaire <u>accounts for / explains</u> the low return rate.

- In 2008 Facebook attempted to acquire Twitter but fierce valuation disagreements <u>ensued / followed</u>.
- <u>Owing to / Because of / As a result of / As a consequence of</u> rises in raw material costs, inflation increases.
- Sometimes <u>there is</u> a global rise in the cost of one or more raw materials. <u>Consequently, / As a consequence, / As a result</u>, general inflation can be affected.
- The cost of raw materials sometimes increases rapidly, <u>thereby</u> <u>leading to</u> economic inflation.
- An election will be held in June, and <u>therefore / thus</u> parties are preparing their campaigns.
- An election will be held next year, <u>hence</u> the campaign preparations.

Effect to cause

- Demand-pull inflation <u>stems from / is a consequence of / results from / is a result of / is due to / is caused by</u> near or full employment in an economy.
- Cost-push inflation <u>occurs as a result of / occurs through / occurs via / arises from</u> firms passing on higher costs.
- I <u>attribute</u> the low return rate of questionnaires <u>to</u> the fact that completing one takes about an hour.

Originating from or obtaining

- A disproportionate number of jobs <u>come from / originate from / can be attributed to</u> new businesses (National Bureau of Economic Research 2016).
- According to the NBER (2016), jobs are disproportionately <u>created by / produced by</u> new businesses.
- Jobs can be <u>generated from</u> a growth in new businesses. / A growth in new businesses can <u>generate</u> jobs.
- Marx <u>derived</u> his theories partly <u>from</u> the German philosophers, particularly Kant and Hegel.

Presenting findings

- This report presents our <u>initial // provisional</u> findings.
- The <u>table // chart</u> <u>shows</u> the <u>data</u> <u>obtained.</u>
- No (significant) change in product performance <u>was detected // was observed</u>.
- I <u>discerned</u> differences in patterns of behaviour between the two groups.
- The data show a <u>statistically significant</u> reduction in project efficiency.
- Middle managers were shown to <u>exhibit</u> generally good levels of delegation skills.
- <u>We find that</u> male–female wage disparity varies with age.

- This review of current research gives / yields useful indicators of potential changes in delivery systems.
- The data accord / agree / are consistent with that of other studies on product reliability.
- The debt distribution pattern conforms to that expected for this type of product.
- At this preliminary stage of analysis the findings are inconclusive / not conclusive.

Problems

- We encountered a problem with the software and so had to do the calculations manually.
- I was unable to replicate the results of previous studies.
- The small dataset meant that I cannot establish / ascertain the cause with certainty.
- We could not (accurately) gauge / assess / measure how employees felt about the new system.
- The sample was too small to produce a measurable outcome.
- I found that I had overestimated // underestimated the effect unemployment has on happiness.
- It seems that the survey was fallible to experimenter bias, so I intend to conduct a second online survey.
- The discrepancy in the results exceeded an acceptable margin of error.

Anomalies and surprises

- There are several anomalies in the data, which means that we might need to repeat the experiment.
- There is an unexplained discrepancy between the expected and actual totals.
- The results are not consistent with / inconsistent with the predicted outcomes.
- A notable exception to rising export prices is Mexico.
- The standard of answers was higher // lower than we had anticipated / expected // predicted.
- The data do not accord with / not agree with earlier observations.
- Contrary to my expectations, the most effective type of bulb is also the cheapest.

19.2   Information to help you use these words correctly

Words you probably already use correctly: *accounts for, anticipate, causal, consequence, derive, due to, ensue, generate, hence, investigate, issue, notable, observation, originate, produce, therefore, thus.*

   Words defined in other sections: *ascertain s2, conform s11, correlation s22, determine s2, establish s2, limit s11, reap s27.*

accord *v / n* **accordance** *n*	*v* – (1) To be consistent with or the same as. (2) To give or grant status or respect to someone. *v* – X accords **with** Y. *n* – X is **in** accordance **with** Y.
affect *v*	To make a difference to or influence something. *Affect* and *effect*. See *effect* below. The word for 'not affected' is *unaffected*. *Disaffected* means 'unhappy with those in authority'.
anomaly *n* **anomalous** *adj*	*n* – Something different from what is usual, expected or normal.
attribute *v / n*	*v* – To think or state as being caused by. For the noun, see section 6.
conclusive *adj*	Providing strong evidence or proof. Opposite of *inconclusive* (see below).
consequence *n* **consequently** *adv* **consequent** *adj*	*n* – Effect or result. *Consequent/ly* and *subsequent/ly*. See section 15.
consistent *adj*	(1) Does not contradict. (2) Unchanging over time. X **is** consistent **with** Y. A consistent **approach** // **standard** // **level**. X is consistent **with the aim** // **data** // **evidence** // **findings** // **objective** // **principle** // **view of** Y. X is **broadly** // **wholly** consistent **with** Y.

data *n*	Statistics, facts or other information to be analysed.
	❗ In formal, scientific writing, *datum* is the singular noun and *data* the plural.
	E.g. This item is important datum. The data are from three different sources.
	However, using *data* as a singular, uncountable noun is now common.
	E.g. The data is/are from three different sources.
detect *v*	To discover the presence of something.
	☹ *Detect* and *discern*
	Can sometimes be interchanged but *detect* is the more general term – see *discern* below.
determine *v*	*v* – To cause in a specific way or to be the decisive factor in.
determinant *n*	
discern *v*	To recognise, find or understand something with some difficulty. People discern things, usually in the context of something visual or intellectual.
	🤝 To discern a (an) **difference** // **change** // **shift** // **link** // **trend** // **relationship** // **pattern** // **theme** // **impact** // **effect** // **influence** // **benefit**.
	For *discernible* see section 13.
discrepancy *n*	A difference between things that are expected to be the same.
effect *n* / *v*	*n* – The change or result caused by someone or something.
	v – To cause or bring about.
	❗ The use of *effect* as a verb is quite formal and not common, except in the phrases *to effect change* and *to effect a cure*.
	☹ *Effect* and *affect*
	Effect is the noun and *affect* is the verb.
	🤝 A **beneficial** / **a positive** // **the desired** // **a profound** // **a serious** // **an indirect** // **an adverse** / **a detrimental** // **a damaging** // **an unintended** // **a cumulative** // **an immediate** // **a short-term** // **a long-term** effect.

elicit *v*	To bring out a response, reaction or answer.
	For *illicit* see section 9.
fallible *adj*	Capable of making mistakes or of containing errors.
findings *n*	Information or conclusion reached by investigation or experiment.
	😞 *Findings*, *data* and *results*
	Findings is the most general term, used to refer to both data and results.
	Data is information (particularly numerical) collected for calculation, analysis and decision making.
	Results is sometimes used to refer to data but should really be used to refer to the observations and conclusions drawn <u>from</u> the data.
gauge *v / n*	*v* – To estimate or determine the amount or level of something.
impinge *v*	To affect, usually in a negative way.
inconclusive *adj*	Not giving definite proof. The opposite word is *conclusive* (see above).
instrumental *adj*	Being chiefly responsible for making something happen or for achieving a goal.
	🤝 Instrumental **in** X / **in doing** X.
prompt *v / n*	*v* – To cause. Used in the context of causing actions or feelings.
	n – To be on time.
provisional *adj*	(1) Not finalised because further analysis is needed.
	(2) Incomplete.
provoke *v*	(1) To cause to have a reaction or response.
	(2) To deliberately anger or annoy.
	🤝 To provoke **a debate // a discussion // a controversy // a crisis // questions // a protest // an attack // violence // a response // a reaction**.
	😞 *Provoke* and *evoke*
	To *evoke* is to cause to bring to mind a particular emotion or memory.
	E.g. The poem evokes memories of childhood.

residual *adj*	Of effects, remaining after the cause has ceased or been removed.
thereby *adv*	'By that means' or 'as a result of that'.
trigger *v / n*	*v* – To make something else happen, usually suddenly.
	✦ To trigger **a rise** // **a fall** // **a crisis** // **an attack** // **a response** // **a memory** // **a collapse** // **an explosion** // **a feeling of** X.
yield *v / n*	*v* – To produce, deliver or give.
	✦ *v* – To yield **a profit** // **an income** // **a return of** X.
	To yield **results** // **outcomes** // **benefits** // **information**.
	n – **A** yield **of** X. A yield **spread of between** X **and** Y.

19.3   Nearly but not quite right

	Incorrect	Correct
1	Unregulated tourism can <u>cause</u> environmental and sociocultural threats.	Unregulated tourism can <u>pose / present / be an</u> environmental and sociocultural threat(s).
2	The product will yield an appropriate return, <u>thereby it</u> satisfying the shareholders.	The product will yield an appropriate return, <u>thereby / thus</u> satisfying the shareholders.
3	Computer games have <u>affected</u> obesity in children.	Computer games have <u>affected</u> obesity <u>rates</u> in children.
4	This legislation will have a <u>higher effect</u> on public transport than on car ownership.	This legislation will have a <u>greater effect</u> on public transport than on car ownership.
5	I hope that the increased bureaucracy does not <u>impinge</u> our delivery speeds.	I hope that the increased bureaucracy does not <u>impinge on</u> our delivery speeds.
6	Short, <u>provisional</u> interviews are next week, followed by more in-depth ones for selected candidates.	Short, <u>preliminary</u> interviews are next week, followed by more in-depth ones for selected candidates.
7	The rise in business tariffs might <u>illicit</u> an angry response from local traders.	The rise in business tariffs might <u>elicit</u> an angry response from local traders.
8	Simon et al. (2000) argue that how a person perceives risk is <u>instrumental to</u> whether and how they decide to start a business.	Simon et al. (2000) argue that how a person perceives risk is <u>instrumental in</u> whether and how they decide to start a business.
9	The Xero software program <u>discerned</u> several errors in the manual accounts.	The Xero software program <u>detected / found</u> several errors in the manual accounts.
10	Despite increased involvement in management decisions, 22% of employees said they still felt <u>unaffected</u> and unhappy.	Despite increased involvement in management decisions, 22% of employees said they still felt <u>disaffected</u> and unhappy.

Analysing and identifying common themes

20 Analysing arguments and ideas

Analysing involves taking something apart and breaking it down in order to examine it. You need to analyse ideas, arguments or data carefully before you can evaluate them.
See also sections 21 and 22 for other useful words and phrases.

20.1 Words in action

Breaking down and examining terms and concepts

▸ We need to <u>break down / separate out / unpick / deconstruct</u> the term 'business ethics' into its <u>constituent parts / components / elements.</u>

▸ <u>Separating / Uncoupling / Disassociating</u> rights from responsibilities gives us a clearer picture of the issue.

▸ The author's use of the word 'freedom' <u>blurs</u> <u>the (crucial) distinction / line between</u> individual and collective choice.

▸ The report's use of the term 'international trade' <u>does not make a distinction between</u> intra and inter industries.

▸ <u>A distinction needs to be</u> <u>made / drawn</u> <u>between</u> specific and ad valorem tariffs.

▸ <u>Superficially, / On the surface,</u> as Surroca et al. (2010) show, corporate responsibility seems to rise with profitability, but on closer <u>examination / inspection / investigation / scrutiny</u> this is not entirely accurate.

▸ It is a <u>common confusion to think / misconception</u> <u>that</u> 'democracy' means everyone has an equal vote.

▸ The paper <u>misuses the term</u> 'Web 2.0' as being synonymous with the technology rather than how it is used.

▸ When discussing poverty <u>we need to be clear on whether</u> we are talking about relative <u>or</u> absolute poverty.

▸ <u>It is important to</u> <u>recognise / acknowledge / realise</u> <u>that some</u> resources <u>are more // less</u> natural <u>than others.</u>

▸ Focus strategies are <u>in fact</u> a <u>combination / hybrid</u> <u>of</u> differentiation and cost strategies.

Examining the nature of concepts, arguments and actions

▸ Netflix <u>embodies / reflects / represents</u> the phenomenon of rapid expansion of an internet company.

▸ The announcement by the government last month <u>denotes / signifies / represents</u> a change in taxation policy.

▸ I suggest that the issue is not the rate of business tax <u>per se</u> but the global trend in declining corporate taxation.

▸ Branding is essential because it <u>conveys</u> a company's values, vision, personality and promise.

▸ For Latoff, a corporate goodwill strategy should be a plan of <u>tangible</u> actions rather than an <u>abstract concept //construct</u>.

▸ I agree with Robinson and Dechant (1997) that thinking of 'diversity' only in <u>literal</u> terms, without understanding its purpose or complexities, often leads to the failure of well-intentioned initiatives.

▸ The charity's report contains <u>implicit</u> criticism of government policy on social housing.

▸ This report shows that the director's inaction was equal to <u>tacit</u> approval for the funding of the project.

▸ According to the World Health Organization, developing regions need more <u>explicit</u> health policies.

▸ Violent acts are only one type of <u>overt</u> aggression in the workplace described by Baron and Neuman (1996).

▸ Corporate <u>euphemisms</u> for firing people include 'involuntary attrition' and 'rebalancing the workforce'.

▸ Business often uses war and sport <u>metaphors</u> such as 'the battle for customers' and 'the ball is in your court'.

▸ The <u>analogy</u> of health care being like the airline industry is an interesting one.

▸ A common <u>paradox</u> is when a company adapts to a new market and gains rapid success and then in turn becomes unwilling or unable to adapt quickly to new challenges.

Identifying flaws in logic

▸ Buchanan offers the <u>truism</u> that to achieve good public health, the whole community needs adequate housing.

▸ Stating that an opt-in email list system ensures only people who choose to join do, is a <u>circular</u> argument.

▸ The MP used the <u>non sequitur</u> that because identity theft is increasing we should introduce identity cards.

▸ The view that as last year's figures were poor we need redundancies is <u>a fallacy / false / illogical / irrational</u>.

- The idea that a new business is like a garden ready for growth is, I think, a <u>false analogy / fallacy</u> because …
- The concept of 'sustainable mining' is <u>an oxymoron / a contradiction in terms</u> used by multinationals in an attempt to make their activities more palatable (Benson and Kirsch 2009).
- The absence of women in the study means that the author's conclusions are an <u>overgeneralisation</u>.

20.2 Information to help you use these words correctly

Words you probably already use correctly: *component, deconstruct, illogical, inspection, investigation, irrational, misuse, represent, separate, uncouple, unpick.*

Words defined in other sections: *analyse* s2, *assumption* s3, *constituent* s4, *distinguish* s21, *element* s1, *interpret* s23, *premise* s3, *reflect* s28, *relative* s23, *scrutiny* s2.

abstract *adj / n / v*	*adj* – Based on ideas or feelings, not physical things (as opposed to 'concrete').
	n – A summary written by the author/s at the start of an academic article or report.
	v – (1) To remove or take something out of something else. Similar to *extract*.
	(2) To think about something in a theoretical or abstract way.
	🤝 *Adj* – An abstract **concept** / **idea** // **theory** // **model** // **principle**.
analogy *n* **analogous** *adj*	*n* – A reasoned and explained comparison between two things to show their similarity. A *false analogy* is when a comparison is used to come to a conclusion that is not supported by the comparison.
	🤝 To **make** / **draw** / **use an** analogy.
	An **apt** // **good** // **close** // **helpful** // **interesting** // **crude** // **poor** // **inappropriate** // **false** analogy.
	😞 *Analogy*, *metaphor* and *simile*
	A *metaphor* is the use of the image of one thing to represent another.
	E.g. She is a lioness stalking her prey in the urban jungle.
	A *simile* also uses images to compare things but uses *like* or *as* + *as*.
	E.g. She is like a lioness stalking her prey. The room was as black as night.

blur *v / n*	*v* – To make or become unclear.
	🤝 To blur **the line** // **distinction between** X **and** Y.
circular *adj*	A mistake of logic whereby an argument is 'empty' because the conclusion is merely a restatement of the premise(s).
	E.g. We should increase staffing levels so that we have a larger workforce.
construct *n / v*	*n* – A complex idea made by combining different pieces of knowledge or different concepts.
	v – To build, develop or create.
	E.g. His argument is carefully constructed.
	🤝 *n* – A **theoretical** // **abstract** // **mental** construct.
contradictory *adj* **contradiction** *n* **contradict** *v*	*adj* – When the elements involved are logically incompatible.
convey *v*	(1) To communicate or express an idea or feeling.
	(2) To transport or carry.
	🤝 To convey **an emotion** // **feelings** // **an idea** // **information** // **a sense of** X.
deconstruct *v*	To take apart and examine.
denote *v*	To indicate or show.
embody *v*	(1) To be a good (or best) example of an idea, principle, belief or quality.
	(2) To contain or include.
euphemism *n* **euphemistic** *adj* **euphemistically** *adv*	*n* – An indirect or mild expression used as a substitute for something embarrassing or offensive.
	E.g. I am in between jobs = I am unemployed.

explicit *adj* **explicitly** *adv*	*adj* – (1) Clear and obvious. (2) Depicting sexual activity. 🤝 An explicit **instruction** // **threat** // **example** // **warning**.
fallacy *n*	(1) A commonly held but in fact false idea or belief. (2) In formal logic, any form of incorrect reasoning that causes an invalid argument. Examples of logical fallacies are *non sequiturs* (see below) and *false analogies*.
implicit *adj* **implicitly** *adv*	*adj* – Expressed, assumed or learnt indirectly rather than being clearly stated or acknowledged. Similar to *tacit*. 🤝 Implicit **knowledge** // **agreement** // **assumption** // **recognition** // **understanding**. Implicit **criticism** // **critique** // **challenge** // **condemnation**. 😟 *Implicit* and *covert* *Covert* means 'hidden' or 'secret' and is only used in political or military contexts.
literal *adj* **literally** *adv*	*adj* – The surface or 'word for word' meaning of something. 🤝 **In a / the** literal **sense**. The literal **meaning of** X **is** Y. 😟 *Literally* and *literary* *Literally* is the adverb of *literal*. E.g. The story should not be interpreted literally but as a metaphor of an idea. *Literary* is an adjective meaning 'related to literature and writing'. E.g. Jane Austen is a famous literary figure. ❗ The adj *literate* has two meanings, (1) 'able to read and write' and (2) 'well-educated'.

metaphor *n* **metaphorical** *adj* **metaphorically** *adv*	*n* – Using the image of one thing to represent another. E.g. He is a lion stalking its prey. ☹ *Metaphor*, *simile* and *analogy*. See *analogy* above.
misconception *n* **misconceive** *v*	*n* – An incorrect belief or opinion caused by a lack of understanding. 🤝 To **have / hold / labour under** a misconception. To **address / tackle / confront // counter / challenge** a misconception. X **reinforces // perpetuates // gives rise to / leads to the** misconception **that** … A **common // popular // prevalent // widespread // damaging // fundamental / basic** misconception.
non sequitur *n*	A statement that does not follow logically from the one before. In formal logic, a *non sequitur* is when a conclusion does not follow from its premise(s). E.g. Clients thought the cats in our car advert were cute, so I think we should switch from selling cars to selling cats.
overgeneralise* *v* **overgeneralisation*** *n*	*v* – To apply a specific case to a wider range of situations (to generalise) too broadly to be justified. E.g. People are healthier now than they were twenty years ago. For *generalise* see section 22. *-*ize* and -*ization* are also acceptable in British spelling and are always used in US spelling.
overt *adj*	Open and obvious rather than hidden. Similar to *explicit*. 🤝 Overt **behaviour // support // racism // hostility // aggression**. ❗ The opposite word *covert* is not used in academic writing (see *implicit* above).
oxymoron *n*	A term or phrase in which the different components seemingly contradict each other.

paradox *n* **paradoxical** *adj*	*n* – A statement or situation where two things are (apparently) correct but which contradict each other. E.g. She is a wise fool. ☹ *Paradox* and *contradiction* Can be interchanged but *paradox* is also more loosely used to mean a problematic or surprising situation which on closer examination can in fact be resolved (i.e. it is not a true paradox). A *contradiction* is when the elements involved are truly incompatible and the situation is truly irresolvable.
per se *adv*	Considered by, of, or in itself. *Per se* is often used with an initial concession. E.g. I am not opposed to guns per se, but I am against private gun ownership.
signify *v* **signification** *n*	*v* – To symbolise or indicate something. Similar to *denote*.
superficial *adj* **superficially** *adv*	*adj* – (1) Existing or happening only on the surface. (2) Lacking authenticity or real / deep understanding. 🤝 (A) superficial **understanding** // **knowledge** // **change** // **difference** // **similarity** // **treatment** // **level** // **way**.
tacit *adj*	Expressed or known in an indirect, informal or hidden way. Similar to *implicit*. 🤝 Tacit **agreement** // **approval** // **acknowledgement** // **consent** // **knowledge** // **support**. To **have** // **gain** tacit **knowledge of** X.
tangible *adj*	Real and concrete, usually able to be seen or touched. The opposite is *intangible*. 🤝 Tangible **goods** // **skills** // **resources** // **assets** // **worth** / **value**.
truism *n*	An obviously true and uninteresting statement.

20.3 Nearly but not quite right

	Incorrect	Correct
1	This essay discusses whether 'business ethics' is a <u>contradiction of terms</u>.	This essay discusses whether 'business ethics' is a <u>contradiction in terms</u>.
2	The report contains too many informal <u>similes</u> such as 'the deal is a slam dunk'.	The report contains too many informal <u>metaphors</u> such as 'the deal is a slam dunk'.
3	The residents group state that they are not <u>per se against fracking</u> but have concerns about how the fracking site will be managed.	The residents group state that they are not against <u>fracking per se</u> but have concerns about how the fracking site will be managed.
4	I will examine how female CEOs are <u>conveyed</u> in the media.	I will examine how female CEOs are <u>portrayed</u> in the media.
5	It is a <u>non sequitur</u> to say that high levels of job satisfaction and happiness lead to a feeling of well-being in employees.	It is a <u>circular argument</u> to say that high levels of job satisfaction and happiness lead to a feeling of well-being in employees.
6	I look at the ways in which use of business social media <u>blurs the lines in between</u> professional and personal communication styles.	I look at the ways in which use of business social media <u>blurs the line between</u> professional and personal communication styles.
7	Tadashi Yanai <u>signifies</u> the image of an innovative and pragmatic company president.	Tadashi Yanai <u>embodies / represents</u> the image of an innovative and pragmatic company president.
8	The website contains several meaningless <u>true ideas</u> such as 'a management team needs to make decisions about how the business is run'.	The website contains several meaningless <u>truisms</u> such as 'a management team needs to make decisions about how the business is run'.
9	According to marketing colour theory, red <u>is significant for</u> action.	According to marketing colour theory, red <u>signifies</u> action.
10	The main <u>covert</u> assumption behind the term 'cultural competence' in business is that one can in fact become truly competent in someone else's culture.	The main <u>hidden / implicit / tacit</u> assumption behind the term 'cultural competence' in business is that one can in fact become truly competent in someone else's culture.

21 Identifying differences, similarities and common themes

21.1 Words in action

Comparing and contrasting

▸ This assignment <u>compares</u> the birth rate of different EU member states.

▸ We conducted a qualitative <u>comparison</u> of consumer attitudes to the three products.

▸ The <u>comparative</u> analysis shows little difference in behaviour between the companies.

▸ Below we <u>contrast</u> the features of the latest Apple and Samsung models.

▸ The two organisations have <u>contrasting</u> public images.

Identifying similarity, uniformity and convergence

▸ There are a number of interesting <u>similarities</u> between the US and UK financial systems.

▸ The US financial system is <u>similar to / comparable to / akin to</u> that of the UK in several respects.

▸ Rinaldi et al. also found that resources were <u>similarly</u> depleted in both countries.

▸ Non-profit administration <u>resembles</u> private-sector management in two important ways.

▸ The current financial crisis <u>has parallels with</u> the problems of some other European countries.

▸ Nastor (2015) <u>draws analogies between</u> starting a business and writing a novel.

▸ Nastor (2015) sees starting a business as <u>analogous</u> to writing a novel.

▸ This idea of significant <u>common ground / overlap</u> in the motivation of the two types of tourist is supported by research conducted by Ooi and Laing (2010).

▸ That happiness should be an economic indicator is a <u>common thread running through / common theme in</u> Oswald's work.

▸ Each subgroup was <u>homogeneous / uniform</u> in terms of age and income.

▸ Van Zoonen (2004) looks at how the <u>convergence of</u> popular culture and politics can be exploited.

▸ The Europa press release outlines the <u>convergent</u> views on the Multiannual Financial Framework.

Identifying difference and divergence

▸ There are a number of interesting <u>differences</u> between the US and UK financial systems.

▸ This report examines how pesticide use in India <u>is different / differs</u> <u>from</u> that of most other countries.

▸ The businesses are quite <u>dissimilar</u>, even though they make the same product.

▸ We have identified <u>disparities</u> in the two sets of data.

- The data shows the <u>relative</u> disadvantage of women (compared to men) as small business owners.
- The current political situation is <u>relatively / comparatively</u> unstable compared with ten years ago.
- Cote and Morgan (2002) <u>differentiate / distinguish / discriminate</u> between amplification and suppression of emotions.
- A <u>distinction</u> needs to be made between the company's strategy and its outcomes and outputs.
- There are two <u>distinct / discrete categories</u> of small business structures in Bengal.
- Foundem is a <u>distinctive</u> search engine because it is the world's 'first and only general-purpose vertical search platform' (Foundem 2016).
- The two economic theories have <u>disparate</u> principles.
- Demir and Nyhan (2008) evaluate the <u>dichotomy between</u> US politics and administration.
- Since the 1990s the approaches of electronics firms in Hong Kong and Taiwan have <u>diverged</u> (Yang 2007).
- Plato and Aristotle developed <u>divergent</u> theories of knowledge.

Identifying diversity and variety

- There are <u>diverse / varied / different</u> opinions as to whether ethics have a valid place in a business.
- Ethnicity tends to be more <u>diverse</u> in larger towns and cities than in rural areas.
- Bowles (2004) argues that cooperation is of evolutionary benefit to <u>heterogeneous</u> populations.
- You need to present a <u>varied</u> portfolio of work in order to gain the award.
- There are a <u>variety of / various</u> leadership styles, and this essay looks at the three most common.
- The polls show significant <u>variation</u> in the voters' opinions.

Identifying common themes, assumptions or characteristics

- The <u>common theme</u> <u>that emerges from / emerging from</u> both arguments is a lack of public funding.
- A <u>common / shared</u> <u>idea / theme / thread</u> <u>running through / in</u> the articles is a questioning of the benefits of non-tariff barriers to developing economies.
- Our analysis of the literature <u>reveals</u> the <u>(general) underlying</u> <u>premise // assumption</u> that ethical business behaviour is desirable.
- <u>Importantly // Interestingly // Arguably</u>, both studies <u>agree that</u> patients are being harmed by online medical advertising.
- The conclusion <u>common to</u> the studies <u>is that</u> patients are being harmed by online medical advertising.

21.2　Information to help you use these words correctly

Words you probably already use correctly: *common, contrast, differentiate, overlap, thread.*
Words defined in other sections: *analogy* s20, *theme* s1.

akin *adj*	(1) Similar in character.
	(2) Related by blood.
	🤝 X **is / are** akin **to** Y.
compare *v* **comparable** *adj*	*v* – To note the similarities and differences between things.
	adj – Similar or equivalent.
	E.g. Teachers' salaries are comparable to those of nurses.
	❗ *Compare* uses *to* or *with*. These are often interchanged but strictly speaking, *compare to* = similarities and *compare with* = differences.
	E.g. A software virus is often compared to a biological one.
	Compared with last year's figures, this year's have been much higher.
	❗ *Incomparable* (adj) has two different meanings.
	(1) Very different and so unable to be compared.
	(2) Unable to be compared because of being the best.
	E.g. She has an incomparable intellect.
comparatively *adv* **comparative** *adj*	*adv* – As compared to other things. When used more loosely, similar to *relatively.*
	E.g. Germany is a comparatively / relatively wealthy country.
	🤝 A comparative **(dis)advantage**. A comparative **analysis // report // survey**.
	🙁 *Comparative* and *comparable*
	These words have different meanings. See *comparable* above.
converge *v* **convergence** *n* **convergent** *adj*	*v* – Of directions or viewpoints, to come or start to come together.

dichotomy *n*	A strict division or difference between two things.
discrete *adj* **discreteness** *n*	*adj* – Being a separate entity. Similar to *distinct*. 😟 *Discrete, discreet and discretion* *Discreet* and one sense of *discretion* means 'to be tactful' / 'tactfulness' (see section 6).
discriminate *v* **discrimination** *n* **discriminatory** *adj*	*v* – (1) To make a distinction between two or more things. Similar to *differentiate*. E.g. Consumers need to discriminate between reliable and fraudulent websites. (2) To treat differently, either favourably or negatively (see section 7).
disparate *adj*	Very different or fundamentally different and therefore unable to be compared. 😟 *Disparate and desperate* Two different words with very different meanings.
disparity *n*	A difference or lack of equality. ❗ Note that unlike the adjective *disparate* above, a *disparity* is a difference between things that also have similarities and can therefore be compared.
distinct *adj*	(1) Recognisable as separate. (2) Noticeable. E.g. There is a distinct absence of evidence in the report.
distinction *n*	A difference. E.g. There is a distinction between relative and absolute poverty. 🤝 To **make** / **draw** / **recognise** // **clarify** // **maintain** a/the distinction **between** X and Y. A **clear** // **important** // **fundamental** distinction.
distinctive *adj*	Different from all others because of a particular characteristic.

distinguish *v*	To recognise a difference between things. Similar to *differentiate* and *make a distinction between*. E.g. She distinguishes between relative and absolute poverty. ❗ The past participle of the verb is *distinguished*. This is the same spelling as the adjective *distinguished* meaning 'looking dignified and/or commanding respect'.
diverge *v* **divergence** *n* **divergent** *adj*	*v* – To go or start to go in different directions. Usually used to describe things that start from a similar point but then separate or to describe things that have both similarities and differences.
diverse *adj*	Varied. Similar to *heterogeneous*. 🤝 A diverse **range** // **group** // **sector** // **market**.
heterogeneous *adj* **heterogeneity** *n*	*adj* – (1) Having elements that are all different. Similar to *diverse*. (2) Of different types.
homogeneous *adj* **homogeneity** *n*	*adj* – (1) Having elements that are all the same or similar. (2) Of the same type.
parallel *n / adj*	*n* – A similarity. *adj* – (1) Side by side or happening at the same time, e.g. Parallel computing. (2) Two lines or surfaces having the same distance continuously between them. 🤝 *n* – To **draw** // **note** // **reveal** // **suggest** a parallel **with** / **between** X and Y. An **obvious** // **striking** parallel.
relative *adj* **relatively** *adv*	*adj* – (1) Having more or less of a particular quality compared with something else. (2) Depending on your position or point of view, rather than being absolute. ❗ Note that the object of comparison is often implied rather than explicitly stated. For example, 'There is a relative lack of information on the website about the company' means as compared to other company websites.

resemble *v*	*v* – To be similar in some way.
resemblance *n*	
reveal *v*	To allow or cause something that exists to be recognised or seen.
	The **data** // **experiment** // **analysis** // **results** // **findings** reveal X.
varied *adj*	Having difference or diversity.
	E.g. The members of the group have varied interests.
variety *n*	*n* – (1) A group or collection of things or occasions that are different. Similar to *range of*.
various *adj*	E.g. You should eat a variety of vegetables.
	(2) A type of.
	E.g. Supermarkets sell only a few varieties of apple.
vary *v*	To make different or to change something.
	E.g. A firm might vary its sales tactics according to the market conditions.

21.3   Nearly but not quite right

	Incorrect	Correct
1	Cote and Morgan (2002) <u>make a difference</u> between amplification and suppression of emotions.	Cote and Morgan (2002) <u>differentiate</u> between amplification and suppression of emotions.
2	I suggest that a <u>parallel can be made</u> between the current global financial downturn and the depression of the 1930s.	I suggest that a <u>parallel can be drawn</u> between the current global financial downturn and the depression of the 1930s.
3	New York has an extremely <u>various</u> population.	New York has an extremely <u>varied / diverse</u> population.
4	My past work experience has been <u>different</u>, involving jobs in four different industries.	My past work experience has been <u>diverse</u>, involving jobs in four different industries.
5	We found a <u>distinctive</u> difference of 8.4 grams between the 'before' and 'after' weights.	We found a <u>distinct</u> difference of 8.4 grams between the 'before' and 'after' weights.
6	As the company had a somewhat <u>varied</u> safety record, their franchise was not renewed.	As the company had a somewhat <u>variable</u> safety record, their franchise was not renewed.
7	Our model proposes that there is no such thing as a <u>heterogeneous</u> workforce – individual differences will always be present.	Our model proposes that there is no such thing as a <u>homogeneous</u> workforce – individual differences will always be present.
8	Sierra Leone is a <u>relative</u> small country.	Sierra Leone is a <u>relatively</u> small country.
9	David, David and David (2011) examine the <u>diversity</u> between what university business schools teach and what business communities want.	David, David and David (2011) examine the <u>disparity</u> between what university business schools teach and what business communities want.
10	It is important to understand the <u>distinction of</u> a business's mission statement and strategy.	It is important to understand the <u>distinction between</u> a business's mission statement and their strategy.

22   Identifying relationships and making logical links

See also sections 19 and 28 for other useful words and phrases.

22.1   Words in action

Dependency and close connections

▸ Many economists argue that a successful society <u>hinges / depends / is dependent</u> <u>on / upon</u> economic growth.

▸ The company operates on the basis that salary increases <u>depend</u> <u>on / upon</u> <u>whether</u> targets are reached.

▸ The company operates on the basis of salary increases being <u>contingent / conditional</u> <u>on</u> reaching the targets.

▸ I agree with Barsoux (1996) that humour is a <u>necessary / requisite</u> part of a successful organisation.

▸ Society and economic performance are <u>interdependent / mutually dependent // interrelated / interconnected</u>.

▸ This essay has argued that economic growth is <u>essential for // an integral part of</u> social happiness.

▸ Harter (2000) claims that there is an <u>inextricable link between</u> physical appearance and self-esteem.

▸ The <u>Integrated</u> Organisation Model (IOM) cannot be usefully applied to all types of organisation.

Other types of connection

▸ I suggest that office configuration <u>is relevant to / has a bearing on / is a factor in / plays a role in</u> productivity.

▸ These case studies demonstrate how revenue <u>relates to</u> elasticity.

▸ Life-prolonging technology and the <u>associated / related</u> business opportunities will be discussed.

▸ Research by Lingard et al. (2001) and others supports the idea that work–life conflict is <u>associated with / linked to</u> mental health issues.

▸ Working-class speech patterns have more favourable <u>connotations / associations</u> for men than for women.

▸ There is <u>a strong / close // direct // positive // negative // significant correlation between</u> advertising <u>and</u> sales.

▸ Online supply enterprises allow a more <u>dynamic</u> network that can <u>react</u> quickly (Grefen et al. 2009).

▸ Our data demonstrates the growth in cross-business <u>synergies</u> in the market since 2000.

▸ There is increasing interest in the <u>reciprocal</u> relationship between humans and their environment.

- This report shows how tourism can be <u>compatible with</u> environmental sustainability if carefully managed.

Being equal to or being the same

- The new national minimum wage rate is <u>equivalent to / corresponds to / amounts to / represents</u> an increase of 2.5% on the previous rate.
- I look at whether the idea that every right has <u>a corresponding</u> duty is applicable to business contexts.
- People tend to <u>equate</u> knowledge with intelligence.
- I will argue that all EU member states should have <u>equal // similar // the same</u> status.
- The strike is over lack of <u>parity</u> in government funding across different regions.
- In the 1980s the Body Shop was <u>synonymous with</u> sustainability.
- Eddy (2016) looks at how business schools in Eastern Europe are catching up with their western <u>counterparts</u>.
- A deeper analysis of these charities' CEO salaries revealed that their pay rates were <u>in proportion to / proportional to / proportionate to / commensurate with</u> their performance (Ribeiro 2013).

Reverse relationships

- As the supply of a currency increases it loses value, and the <u>converse / reverse</u> is also true.
- The students in group A were asked to mix with the students in group B and <u>vice versa</u>.

Non-dependency and lack of relationship

- Several studies suggest that the <u>link between</u> business plans and performance is <u>not</u> necessarily <u>causal</u>, and can in fact be <u>tenuous</u> (Phillips 1996, Pearce, Freeman and Robinson 1987, Gibson and Cassar 2005).
- Despite the media hype, identity cards are in fact <u>tangential / peripheral to</u> national security.
- Table 1 shows the number of <u>incidental</u> injuries to marine mammals during commercial fishing operations.

Making logical links and inferences

- This evidence suggests that intention to quit is <u>causally linked to</u> job satisfaction.
- From the analysis it can be <u>inferred</u> that having a job has a greater impact on happiness than salary received.
- The <u>inference we can make / conclusion we can draw</u> from the survey is that SMEs need more support.
- People are now richer but less happy, and so we <u>come to / arrive at the conclusion that</u> wealth does not increase happiness.
- People are now richer but less happy, which <u>implies</u> that wealth is not a key contributor to happiness.

- Higher returns on investment <u>entail / involve</u> higher risks.
- The aggregate data enables us to <u>deduce</u> the function sequence of individual organisations.
- The employees who responded to our survey were dissatisfied, therefore (<u>via induction</u>) we can assume that there is a lack of job satisfaction across the organisation.
- We can <u>generalise</u> from our data and suggest a link between laissez-faire style leadership and productivity.
- By <u>extrapolating</u> current trends, this report <u>concludes</u> that continued growth is possible but at a slower rate.

22.2   Information to help you use these words correctly

Words you probably already use correctly: *amount to, associated, bearing on, conclude, conditional, connection, equal, equate, equivalent, essential, extrapolate, link, necessary, react, relevant, represent, reverse, via.*

Words defined in other sections: *asssume* s3, *attribute* s6, *constitute* s4, *factor* s1, *hypothesis* s3, *proportionate* s13, *role* s1.

commensurate *adj*	Corresponding in degree, extent or size. Similar to *proportionate*.
	🤝 X is commensurate **with** Y.
compatible *adj*	Existing and/or operating together without problems or conflict.
connotation *n*	An emotion or idea associated with a word or phrase in addition to its literal meaning. Similar to *association*.
	🤝 A **positive** // **negative** // **strong** // **obvious** // **subtle** connotation.
contingent *adj / n*	*adj* – (1) Dependent on other events. Similar to *conditional*.
	(2) Dependent on chance.
	(3) In philosophy, dependent on the truth values of the proposition.
	n – A representative group or portion, e.g. A contingent force of soldiers.
	❗ The noun meaning 'a possible future event' is *contingency* (see section 30).

converse *n* **conversely** *adv*	*n* – When elements are reversible or interchangeable. Similar to *vice versa*. ☹ *Converse* and *opposite* A *converse* relationship is when the different parts are interchangeable, for example, the converse of 'All Ys are Xs' is 'All Xs are Ys'. This is not the same as an *opposite* relationship, in which the terms are incompatible, sharing no common ground. Examples of opposites are *long – short* and *happy – sad*. ☹ *Conversely*, *in contrast* and *however* *In contrast* and *however* introduce differences or opposites.
correlation *n* **correlate** *v*	*n* – An interdependent link or relationship. In statistics, a correlation is where if one thing increases / decreases, the other also increases / decreases. Importantly, a correlation does not necessarily mean that one thing causes the other. 🤝 A **strong** // **direct** // **significant** // **high** // **positive** // **negative** // **weak** correlation.
correspond *v* **corresponding** *adj* **correspondingly** *adv*	*v* – (1) To have a directly matching relationship or link. (2) To communicate in writing with someone. ☹ *Correspondingly* and *similarly* *Correspondingly* means having a linked or matching relationship to something else. E.g. Oil reserves have increased and the price of cars has dropped correspondingly. *Similarly* is used when one thing is done in a similar way to the other. E.g. The E9 model will be launched at a large media event in the US next May, and the T9 model will be similarly launched in Germany.
counterpart *n*	A corresponding thing or person, often with the same or similar function.

deduce *v* **deduction** *n* **deductive** *adj*	*v* – A process of logic in which general facts or premises are used to arrive at a specific conclusion. If your premise is correct then your conclusion must be correct. E.g. All mammals are warm-blooded. A cow is a mammal, therefore a cow is warm-blooded. Compare with *induce / induction* below. **!** In academic writing the more general terms *conclude / conclusion* are much more commonly used than *deduce / deduction*.
depend *v* **dependent** *adj*	*v* – (1) To be determined by. (2) To need or rely on. 😟 *Dependent* and *dependant* A *dependant* is someone for whom another family member is responsible.
dynamic *adj / n*	*adj* – (1) A continuously changing and developing process or system, often in the context of a two-way relationship. (2) Full of ideas and/or energy. *n* – A force that causes change.
entail *v*	(1) To be a necessary part or result of. Similar to *necessitate*. (2) To logically follow. In logic, A is said to entail B if it is the case that if A is true, B must be true, and that if A is false, B must be false.

generalise* *v* **generalisation*** *n*	*v* – To use specific data or specific case/s to arrive at a general statement. E.g. The shops in this street have high prices so all the shops in town have high prices. *adj* – A generalisation can be: Universal – forms a premise of a deductive argument (see *deduction* above). E.g. All mammals are warm-blooded. Partial – forms a premise of an inductive argument (see *induction* below). E.g. The shops in this street have high prices. 🤝 To **make a** generalisation. *-ize* and *-ization* are also acceptable in British spelling and are always used in US spelling.
hinge on *v*	When one action or event depends on another.
imply *v* **implication** *n*	*v* – (1) To enable to arrive at a conclusion. E.g. The data implies that employee well-being has increased in the company. (2) To logically necessitate a consequence, e.g. Life implies death. Similar to *entail*. (3) To suggest something indirectly. E.g. The tone of her email implied that I wasn't working hard enough. 😟 *Imply* and *infer* – see *infer* below.
incidental *adj*	(1) Occurring by chance as part of something else. (2) Of minor importance or with minor effect.

induction *n* **inductive** *adj*	*n* – The everyday reasoning process used for making generalisations, using specific cases to arrive at a more general conclusion. A conclusion arrived at through induction is only as sound as the evidence used, and cannot be proven with absolute certainty. E.g. The shops in this street have high prices so probably most shops in the town do. (!) In writing the more general terms *conclude / conclusion* are more commonly used. The verb *to induct* has a different meaning (e.g. student induction).
inextricable *adj* **inextricably** *adv*	*adj* – Impossible to separate. 🤝 *adj* – There **is an** inextricable **link** between X and Y. *adv* – X **and** Y **are** inextricably **linked**.
infer *v* **inference** *n*	*v* – To reach a conclusion (through any type of reasoning process). 😞 *Infer* and *imply* Only people infer things. E.g. From the data we can infer that having a job is more important than the salary. Data and other information imply things (see meanings (1) and (2) of *imply* above). E.g. The data implies that having a job is more important than the salary.
integral *adj*	Essential as a part of something. Necessary in order to make complete.
integrate *v* **integrated** *adj* **integration** *n*	*v* – To combine two or more things to form one entity. 🤝 To integrate X **with** Y. To integrate X **into** Y.
interconnected *adj*	When parts are linked to each other, often in a physical way.
interdependent *adj*	Where things are essential to each other in order to function properly.

interrelated *adj*	When things have a relationship to each other.
	😟 *Interrelated, interconnected* and *interdependent*
	Interrelated is the most general term, followed by *interconnected*, and the two words can usually be interchanged. *Interdependent* is used for closer relationships, often in the context of people and societies.
parity *n*	The state or condition of being equal, usually in the context of pay or status.
peripheral *adj*	On the outer edges, marginal or of minor importance.
	🤝 X **plays a** peripheral **role in** Y.
reciprocal *adj*	*adj* – Having mutual exchange and benefit between two things or groups.
reciprocity *n*	❗ Having a reciprocal relationship does not necessitate dependency.
relate *v*	*v* – (1) To connect with or refer to.
related *adj*	(2) To give an account of/ tell a story.
	For *relative* see section 21.
relevant *adj*	Connected or appropriate to.
relevance *n*	😟 *Relevant* and *related*
	Related means that there is a connection between X and Y.
	Relevant means that X is of a similar (or appropriate) subject or type as Y.
requisite *adj / n*	*adj* – Necessary.
	n – A thing that is necessary in order for something else to happen.
	🤝 The requisite **funds // skills // structures // parts // machinery // client base // market share // permission**.
	😟 *Requisite* and *requisition*
	A requisition is an official document or order to take goods from someone else.
	The verb *to requisition* has this same sense.

synergy *n*	The combined energy and activity produced when two or more things work together.
synonymous *adj*	(1) Of words and phrases, having the same meaning.
	(2) Closely associated with.
tangential *adj*	(1) Of little or no relevance.
	(2) In geometry, touching but not crossing.
tenuous *adj*	Weak and/or lacking a strong basis.
	🤝 A tenuous **link** // **argument**.
vice versa *adv*	Also true in reverse order. Similar to *conversely*.

22.3 Nearly but not quite right

	Incorrect	Correct
1	A business model is the overall operational approach an organisation takes. <u>Conversely</u>, its strategy is a plan of how to put this model into practice.	A business model is the overall operational approach an organisation takes. <u>In contrast</u>, its strategy is a plan of how to put this model into practice.
2	Many Spanish business schools have <u>reciprocity</u> relationships with overseas universities.	Many Spanish business schools have <u>reciprocal</u> relationships with overseas universities.
3	A referral partnership is when one company refers customers to another and <u>then visa versa</u>.	A referral partnership is when one company refers customers to another and <u>vice versa</u>.
4	One advantage of having <u>conditional</u> workers is only having to pay them when they are needed.	One advantage of having <u>contingent</u> workers is only having to pay them when they are needed.
5	The evidence Paling (2012) presents suggests that although the picture is complex, Cambodia is still clearly <u>depends on</u> donor finance.	The evidence Paling (2012) presents suggests that although the picture is complex, Cambodia is still clearly <u>dependent on</u> donor finance.
6	This essay has demonstrated that written role descriptors are important because different people tend to <u>imply</u> different things from informal meetings.	This essay has demonstrated that written role descriptors are important because different people tend to <u>infer</u> different things from informal meetings.
7	We conducted a survey on consumer trust. The table below gives firstly the responses from ten online companies, followed by the <u>similar</u> answers from local physical outlets.	We conducted a survey on consumer trust. The table below gives firstly the responses from ten online companies, followed by the <u>corresponding</u> answers from local physical outlets.
8	An organisation's business model is <u>relative to</u> its strategy in that the latter is a plan for the realisation of the former.	An organisation's business model <u>is related to / relates to</u> its strategy in that the latter is a plan for the realisation of the former.
9	These 'coupled companies' (Schonsleben 2016) need to further co-ordinate, as they are <u>dependent to</u> each other for efficiency along the supply chain.	These 'coupled companies' (Schonsleben 2016) need to further co-ordinate, as they are <u>dependent on</u> each other for efficiency along the supply chain.
10	The Bain & Company survey demonstrates that it is extremely common to overestimate merger <u>energy</u> benefits.	The Bain & Company survey demonstrates that it is extremely common to overestimate merger <u>synergy</u> benefits.

23 Identifying points of view and position

To write successful assignments you need to show clearly what your position is on the topic or issue, and what position your source authors hold.

23.1 Words in action

Point of view and position

▸ This essay <u>takes / holds / subscribes to</u> <u>the view that</u> earning money from money is unethical.

▸ The <u>view</u> that all research should help develop theory is debatable, <u>according to</u> May (2000).

▸ Kirsch (2010) <u>thinks / holds the opinion / is of the opinion</u> <u>that</u> mining cannot be sustainable.

▸ Adam Smith is <u>widely</u> <u>regarded as / viewed as / seen as / thought of as / considered to be / deemed to be</u> the father of free-market capitalism.

▸ The article criticises the government's <u>stance / position on</u> potential strike action.

▸ Increasingly, schools in Australia are <u>positioning</u> themselves within a free-market economy.

▸ I use Gordijn and Akkermans (2001) to look at e-business <u>from</u> an economic <u>perspective / viewpoint / standpoint.</u>

▸ Harris (2016) argues that law should be viewed <u>through the lens of / through the prism of</u> social practices.

▸ Increasingly, schools are <u>orientating</u> themselves <u>towards</u> a free-market economy.

Interpretation, perception and connotation

▸ Sloboda and Lehmann (2001) investigate how listeners <u>interpret</u> the same piece of music differently.

▸ Legislation is often <u>open to interpretation</u>, and so the principle of statutory construction is important.

▸ Avoiding eye contact can be <u>perceived as / seen as</u> a sign of dishonesty in western business cultures.

▸ It is important to agree meeting minutes, because people's memory and <u>perception of</u> what was said can vary.

▸ As Harris (2016) argues, morality is a <u>relative</u> concept, as its parameters change across social groups.

Impartiality and bias

▸ I will argue that good business journalism should be <u>impartial / disinterested</u>.

▸ People have various cognitive and emotional <u>biases</u>, which can affect the quality of business decisions.

- Our report shows that food labelling is heavily <u>biased towards</u> the producer rather than the consumer.
- I will argue that aid charity advertising can encourage a <u>distorted view</u> of developing countries.
- Business blogs are often written from a <u>subjective</u> rather than <u>objective</u> perspective.

Ways of thinking and ideologies
- Many business psychologists today do not adhere closely to any one <u>school of thought</u>.
- Marxist Communism is still an influential <u>ideology</u> despite the breakup of the Soviet Union.
- Gibson's view is that innovators, by definition, challenge <u>orthodoxy / received wisdom // dogma</u>.
- The <u>paradigm</u> shift from organisation to customer-centric practices is not as radical as is being claimed.
- This essay challenges two of the core <u>tenets / beliefs</u> of high-performance companies.
- The Peter <u>Principle</u> states that successful staff are eventually promoted to a level beyond their capability.

Supporting or accepting viewpoints
- Recent studies <u>support</u> the idea that a successful organisation is one that <u>embraces</u> change.
- The government has received significant <u>backing</u> from the industrial sector over its tariff reforms.
- The company's CEO is a <u>proponent / advocate / supporter of</u> the civil liberties movement in Chile.
- In this report an alliance is defined as businesses <u>aligned with</u> each other for the duration of a project.
- Steve Jobs was an <u>exponent of</u> Zen meditation.
- I argue that the notion that a leader must <u>stick / adhere to</u> their business plan is flawed.
- Diehm and Armatas (2004) look at how surfing is a high-risk business that has been <u>accepted by</u> society.
- Most self-employed workers <u>acknowledge / concede / accept the need to</u> complete a tax evaluation form.
- We ask whether the board should <u>condone</u> the organisation's current practice of cold calling.

Inflexible, indifferent, rejecting and opposing viewpoints
- The article criticises the government's <u>rigid stance / inflexible position / intransigence</u> on strike action.
- Puffer and McCarthy (1995) identified <u>ambivalence</u> about ethics as highly stressful for businesspeople.
- Recent human rights violations indicate the government is <u>indifferent to / uninterested in</u> international opinion.
- The owner of a business should check that their board's legal advisers are <u>disinterested</u> parties.
- Many economists remain <u>sceptical</u> about the reliability of qualitative research data.
- Honesty and even <u>dissent</u> should be encouraged in management groups in order to reach informed decisions.

- Svensson and Wood (2007) <u>disagree with / counter / contest / rebut / refute</u> Friedman's claim that businesses do not need to consider social issues, and state that, <u>on the contrary</u>, they have a huge impact on society.
- Ainsworth <u>disagrees with / rejects / dismisses</u> Dawkins' claim that faith schools are discriminatory.
- Market socialists <u>object to</u> <u>the concept of</u> capitalism <u>on the grounds that</u> it leads to inequality.

23.2   Information to help you use these words correctly

Words you probably already use correctly: *backing, bias, contrary, on the grounds that, regard, reject, school of thought, standpoint.*
    Words defined in other sections: *according to* s4, *counter* s25, *paradigm* s18, *radical* s17, *relative* s21.

adhere *v* **adherence** *n*	*v* – (1) To agree with or support an idea, belief, principle, policy or point of view. (2) To stick to something.
advocate *v / n*	*v* – To actively support. *n* – A (strong) supporter of something. 🤝 *v* – To **actively // openly // strongly** advocate X. *n* – An advocate **of** / advocate **for** X. To be a **keen // passionate** advocate of X.
align *v*	(1) To support and/or agree with. (2) Place in a straight line.
ambivalent *adj* **ambivalence** *n*	*adj* – Having mixed or contradictory feelings or ideas about something. 🙁 *Ambivalent* and *indifferent* These words have different meanings. See *indifferent* below.
averse *adj*	Opposed to. 🙁 *Averse* and *ad**verse*** *Ad**verse*** means unpleasant and/or harmful (see section 7).

condone *v*	To accept (reluctantly), agree with or approve of behaviour usually viewed as morally wrong.
	🤝 To condone **behaviour** // **the practice of** // **the action of** // **violence** // **abuse** // **torture** // **murder**.
contest *v / n*	To argue against. Similar to *challenge*, *refute* and *rebut*.
deem *v*	To consider or regard as.
disinterested *adj*	(1) Unbiased.
	(2) Having no interest in.
	😟 *Disinterested* and *uninterested*
	Note that as shown by (2) above, *disinterested* is sometimes used interchangeably with *uninterested*. However, only *disinterested* means 'unbiased' / 'impartial'.
dismiss *v* **dismissive** *adj*	*v* – (1) To regard as unimportant or not valuable.
	(2) To order to leave.
	🤝 *v* – To dismiss X **as** Y.
	adj – To be dismissive **of** Y.
dissent *n*	Disagreement, often in the context of official debates or judgements.
dogma *n* **dogmatic** *adj*	*n* – A system of principles or beliefs that supporters view as undeniably true. *Dogma* is also sometimes used more loosely to mean 'strong political views'.
	adj – (1) Relating to dogma.
	(2) The characteristic of being stubborn and opinionated (see section 5).
embrace *v*	To accept and welcome something.
	🤝 To **willingly** // **actively** // **wholeheartedly** // **fully** embrace X.
	To embrace (a) **change** // **a challenge** // **a concept** / **a notion** / **an idea** // **an opportunity**.
endorse *v*	To publicly support and recommend an idea, belief, action or product.

exponent *n*	(1) An example, practitioner or representative of something.
	(2) A skilled artist or performer, usually a musician.
	☹ *Exponent* and *proponent*. See *proponent* below.
ideology *n* **ideologically** *adj* **ideologically** *adv*	*n* – A set of ideas held by a social or political group used to promote and/or protect their interests.
	🤝 A **political** // **liberal** // **extremist** // **free-market** // **economic** // **business** // **secular** // **racist** // **totalitarian** ideology.
	The **dominant** / **ruling** / **prevailing** ideology.
	To **adopt** // **embrace** // **share** // **challenge** // **oppose** an ideology.
impartial *adj* **impartiality** *n*	*adj* – Not influenced by any particular side or not favouring one side or view. Similar to *neutral*, *unbiased*, *balanced* and *disinterested*.
	🤝 To **offer** / **give** impartial **advice** / **guidance**.
interpret *v* **interpretation** *n*	*v* – To explain or understand something from a particular perspective.
lens *n*	A particular way of thinking. Similar to *perspective* and *prism*.
	🤝 **Discuss** / **examine** / **analyse** / **see** X **through the** lens **of** Y.
objective *adj*	Based only on facts and not influenced by feelings or beliefs.
orthodoxy *n* **orthodox** *adj*	*n* – A generally accepted viewpoint, doctrine or way of doing things.
	🤝 *n* – **Economic** / **monetarist** orthodoxy.
	adj – Orthodox **economic** / **social** / **business theory**.
perceive *v* **perception** *n*	*v* – (1) To see or become aware of something.
	(2) To understand or realise something in a particular way.

perspective *n*	(1) Point of view or particular understanding.
	(2) Representing three-dimensional objects on a two-dimensional surface.
principle *n*	A belief, idea, theory, rule or moral code.
	😟 *Princip**le*** and *princip**al***
	*Princip**al*** means 'the main and/or most important'.
prism *n*	A particular way of thinking. Similar to *perspective* and *lens*.
	🤝 **Discuss / examine / analyse / see** X **through the** prism **of** Y.
proponent *n*	Someone who agrees with a plan, idea or theory. Similar to *advocate* and *supporter*.
	😟 *Proponent* and *exponent*
	Sometimes used interchangeably but there is a difference in meaning.
	A *proponent* does not necessarily make their support public or active.
	An *exponent* is in favour of something and puts their support into practice.
rebut *v* **rebuttal** *n*	*v* – To argue against a statement and to attempt to prove it is false. Similar to *contest* and *refute* but less commonly used.
received wisdom *n*	A generally accepted viewpoint, doctrine or way of doing things. Similar to *orthodoxy*.
refute *v* **refutation** *n*	*v* – To oppose a statement and attempt to prove that it is false. Similar to *contest* and *rebut*.
	🤝 To refute **the claim // suggestion // accusation // idea // theory that** …
sceptical* *adj* **sceptic*** *n*	*adj* – (1) Doubtful about something.
	(2) Questioning. In philosophy, *scepticism* is the approach whereby all knowledge and belief is questioned.
	* The US spellings are *skeptical* and *skeptic*.

stance *n*	A clear position on an issue.
	🤝 A **hardline** / **tough** // **firm** // **ethical** // **moral** stance **on** X.
	To **adopt** // **hold** // **take a** stance.
subjective *adj*	Based on feelings and beliefs rather than fact.
	🤝 **Highly** / **extremely** / **largely** // **somewhat** subjective.
	A subjective **opinion** // **viewpoint** // **response** // **assessment** // **judgement**.
subscribe *v*	(1) To agree with a particular idea or way of thinking.
	(2) To make regular payments for a magazine, newspaper, book club etc.
tenet *n*	A key principle or belief.
	🤝 A **core** tenet.
view *n / v*	*n* – An opinion, belief or attitude, often not based on evidence.
	v – (1) To think of in a particular way.
	(2) To look at or inspect.
	🤝 *n* – A **personal** // **broad** // **narrow** // **simplistic** // **orthodox** // **traditional** view.
	To **subscribe to** / **hold the** view **that** … .
viewpoint *n*	A particular way of thinking about something. Similar to *standpoint* and *perspective*.
	😦 *Viewpoint*, *view* and *point of view*
	These words are usually interchangeable but strictly speaking, a *viewpoint* is a more general position from which a specific *view* / *point of view* / *opinion* is formed.
	🤝 An **alternative** // **a different** // **an opposing** // **a subjective** // **an objective** viewpoint.

23.3   Nearly but not quite right

	Incorrect	Correct
1	It is common for different stakeholders to have <u>disagreements</u> about what is best for the business.	It is common for different stakeholders to have <u>different opinions / views / points of view</u> about what is best for the business.
2	A court judge should remain <u>indifferent</u> throughout a trial.	A court judge should remain <u>impartial</u> throughout a trial.
3	The trade union is <u>contrary</u> to widespread use of zero hours contracts.	The trade union <u>opposes / is opposed to</u> widespread use of zero hours contracts.
4	In his 1991 article 'The Thriving Cult of Greed and Power', Behar discusses his strong <u>views against</u> scientology.	In his 1991 article 'The Thriving Cult of Greed and Power', Behar discusses his strong <u>views on / about</u> scientology.
5	I suggest that if a manager does not deal with unacceptable behaviour from an employee, they are, in effect, <u>condoning with it</u>.	I suggest that if a manager does not deal with unacceptable behaviour from an employee, they are, in effect, <u>condoning it</u>.
6	Karl Marx <u>refuted</u> capitalism.	Karl Marx <u>rejected</u> capitalism. Karl Marx <u>refuted</u> capitalism <u>by arguing that</u> …
7	The idea of using a computer program to collectively edit a website was <u>perceived</u> by Beck in the 1990s.	The idea of using a computer program to collectively edit a website was <u>conceived</u> by Beck in the 1990s.
8	Rinzai Zen is a <u>way of thinking</u> based in the Japanese rather than the Chinese tradition.	Rinzai Zen is a <u>school of thought</u> based in the Japanese rather than the Chinese tradition.
9	Cognitivism is one of the most influential <u>schools of thinking</u> within business psychology.	Cognitivism is one of the most influential <u>schools of thought</u> within business psychology.
10	Storey (2016) looks at current issues in organisational leadership <u>from a critical lens</u>.	Storey (2016) looks at current issues in organisational leadership <u>through a critical lens / from a critical perspective.</u>

Evaluating ideas, evidence and impact

24 Evaluating ideas and evidence positively

When you analyse and evaluate source material it is important to use the right verbs, in order to show your tutor that you have correctly identified what the author is doing (e.g. stating, questioning or arguing). It is also important to use the right verbs, adjectives and nouns to show your tutor what *you* think of the author's ideas.

24.1 Words in action

Using 'neutral' verbs to introduce a source and then give a positive comment

▶ In 1984, Levitt <u>stated // suggested // asserted / contended / claimed / maintained / proposed</u> that the world was becoming a 'global village', and this concept is now well established.

Using 'positive' verbs to comment on a source

▶ Milanovic (2002) <u>explains // demonstrates / illustrates / shows</u> how globalisation can affect income distribution.

▶ Martin and Thompson (2010) <u>examine // cover in detail // consider / take into account</u> the different definitions and types of social enterprises.

▶ Keegan and Bosilie (2006) <u>found that // observed that / made the observation that / noted that // established that</u> HRM journals tend to exclude articles that are highly critical of HR practices.

▶ Purdue and Gurtman (1990) <u>identified</u> important economic consequences of ageism.

▶ The author's argument is <u>validated by / supported by / justified by</u> the data presented in my report.

▶ Martin and Thompson (2010) <u>investigate</u> and <u>clarify / elucidate</u> the nature of social enterprises.

▶ Miller (1991) <u>explicates / expounds / delineates</u> the process by which people develop mental models of relationships.

▶ The examples used by the authors <u>encapsulate</u> how transactional leaders can create a better society.

▶ The article successfully <u>simplifies</u> the complex phenomenon of asset bubbles.

Using 'positive' adjectives, adverbs and nouns to comment on a source

▸ The article contains <u>overwhelming // compelling // convincing // objective // hard / strong / clear // ample</u> evidence for …

▸ Their research <u>conclusively // convincingly</u> shows / establishes that environment affects mental health.

▸ Crane and Matten (2015) give a <u>comprehensive / thorough // extensive</u> overview of business ethics, and <u>give / offer</u> <u>clear // useful insights</u> into …

▸ The report provides <u>important // interesting // reliable / sound</u> data on small business growth in India.

▸ He provides a <u>cogent / coherent / logical / rational // sound / valid / legitimate // grounded // reasonable / tenable // considered</u> argument to support his theory that …

▸ Chesbrough puts forward <u>innovative // convincing / persuasive / plausible / credible</u> ideas about how to overcome barriers to business model innovation.

▸ The logic of Brigham's argument is <u>unquestionable / unassailable // remarkable // impressive</u>.

▸ In my view, Perdue and Gurtman (1990) <u>correctly identify</u> an important and previously overlooked factor in ageism, and their insights have <u>currency / relevance</u> for other areas of work discrimination.

▸ This comprehensive study on 20th-century fiscal policies is often seen as <u>definitive</u>.

▸ The 2015 EU report is an <u>exceptional / singular</u> analysis of the migration issue.

▸ Stich (1985) provides some <u>illuminating</u> examples of human irrationality.

▸ The report benefits from a <u>robust</u> methodology, <u>rigorous</u> research, a <u>succinct</u> style and a <u>readable</u> format.

▸ A clear <u>strength</u> of the survey is the very large sample size.

Stating that a source is supported by other research or has contributed to the field

▸ The proposition that ICT is largely responsible for the growth of interest in business models is <u>supported / corroborated / confirmed / verified / validated / substantiated by</u> several other studies in this area.

▸ Importantly, the findings are <u>consistent with</u> those of previous studies.

▸ Kramer's article is a <u>noteworthy // valuable // substantive</u> contribution to the debate on corporate responsibility.

Showing how one author comments positively on another

▸ Barrick et al. (2002) <u>cite</u> Bakan as a proponent of the idea that achieving status is a key social goal.

▸ Mass and Tucci <u>paraphrase // quote</u> Amit, Zott and McGrath <u>to support</u> their argument that business models are necessarily discovery-driven.

▸ Burns (2011) uses <u>extracts / excerpts</u> from various newspapers <u>to illustrate // defend / justify</u> his ideas.

- ▸ According to Schumpeter, Adam Smith purposely used a 'common sense' style of writing.
- ▸ Berlin acknowledged Marx as the founder of sociology and that all subsequent theorists are indebted to him.
- ▸ Berlin credited Marx with being the founder of sociology.

24.2   Information to help you use these words correctly

Words you probably already use correctly: *according to, appealing, cite, clarify, considered, convincing, impressive, noteworthy, overwhelming, paraphrase, persuasive, quote, shed light, sound, unquestionable.*
  Words defined in other sections: *assert s2, consistent s19, contend s3, justify s30, legitimate s30, valid s9.*

acknowledge *v* **acknowledgment** *n*	*v* – (1) To accept, admit or show gratitude for something. (2) In academic writing, to reference / cite an author.
claim *v / n*	*v* – To state something clearly and confidently, with or without evidence. Similar to *maintain*. 🤝 To **make a / the** claim.
cogent *adj*	Logical, clear and convincing. Usually used in the context of an argument. 🤝 A cogent **argument // case**. To **put forward / propose** a cogent **argument // case**.
coherent *adj*	Logical, well structured and consistent. 🤝 A coherent **argument // article // framework // strategy // policy // system // theory**. To do X **in a** coherent **way / manner**. 😟 *Coherent, cogent* and *cohesive* *Coherent* and *cogent* are often used interchangeably but strictly speaking, a *coherent* argument is well structured but not necessarily *cogent* (convincing). *Cohesive* means 'sticking together' and is used in the context of physical things rather than argument, e.g. They are a cohesive team.
compelling *adj*	Very convincing.

comprehensive *adj*	Covering all or nearly all aspects, very wide ranging. Similar to *thorough*.
	🤝 (A) comprehensive **review** // **examination** // **study** // **account** // **coverage** // **survey**.
conclusive *adj*	Of an argument or evidence, very strong and convincing.
	🤝 X **is** / **provides** / **gives** / **shows** conclusive **proof** / **evidence** // **results**.
	For *inconclusive* see section 25.
corroborate *v*	To confirm or give support to something else.
credible *adj*	Authoritative and convincing.
	🤝 (A) credible **source** // **evidence** // **data** // **argument** // **explanation** // **threat** // **deterrent**.
	Scientifically // **politically** // **academically** credible.
credit *v / n*	*v* – To acknowledge someone's achievement or contribution.
currency *n*	(1) Relevance and usefulness.
	(2) Thing used as a value-exchange system, e.g. gold.
definitive *adj*	The best.
elucidate *v*	To explain and clarify. *Elucidate* is more formal than *clarify*.
encapsulate *v*	To express or show the essential aspects of something.
exemplary *adj*	Acting as an excellent example or model. For *exemplify* see section 4.
exhaustive *adj*	Covering absolutely all aspects with nothing left out.
explicate *v* **explication** *n*	*v* – To analyse and develop an idea, theory or argument.

expound *v*	To explain an idea, theory or argument clearly and in detail.
	😞 *Explain, explicate* and *expound*
	There is overlap but also some difference in meaning.
	Explain = to give reasons or to make clear.
	Expound = to give reasons or to make clear in a detailed and systematic way.
	Explicate = to analyse deeply and develop further.
extensive *adj*	(1) Covering many aspects of an issue or idea, e.g. An extensive survey.
	(2) Covering a wide area.
	😞 *Extensive, comprehensive* and *exhaustive*
	There is overlap but also some difference in meaning.
	Extensive = covering many aspects.
	Comprehensive = covering all or nearly all aspects.
	Exhaustive = covering absolutely all aspects.
grounded *adj*	Based on solid theory, logic and/or evidence.
illuminating *adj* **illuminate** *v*	*adj* – (1) Providing clarity and understanding. Similar to *insightful*.
	(2) Providing light.
	🤝 An illuminating **example** // **discussion** // **piece of research** // **experience**.
indebted *adj*	Owing gratitude or money to someone.
insight *n* **insightful** *adj*	*n* – A new understanding or piece of new knowledge.
	🤝 **Fresh** // **further** // **new** // **rare** // **unique** // **profound** // **clear** // **useful** // **important** // **valuable** insight(s).
	To **give** / **provide** // **offer** // **acquire** // **obtain** // **present** // **provide** // **offer** // **afford (an)** insight(s) **into** X.
maintain *v*	*Maintain* has several different meanings. In the context of evaluating sources, *maintain* means to state something clearly and confidently (with or without evidence) often in the face of criticism. Similar to *claim*.

plausible *adj*	Seeming to be reasonable and believable.
	🤝 A plausible **explanation** // **theory** // **argument** // **hypothesis** // **idea** // **interpretation**.
rational *adj*	Sound, logical. For *rationale* see section 18.
remarkable *adj*	Highly impressive, unusual or surprising.
	🤝 A remarkable **achievement** // **success** // **progress** // **recovery**.
rigorous *adj* **rigour*** *n*	*adj* – Thorough and accurate.
	*The US spelling is *rigor*. Note that the adjective is spelt the same way in both UK and US spelling.
robust *adj*	Logically strong / well designed and effective.
singular *adj*	(1) Unusually excellent and/or impressive. Similar to *exceptional* (see section 13).
	(2) Very unusual, unique.
	(3) Referring to just one.
substantiate *v*	To provide supporting evidence or information. Similar to *corroborate* and *support*.
substantive *adj*	(1) Dealing with real-world issues and facts, and having importance and impact.
	(2) Important, main.
	🤝 A substantive **issue** // **body of work** // **report** // **piece of research**.
	😟 *Substantive* and *substantial*
	Substantial means of a large size or quantity.
tenable *adj*	(1) Logically valid.
	(2) Able to be defended.
unassailable *adj*	(1) Of logic, so correct that it cannot be questioned. Similar to *unquestionable*.
	(2) Of a position, so powerful that it cannot be attacked.
	❗ *Assailable* is not commonly used.
valid *adj*	(1) Having sound logic.
	(2) Legally correct and binding.

24.3 Nearly but not quite right

	Incorrect	Correct
1	Smith <u>alleges</u> that the company has always evaded declaring its domestic profits.	Smith <u>claims / maintains / suggests / states / proves</u> that the company has always evaded declaring its domestic profits.
2	<u>According to</u> Green (2015), <u>he suggests that</u> the lack of available 4D film content is hampering sales of 4D televisions.	<u>According to</u> Green (2015), the lack of available 4D film content is hampering sales of 4D televisions. Green (2015) <u>suggests that</u> the lack of …
3	Oswald gives us <u>insightful insights</u> into how we can measure happiness.	Oswald <u>gives / offers us (some) profound / useful / important</u> insights into how we can measure happiness. Oswald's ideas on how to measure happiness are <u>insightful</u>.
4	Carr (1968) uses the <u>illustrating</u> analogy of a poker player to demonstrate his position on business ethics.	Carr (1968) uses the <u>illuminating</u> analogy of a poker player to demonstrate his position on business ethics.
5	Importantly, the findings are <u>consistent to</u> those of previous studies.	Importantly, the findings are <u>consistent with</u> those of previous studies.
6	As Collins (1994) <u>cites</u>, 'good ethics is synonymous with good management' (p. 2).	As Collins (1994) <u>states</u>, 'good ethics is synonymous with good management' (p. 2).
7	Although the survey is <u>exhaustive</u>, it fails to look at applications of learning curve theory.	Although the survey is <u>extensive / wide ranging</u>, it fails to look at applications of learning curve theory.
8	Although only a small study, Whiteley and Faria's work is <u>substantial</u> because it sheds light on a key student success factor in one of the fastest growing degree subjects.	Although only a small study, Whiteley and Faria's work is <u>substantive</u> because it sheds light on a key student success factor in one of the fastest growing degree subjects.
9	Hook and Tang (2013) <u>demonstrate</u> that climate change models are based on incorrect assumptions. I disagree with their statement because …	Hook and Tang (2013) <u>state // suggest // assert</u> that climate change models are based on incorrect assumptions. I disagree with their statement because …
10	The first section of the report briefly <u>explicates</u> what happens in a normal business cycle.	The first section of the report briefly <u>explains</u> what happens in a normal business cycle.

25 Evaluating ideas and evidence negatively and disagreeing

When you analyse and evaluate ideas and source material it is important to use the right verbs, in order to show your tutor that you have correctly identified what the author is doing (e.g. stating, questioning or arguing). It is also important to use the right verbs, adjectives and nouns to show your tutor what *you* think of the author's ideas.

25.1   Words in action

Using *not* with 'positive' verbs to give a negative comment

▸ Jones does <u>not</u> <u>consider // cover // show / demonstrate // establish // take into account</u> the rights of employees in her argument.

Using 'neutral' verbs to introduce a source and then give a negative comment

▸ In 1984, Levitt <u>stated // suggested // asserted / contended / claimed / maintained / proposed</u> that the world was becoming a 'global village'. Our proposition is that this term is <u>not</u> useful because …

▸ The report <u>proposes // states // suggests</u> that all students should do an internship. This is <u>not</u> a sensible policy because …

▸ Shaw (2016) <u>tends to</u> <u>overcomplicate</u> some aspects of business ethics. For example, he …

Using 'negative' verbs to comment on a source

▸ Keegan and Bosilie (2006) <u>neglect / overlook / omit // ignore</u> the fact that critical views about business models might be contained within articles whose titles <u>purport</u> to be uncritical.

▸ The article <u>fails to</u> successfully convey the complex phenomenon of asset bubbles.

▸ The study <u>complicates</u> what is in fact a relatively simple concept.

▸ The report <u>suffers from</u> a lack of detailed analysis.

▸ Miller's (1991) model of mental models of relationships has been <u>disproved / discredited</u> by …

▸ The fact that there are several digressions <u>detracts</u> from the main argument.

▸ The diagrams and tables <u>distract</u> the reader from the main point of the text.

▸ The study <u>manipulates / distorts</u> the findings to fit in with the author's initial proposition.

▸ In my view, we can <u>disregard / discount</u> the author's idea that pay rate is only a small factor in job satisfaction.

- The small sample size should <u>alert</u> us to the fact that the findings may be <u>unreliable</u>.
- Alwald's conclusion <u>conflicts with / contradicts</u> his earlier point that we need new legislation on business taxation.
- I suggest that the Copyright Amendment Act is <u>misconceived</u> because …
- Batiste's view that discoveries are made by developing and then testing a theory <u>oversimplifies</u> the process.

Using adjectives and adverbs to comment negatively on a source

- Smith's argument is <u>invalid / flawed / unsound / irrational // inconsistent // incoherent // contradictory // problematic // circular // unconvincing // misguided</u> because …
- Smith's study is <u>inconclusive // limited // questionable // unreliable // unsatisfactory</u> because …
- Alwald's evidence seems <u>subjective // anecdotal // contradictory // incomplete</u>. He fails to …
- The questions in the survey used to gather the data seem somewhat <u>arbitrary // simplistic // obscure // opaque</u>.
- The report's conclusion is <u>vague</u>. It does not specify …
- Patel's model has <u>limited application</u> because it only deals with small-sized businesses.
- The company's so-called 'innovative and coherent' strategy is in fact <u>formulaic // derivative // discursive</u>.
- I will show that Peccori <u>wrongly</u> assumes that the correlation between work stress and drug use is a causal one.

Using nouns to comment negatively on a source

- There are practical <u>objections to / problems with</u> Noah and Gee's idea of rewarding regulatory compliance.
- A <u>weakness in / limitation of</u> the argument is that it does not distinguish between volunteers and employees.
- A (common) <u>criticism</u> of Clark and Oswald's study is that any measurement of happiness is largely subjective.
- <u>The problem with</u> Kohil's argument is that it does not cover all possible situations.
- One <u>flaw</u> in the study is that it is biased towards Western cultures.
- The argument that business and society are separate is, as I will demonstrate, a <u>fallacy</u>.
- The research team seem to <u>show a disregard for</u> proper contamination control.
- Tse <u>offers no explanation</u> as to how employees might benefit from rationalisation.

- The report <u>suffers from</u> <u>a lack of / absence of</u> detailed analysis.
- A <u>conspicuous / noticeable</u> <u>omission</u> is that the report's analysis does not include children.
- There are several <u>digressions</u>, and the many anecdotes are <u>a distraction</u> from the main point of the paper.
- The authors <u>make no attempt to</u> present or evaluate the counterarguments.

Stating that an argument is not supported by other research

- Lock's idea is <u>not supported by / not corroborated by // contradictory to // undermined by</u> other research.
- This claim <u>is called into question by / conflicts with / is contradicted by / is inconsistent with</u> later studies.

Stating how research or an argument could have been better

- The report <u>would have been more</u> <u>convincing // persuasive // effective</u> <u>if it had</u> used more recent data.

Conceding up to a point but then disagreeing

- Unions are <u>necessary for</u> employee rights <u>but</u> can lead to undemocratic practices and lower productivity.
- <u>Although</u> unions are necessary, <u>I have shown that</u> they can lead to undemocratic practices and lower productivity.
- <u>Notwithstanding the fact that / Despite the fact that</u> workers need them, unions can cause …
- In my view unions are essential. <u>Nonetheless, / Nevertheless, / However,</u> they can cause …
- <u>While I don't agree with</u> Riley that unions are not beneficial to employees in the long term, <u>I do think that</u> he has a valid point when he says that …
- <u>Although I think it is going too far to say that</u> unions are redundant, <u>we should be willing to concede / accept / acknowledge that</u> …
- <u>I disagree with</u> Collins <u>on the extent to which</u> businesses should be ethical <u>but I do agree with</u> his basic proposition.

Stating clearly that you disagree (For information on *reject, contest, refute* and *rebut* see section 23.)

- I <u>do not agree with / disagree with / reject // contest / refute / rebut</u> Lei's claim and offer the alternative suggestion that …

Suggesting counterarguments

▸ An argument against / An argument that counters / A counterargument to the proposition that we do not need continued economic growth is that humans have an in-built need to invent, innovate, grow and change.

▸ A challenge to pro-capitalism ideology is that it results in the rich getting richer and the poor getting poorer.

▸ There is evidence for man-made causes of global warming but an alternative theory is that …

▸ I counter Wolf's hypothesis with the suggestion that businesses and society are interdependent.

▸ My rebuttal of the argument that Type B personalities are better than Type A is based on the fact that …

▸ The main problem with Bernhard's hypothesis is that it is too restrictive. I therefore / thus offer an / the alternative suggestion / view, which is that …

▸ I would argue that the opposite is probably / likely to be the case because …

25.2   Information to help you use these words correctly

Words you probably already use correctly: *absence, alternative, challenge, conflict, disprove, flaw, inconsistent, invalid, irrational, omission, overlook, oversimplify, questionable, reject, suffer, tend, unsound, unreliable, vague.*

Words defined in other sections: *assert* s3, *circular* s20, *claim* s24, *conceed* s12, *consistent* s16, *contradict* s20, *corroborate* s24, *effective* s30, *fallacy* s20, *limitation* s11, *maintain* s24, *misconception* s20, *subjective* s4, *superficial* s20, *undermine* s27.

anecdotal *adj*	Coming from personal observations rather than more objective data.
	❗ The noun *anecdote* means 'a short entertaining story'.
arbitrary *adj*	Not logical and/or not planned.
	❗ *Arbitration* and *to arbitrate* have a different meaning (see section 12).
	🤝 (An) arbitrary **decision** // **limit** // **rules**.
conspicuous *adj*	Clearly visible, noticeable. Often used in a negative context.
	🤝 A conspicuous **flaw** // **deficiency** // **absence**.

counter *v*	To respond with an opposing argument, view or action.
	🤝 To counter **a claim** // **an argument** // **a threat** // **a criticism**.
	❗ The phrase 'X **is counter to** Y' / 'X **runs counter to** Y' is when an action (accidentally or purposely) goes against something else.
	E.g. Building on this site would run counter to the government's policy of maintaining green spaces.
counterargument *n*	An argument that opposes another one.
	🙁 *Counterargument* and *counterclaim*
	In academic study you can counter a claim someone makes. However, *counterclaim* is usually only used in legal and insurance contexts. For example, after a car crash, the car owner claims for damages and the other person then counterclaims (or makes a counterclaim) for personal injury.
derivative *adj / n*	*adj* Unoriginal.
detract *v*	To reduce the value of something or to make it seem less impressive.
	🤝 X detracts **from** Y.
	🙁 *Detract* and *distract*. See *distract* below.
digress *v* **digression** *n*	*v* – To move away from the main topic or issue.
	🙁 *Digress* and *divert*
	To *divert* is to change or cause to change direction or purpose from one thing to another (see section 17).
discount *v / n*	*v* – (1) To disregard or leave something out because it lacks validity or importance.
	(2) To deduct from the original price.
discredit *v*	(1) In academic study, to cause ideas or evidence to seem unreliable or false.
	(2) To damage someone's reputation in some way.
	🤝 To discredit **an argument** // **an idea** // **a theory** // **research**.

discursive *adj*	(1) Of written texts, moving between different subjects in an incoherent way.
	(2) Consisting of or including discussion.
disregard *v*	To ignore and/or regard as unimportant.
distort *v* **distortion** *n*	*v* – To give a misleading or false impression or to misrepresent. 🤝 To distort (the) **facts** // **evidence** // **findings** // **results** // **truth**.
distract *v* **distraction** *n*	*v* – To use something to prevent someone from paying attention. ☹ *Distract* and *detract*. See above for *detract*.
formulaic *adj*	Not original or interesting because it uses a standard and much-used format.
incoherent *adj*	(1) Of speech or writing, very difficult to understand.
	(2) Illogical.
inconclusive *adj*	Not producing a definite result or conclusion. 🤝 To **be** // **prove** inconclusive.
misguided *adj*	Incorrect due to faulty ideas or opinions.
obscure *adj*	(1) Not known about by many people.
	(2) Difficult to understand. Similar to *opaque*.
opaque *adj* **opacity** *n*	*adj* – (1) Not able to be seen through.
	(2) Difficult to understand. Similar to *obscure*.
simplistic *adj*	Being described or treated in a way which is simpler than is actually the case and therefore unhelpful or misleading. 🤝 A simplistic **approach** // **argument** // **assumption** // **description** // **explanation** // **view**. ❗ The noun and verb with a similar meaning to *simplistic* are *oversimplification* and *oversimplify*. The verb *simplify* and noun *simplification* both have the positive meaning of 'simple and therefore clear'.

25.3 Nearly but not quite right

	Correct	Incorrect
1	Her conclusion is <u>contradicted with</u> the data given earlier in her paper.	Her conclusion is <u>contradicted by</u> the data given earlier in her paper.
2	Amin and Amin (2013) <u>fail to neglect</u> the fact that in urban areas rich and poor often live in proximity.	Amin and Amin (2013) <u>fail to consider</u> the fact that in urban areas rich and poor often live in proximity.
3	The arguments in Bazer's article have a strong <u>bias of</u> Eurocentric.	The arguments in Bazer's article have a strong Eurocentric <u>bias</u>. The arguments in Bazer's article <u>are strongly biased towards</u> Europe.
4	Oswald's argument <u>is more convincing if he has</u> included more women in his survey.	Oswald's argument <u>would be more convincing if he had</u> included more women in his survey.
5	Smith's study <u>is limiting</u> because the sample size is too small.	Smith's study <u>is limited</u> because the sample size is too small.
6	Joffe (2013) claims that Irish textbooks still teach theories that have been <u>unproved</u> by what happened in the 2008 financial crash.	Joffe (2013) claims that Irish textbooks still teach theories that have been <u>disproved / discredited</u> by what happened in the 2008 financial crash.
7	The report <u>is suffering from</u> lack of evidence.	The report <u>suffers from</u> lack of evidence.
8	Various models have <u>established</u> that the most powerful motivator for employees is financial incentive. However, Amabile and Kramer's study has shown this to be incorrect.	Various models have <u>stated // suggested // asserted / contended / claimed / maintained / proposed</u> that the most powerful motivator for employees is financial incentive. However, …
9	The author gives only a <u>surface level</u> analysis of Lewin's three-step model of change.	The author gives only a <u>superficial</u> analysis of Lewin's three-step model of change.
10	In my view, we can <u>have disregard for</u> the results because the survey does not have a mix of ages and genders.	In my view, we can <u>disregard</u> the results because the survey does not have a mix of ages and genders.

26   Evaluating importance and significance

26.1   Words in action

Importance and significance

▸ This essay has argued that understanding your market is <u>paramount / imperative</u>.

▸ Reaching a state of positive cash flow is <u>crucial / critical / vital</u> <u>for / to / pivotal to</u> a new business.

▸ Cash flow <u>plays a</u> <u>crucial / a critical / a vital</u> <u>role / part</u> <u>in</u> a new business.

▸ We show that innovative business models are <u>essential / indispensable / invaluable</u> for success.

▸ World War II had <u>a significant / a great // an overwhelming // a profound impact</u> <u>on</u> the breakdown of the class system.

▸ World War II was <u>(highly) significant</u> in the breakdown of the class system.

▸ I agree with Branson that employee well-being <u>warrants attention / merits attention / is worthwhile / is worth taking care of</u> because it leads to high productivity, profitability and customer satisfaction.

▸ Ratan Tata remains <u>an eminent // a prominent</u> and influential business figure in India.

▸ This report examines how recent <u>advances</u> in mobile computing have affected the small business environment.

▸ A <u>milestone / landmark // historic moment</u> in the development of personal finance was the Bank of America's 1946 credit card.

Dominance

▸ The chief executive <u>presided over</u> and, unhelpfully, <u>dominated</u> the meeting.

▸ The <u>prevailing</u> opinion among the respondents was that they did not receive sufficient compensation.

▸ The pursuit of wealth tends to <u>override / have priority / take precedence over</u> that of happiness (Oswald 1997).

▸ This essay looks at how Folorunsho Alakija has become <u>pre-eminent</u> in the Nigerian oil sector.

Of less, little or no importance or dominance

▸ The new sick leave policy was found to have (only) <u>a marginal / a minor</u> effect on absenteeism.

▸ Oswald and Blanchflower (2004) argue that economic wealth should be <u>subsidiary to</u> social well-being.

▸ Results show that the price rise was <u>insignificant / of no consequence / inconsequential</u> in terms of revenue.

▸ We recommend that a root and branch review is carried out to identify any <u>redundant / superfluous // dispensable</u> activities or areas of expenditure.

▸ The fact that many Web 2.0 services are free to the end-user has made traditional business models <u>obsolete</u>.

Influence

▸ Marxist Communism is still an <u>influential</u> ideology, despite the breakup of the Soviet Union.

▸ The data suggests that YouTube advertising <u>influences / has a (direct) bearing on</u> what 10–12-year-olds buy.

▸ Research suggests that the new EU regulations will be <u>a catalyst for</u> change in fund management.

▸ This essay argues that business hierarchies need to become much more <u>informed by</u> a feminist perspective.

▸ It is clear that the board need to be wary of allowing a large bonus rate to <u>set a precedent</u> in the business.

▸ The analysis above shows how toy adverts <u>reinforce</u> gender stereotypes.

▸ As Mason and Harrison (2011) show, the geography of investment opportunities <u>perpetuates</u> the economic north–south divide.

▸ It is likely that increased investment will <u>underpin</u> continued growth in African economies in the medium term.

26.2   Information to help you use these words correctly

Words you probably already use correctly: *crucial, influential, inform, reinforce, vital.*
Words defined in other sections: *distinctive* s21, *exceptional* s13, *merit* s7, *predominant* s13, *superfluous* s14.

advance *n / v*	*n* – A positive development or invention.
	v – To develop or progress.
	🤝 *n* – A/An **considerable / major / significant / important** advance in **science // medicine // technology // (our) understanding // (our) knowledge**.
	v – To advance **an agenda // a career // knowledge / (our) understanding**.
	🙁 *Advance* and *advancement*
	Advancement means professional promotion or other recognised forms of career development.
catalyst *n*	Something or someone that causes change, often suddenly.
	🤝 To **act as a** catalyst **for change**. To **be a** catalyst **for change**.
dispensable *adj*	Not essential. Able to be done without or replaced.

dominant *adj* **dominate** *v*	*adj* – The most powerful. 😟 *Dominant* and *predominant* There is overlap, as *predominant* means 'the main / most common element' (see section 13) and might therefore sometimes also be the most powerful. However there is a difference in meaning. E.g. Pink is the predominant colour in the wallpaper but does not dominate.
eminent *adj*	Of people, admired and respected in their field.
historic *adj*	Interesting and important because of its history. 😟 *Historic* and *historical* *Historical* merely means 'relating to history', not 'important and interesting'. E.g. I am doing a small amount of boring historical research.
imperative *adj / n*	*adj* – Of vital importance. *n* – (1) An essential thing. (2) An order.
inconsequential *adj*	Of little or no importance.
indispensable *adj*	Essential in order for something to be done or to exist.
invaluable *adj*	Extremely helpful and/or useful. ❗ The prefix *in-* here means 'so useful that a value cannot be given'.
landmark *n*	(1) An event that is significant because it develops or changes something. (2) An easily recognisable feature of the landscape. 🤝 X **is / represents a** landmark **deal // decision // event // ruling // study // discovery // essay**.
milestone *n*	An event that marks an important point in a process. 🤝 To **reach a** milestone.

obsolete *adj*	No longer of use because it has been replaced by something newer or better. Usually used in the context of technology, machinery and gadgets.
overriding *adj* **override** *v*	*adj* – More important than the others. *v* – (1) To use authority to cancel or reject something. (2) To be more important than anything else. 🤝 The overriding **aim / goal / objective // factor // principle // concern // consideration // priority is** X. X **is of** overriding **importance // significance**.
perpetuate *v* **perpetuation** *n*	*v* – To cause to continue.
pivotal *adj*	Very significant and/or leading to great change. 🤝 X **plays a** pivotal **role in** Y.
precedence *n*	Having more importance than something else. 🤝 X **takes** precedence **over** Y.
precedent *n*	An act that is an example, standard or decisive ruling. 🤝 To **set a** precedent. A **legal // historical // historic // constitutional** precedent. The **ruling is / provides / serves as / constitutes a** precedent. ❗ The adj *unprecedented* means 'never happened before' (see section 15).
pre-eminent *adj*	The best, most important or most influential. Usually applied to people.
preside *v*	To be officially in charge at a meeting or event. 🤝 To preside **over** X.
prevailing *adj*	(1) The most influential or dominant behaviour or attitude. (2) Existing at a particular place and time (often the present). 🤝 The/A prevailing **attitude // custom // trend // belief // ideology // mood // opinion // assumption**. The prevailing **circumstances // conditions // climate**.

profound *adj* **profundity** *n*	*adj* – Very great, deep and/or significant. 🤝 A profound **effect** / **impact** // **consequence** // **implication** // **influence**. A profound **change** // **shift** // **transformation** // **problem** // **understanding** // **knowledge**. Profound **repercussions** // **shock** // **sadness**.
prominent *adj*	Famous and/or important.
redundant *adj*	(1) Not needed any longer or no longer useful. (2) Having lost your job. 🤝 To **be made** redundant. A redundant **process** // **system** // **idea** // **model** // **theory**.
significance *n* **signify** *v*	*n* – The meaning or implication of something. 🤝 The report **has** / **holds** great significance **for** the company. X **is** / **are of** minor significance **to** the company. **Considerable** / **great** / **major** // **profound** / **special** / **real** / **general** / **wider** / **little** / **limited** / minor // **no** significance. **Strategic** / **practical** / **economic** / **political** / **statistical** significance.
significant *adj*	Very important or large.
subsidiary *adj*	(1) Of secondary or less importance. (2) Owned by the parent or holding company.
underpin *v*	(1) To provide essential support from below. (2) To form the basis of. For the difference between *underpin* and *underlie* see section 3.
warrant *v*	To necessitate, justify or deserve.
worth *n*	Importance, usefulness, goodness or monetary value.

26.3 Nearly but not quite right

	Incorrect	Correct
1	The discovery of the Canterell Oil Field in 1968 was an <u>historical</u> event for the Mexican economy.	The discovery of the Canterell Oil Field in 1968 was an <u>historic</u> event for the Mexican economy.
2	The report emphasised that a desire for results should not <u>preside</u> over accuracy.	The report emphasised that a desire for results should not <u>take precedence</u> over accuracy.
3	Although he is becoming a fairly <u>pre-eminent</u> figure, he is certainly not yet <u>prominent</u> in Brazilian politics.	Although he is becoming a fairly <u>prominent</u> figure, he is certainly not yet <u>pre-eminent</u> in Brazilian politics.
4	Clinical trials <u>are a pivotal role for</u> the development of treatment drugs.	Clinical trials <u>play a pivotal role in</u> the development of treatment drugs.
5	After the crash the shares became <u>invaluable</u> and so the shareholders lost all the funds they had invested.	After the crash the shares became <u>worthless</u> and so the shareholders lost all the funds they had invested.
6	The army <u>predominated</u> the region for 15 years.	The army <u>dominated</u> the region for 15 years.
7	Medical journalists often fail to explain <u>advances of</u> pharmaceuticals clearly.	Medical journalists often fail to explain <u>advances in</u> pharmaceuticals clearly.
8	The judge's ruling sets a <u>president</u> for future libel actions.	The judge's ruling sets a <u>precedent</u> for future libel actions.
9	Mobile learning is already proving to be a huge <u>catalyst of</u> change in the education industry (Kukulska-Hulme 2010).	Mobile learning is already proving to be a huge <u>catalyst for</u> change in the education industry (Kukulska-Hulme 2010).
10	The co-development outlined above <u>signifies</u> potential for creating an innovative business model.	The co-development outlined above <u>has significant</u> potential for creating an innovative business model.

27 Suggesting impact and implications

See also sections 19, 24, 25 and 26 for other useful words and phrases.

27.1 Words in action

Impact and implication

▸ Gurtman (1990) showed that ageism can have a <u>profound</u> <u>impact on / effect on</u> people's behaviour.

▸ Business leaders in the sector need more training in how to consider the possible <u>consequences // repercussions // ramifications // implications</u> of their decisions.

Positive impact

▸ Lowering the regional business tariff will <u>have a positive impact on</u> local traders.

▸ Cognitive theory <u>enhances / helps / improves / facilitates // expands</u> our understanding of workplace stress.

▸ I agree with Fink and Scholl's 2016 proposition that IMF loans can <u>alleviate / relieve / ease / ameliorate / mitigate</u> a country's debt situation in the short term.

▸ Rowledge (2011) suggests that having a sustainability policy can promote a <u>virtuous cycle / upward spiral</u> of effective resource use in an organisation.

▸ The examples above illustrate how using value-added planning can <u>enrich</u> the business environment.

▸ Steve Jobs often spoke about <u>reaping</u> the rewards of risk-taking.

▸ Risk-taking can be daunting but if properly assessed and planned for usually <u>pays dividends</u>.

▸ The company's success has been <u>consolidated</u> by a continuing increase in demand.

Negative impact

▸ The media coverage is likely to <u>have a negative impact / be detrimental to / damage / impair</u> the negotiations.

▸ Financial bailouts can in fact <u>worsen / aggravate / exacerbate</u> a country's long-term sovereign debt.

▸ The higher the conditionality of a loan, the <u>more difficult / harder</u> it is to repay the debt (Fink and Scholl 2016).

▸ Kodak's fortunes quickly <u>deteriorated / went downhill</u> because of the development of digital photography. Their problems <u>escalated</u> further in 2010, and in 2012 they filed for bankruptcy.

▸ This report recommends that the company substantially reduces its dividend in order to halt the <u>vicious cycle / downward spiral of</u> underinvestment and price reduction.

- Being excluded from the workforce can <u>erode / undermine</u> self-confidence.
- As Kwok and Tadesse (2006) point out, systemic corruption can have a <u>pernicious / insidious</u> effect on a country's economy.
- Consumer <u>backlash</u> after the Volkswagen 'emissions scandal' in 2015 resulted in a drop in sales of nearly 20%.
- This essay shows how a free market <u>subjects</u> all aspects of society <u>to</u> the negative effects of market failures.
- The main objection is that the superstore will be <u>prejudicial</u> to smaller, local shops.
- The performance targets had the effect of <u>diverting</u> attention and resources <u>away from</u> new safety regulations.
- A <u>caveat</u> to using activity-based costing <u>is that</u> central costs should not be included when assessing profitability of a specific programme.

Restoring and compensating

- The IMF is predicting that quantitative easing will help <u>restore / regain</u> confidence in the market.
- The team decided to <u>resurrect</u> the project and present an implementation strategy at the meeting.
- Our data suggest that the new stadium has been shown to have helped <u>revitalise</u> the neighbourhood.
- I examine whether colleague outcome interdependency makes it easier to <u>redeem</u> a bad first impression.
- I have shown how team building exercises, if done well, can <u>rectify / redress / remedy</u> poor colleague relationships.
- We <u>compensated for</u> lack of data <u>by</u> improving the analysis and limiting our scope to multinationals.

27.2   Information to help you use these words correctly

Words you probably already use correctly: *compensate, consequence, damaging, downhill, downward spiral, ease, enhance, enrich, impact, regain, restore, upward spiral.*
Words defined in other sections: *divert s17, effect s19, escalate s16, peripheral s22, profound s26, subject to s18.*

aggravate v	(1) To make worse.
	(2) To annoy.
	🤝 To aggravate **a situation** // **a condition** // **an illness** // **a symptom** // **a problem**.

alleviate *v* **alleviation** *n*	*v* – To make less painful, harmful or difficult. 🤝 To alleviate **pain** // **symptoms** // **anxiety** // **pressure** // **depression** // **hardship** // **poverty** // **hunger**.
ameliorate *v* **amelioration** *n*	*v* – To improve a painful, harmful or difficult situation.
backlash *n*	A strong, negative reaction to an action or event. 🤝 **Political** / **consumer** / **financial** / **public** backlash.
caveat *n* / *v*	*n* – (1) A warning or qualification. (2) A formal, legal notice to prevent someone acting without prior warning to the other party. *v* – To qualify with a condition. 😞 *Caveat* and *proviso* A *proviso* is a legal and/or contractual condition (see section 9). ❗ *Caveat emptor* is the legal principle that the buyer is responsible for any problems with their purchase.
consolidate *v*	(1) To make or become more effective, successful and/or stronger. (2) To join or group parts of a business or market. 🤝 To consolidate **a position** // **power** // **a reputation** // **a hold on the market** // **skills** // **knowledge** // **learning**.
deteriorate *v* **deterioration** *n*	*v* – To get progressively worse.
detrimental *adj*	Damaging and/or harmful.
dividend *n*	(1) A benefit. (2) A proportion of profit paid to shareholders or policy holders. 🤝 X **will pay** dividends.

erode *v* **erosion** *n*	*v* – To decrease or wear away gradually. 🤝 To erode **trust** // **support** // **confidence** // **value**.
exacerbate *v*	To make a situation, pain or feeling worse. Similar to *worsen* and *aggravate*. 🤝 To exacerbate **a/the situation** // **problem** // **symptom** // **cough** // **headache**.
facilitate *v*	To help, make easier or to make possible. ❗ The noun *facility* has a different meaning (see section 6).
impair *v* **impaired** *adj* **impairment** *n*	*v* – To damage, weaken or make less. ❗ *Impairment* has a different and specialised meaning in finance and accounting.
implication *n*	(1) A likely consequence or effect. (2) A conclusion that is not stated explicitly (see section 22). (3) A conclusion that follows logically from the premise (see section 22). 🤝 **Important** // **profound** // **considerable** // **serious** // **wide** // **far-reaching** // **long-term** implications.
insidious *adj*	Having a gradual, harmful effect. Similar to *pernicious*.
mitigate *v* **mitigation** *n*	*v* – To make something less harmful, painful or serious. E.g. The food aid helped to mitigate the effects of the famine.
pernicious *adj*	Having a harmful effect, often gradually. Similar to *insidious*.
prejudicial *adj*	Harmful. Similar to *detrimental*.
ramification *n*	Many and/or complex consequences. 😟 *Ramification* and *implication*. See *repercussion* below.
reap *v*	To receive the benefits from doing something or from a particular situation. 🤝 To reap **the rewards / benefits of** X.

rectify *v*	To find a solution or put right. Similar to *redress* and *remedy*.
	🤝 To rectify **the problem** // **situation** // **balance**.
redeem *v*	To make up (compensate) for a previous fault, error or bad situation.
	🤝 To redeem **the situation**.
	❗ *Redeem*, *redemption* and *redeemable* also have another meaning in business – that of exchanging or buying shares, bonds or other assets.
redress *v / n*	*v* – To find a solution to or put right. Similar to *remedy* and *rectify*.
relieve *v* **relief** *n*	*v* – To make less painful, harmful or difficult. Similar to *alleviate*.
	🤝 To relieve **pain** // **symptoms** // **anxiety** // **boredom** // **suffering** // **poverty**.
remedy *v / n*	*v* – To find a solution to or to put right. Similar to *rectify* and *redress*.
repercussion *n*	Unintended consequence. Usually used to refer to negative effects.
	E.g. The repercussions of the strike are still being felt by the sector.
	😞 *Repercussion*, *ramification* and *implication*
	There is some overlap and these words are often interchanged, but there are differences in meaning.
	A *repercussion* is unintended, negative and refers to just one consequence.
	Ramifications (usually plural) means several or many 'branching or spreading' consequences.
	An *implication* is a likely, future logical consequence, as in 'if A happens, B will happen'.
resurrect *v*	To bring back to life or restore something which was forgotten or 'dead'.
revitalise* *v* **revitalisation*** *n*	*v* – To cause something to come back to a previous position of success and growth.
	*-ize and *-ization* are also acceptable in British spelling and are always used in US spelling.

undermine *v*	To cause something to become less confident, successful or powerful.
	🤝 To undermine **(self-) confidence** // **credibility** // **trust** // **validity** // **power** // **effectiveness** // **competitiveness** // **growth** // **stability**.
	☹ *Undermine* and *underpin*
	Underpin is a positive word meaning 'fundamentally supportive' (see section 26).
	For *underlie* see section 3. For *undergo* see section 17.
vicious cycle/ circle *n*	A situation in which one negative event causes another. Similar to a *downward spiral*.
virtuous cycle *n*	A situation in which one positive event causes another. Similar to an *upward spiral*.

27.3 Nearly but not quite right

	Incorrect	Correct
1	The aim of the meeting is to discuss how to <u>relieve</u> consumer confidence in the banking system.	The aim of the meeting is to discuss how to <u>restore</u> consumer confidence in the banking system.
2	This final agreement will hopefully <u>alleviate</u> the dispute.	This final agreement will hopefully <u>resolve</u> the dispute.
3	Focusing on customer problems will <u>increase</u> the user-friendliness of the business.	Focusing on customer problems will <u>enhance / improve / develop</u> the user-friendliness of the business.
4	Not consulting with staff about organisational change is likely to <u>exaggerate</u> fears and dissatisfaction.	Not consulting with staff about organisational change is likely to <u>exacerbate / aggravate / worsen</u> fears and dissatisfaction.
5	We hope that the seminars have had a positive <u>impact for</u> hygiene practices in the company.	We hope that the seminars have had a positive <u>impact on</u> hygiene practices in the company.
6	Poor management gradually <u>deterred</u> morale within the organisation.	Poor management gradually <u>undermined / eroded</u> morale within the organisation.
7	Humour can be effective <u>to relief</u> tension.	Humour can be effective <u>in relieving</u> tension.

	Incorrect	Correct
8	Pearson and Porath (2009) show how deteriorating impolite behaviour in the workplace can be.	Pearson and Porath (2009) show how detrimental / damaging impolite behaviour in the workplace can be.
9	I outline a work placement programme that will help improve the lack of joined-up thinking between the college and local businesses.	I outline a work placement programme that will help remedy / redress the lack of joined-up thinking between the college and local businesses.
10	The impacts of mobile computer technology are only just starting to be fully realised.	The effects of mobile computer technology are only just starting to be fully realised. The impact of mobile computer technology is …

Concluding, applying ideas and making recommendations

28 Drawing conclusions, generating ideas and clarifying your position

See also sections 24–27 for other useful words and phrases.

28.1 Words in action

Giving initial summary remarks

▸ This report <u>has</u> <u>assessed // evaluated // argued // clarified // highlighted // given an account of</u> …

▸ To summarise, our analysis <u>has</u> <u>exposed / revealed / identified // shown</u> <u>that</u> …

Drawing specific conclusions

▸ The <u>conclusion we can draw</u> from the survey is that students prefer seminars.

▸ As people are on average richer but not happier than forty years ago, we can perhaps <u>conclude that</u> …

▸ These findings <u>corroborate / confirm / are consistent with / support / verify</u> <u>the idea that</u> …

▸ <u>This evidence helps to validate my hypothesis // These results testify to the fact</u> <u>that</u> many women …

▸ My <u>reflections on</u> managing this project have drawn my attention to the importance of rigorous risk assessment.

Expressing degrees of certainty or caution
Being certain about your conclusion

▸ <u>It is</u> <u>clear / evident / apparent</u> <u>that</u> …

▸ <u>The findings</u> <u>clearly // almost certainly show that</u> …

▸ <u>The data</u> <u>strongly / clearly</u> <u>suggest a causal link between</u> …

▸ <u>X has almost certainly</u> …

- It is highly probable / highly likely that …
- I have shown that there is a good / strong / definite possibility that …

Being fairly certain about your conclusion
- It is debatably / arguably the case that …
- This would seem / appear to show / indicate that …
- It is probable / likely / possible / conceivable that …
- The data suggest / indicate that

Being cautious about your conclusion
- The data seem / appear to suggest …
- The findings perhaps suggest / might suggest / could suggest that …
- The findings suggest that there might be …
- I can draw only tentative conclusions from the data because …
- There is (only) a small // slight // remote possibility that …

Qualifying your conclusion to avoid overgeneralisation
- On the whole, / By and large, / With a few exceptions, / The majority of Chinese businesses …
- In general / Generally / To a large extent this framework is applicable to other areas of the market.
- I have shown that the majority of / most // many // some // a small number of adverts are (to some extent) …
- (Most // Many // Some) adverts have a tendency to / tend to misuse the word 'free'.
- The legislation has been effective, although this is not always the case.

Qualifying your conclusion by stating its limitations
- I should qualify my position // statement // argument // conclusion by stating that …
- The legislation is effective up to a point but, as I have shown, …
- We need to be cautious in applying these findings to other situations because …
- These advantages are not necessarily transferable to all other types of organisation such as …
- I have looked only at this specific piece of legislation and so cannot generalise to other areas of law.
- Businesses need to be profitable; however, they still / also need to take account of social norms.
- Businesses need to be profitable. Having said that, / Even so, / Despite this, / Nevertheless, / Nonetheless, / Notwithstanding this, they (also) need to act within ethical boundaries and so …
- We have shown that the two firms use similar strategies, albeit / although / though with one or two differences.

- In spite of / Notwithstanding <u>the fact that</u> this is an aggressive sales tactic, it seems to be effective in …
- <u>Even though / Although / Though</u> this is an aggressive sales tactic, it would seem that …
- <u>Despite</u> <u>being</u> an aggressive sales technique, it seems to be effective in …

Repositioning, clarifying and emphasising your point

- <u>The evidence has caused me to</u> <u>modify / alter / shift // change</u> <u>my original position (slightly)</u> because …
- <u>I have justified</u> <u>my position / my initial proposition / my claim</u> by presenting specific, real-life examples to expose the flaws in the total quality management system.
- <u>To</u> <u>clarify // summarise</u> my position, I recommend that …
- This research has helped <u>clarify // emphasise // accentuate</u> <u>the issues</u> and <u>reach the informed position that</u> …
- To <u>repeat / reiterate</u>, this report strongly suggests that …
- <u>It is worth noting / It should be noted / It is worth remembering / It is important to remember / It is important to bear in mind / We should bear in mind</u> <u>that</u> markets are never static.
- What I <u>wish to</u> <u>stress / emphasise / underline</u> <u>is that</u> …
- <u>The</u> <u>fundamental / essential / primary</u> <u>point is that</u> …
- <u>Of paramount importance // Of particular importance / Of particular significance</u> <u>is that</u> …
- <u>Most importantly</u>, many new businesses collapse due to overly rapid growth at the expense of cash flow.
- <u>This study has contributed to the debate on</u> food labelling <u>in that it has</u> provided data to show that …
- In summary, start-ups are more important to the economy than is often realised, <u>in particular / particularly, especially</u> as they create a disproportionate number of secure jobs relative to their size.
- The findings show that business ethics is, <u>in essence</u>, part and parcel of good business practice.
- <u>Ultimately</u>, a CEO's role is to <u>inspire / provide inspiration</u>.

Going further: generating your own ideas, creating new concepts and establishing new ground

- <u>By looking at the issue in this way, we reach the</u> <u>novel // interesting // important // disturbing</u> <u>conclusion</u> <u>that</u> …
- <u>I would go even further / I would take an even stronger position</u> <u>and suggest that (crucially)</u> …
- <u>I would like to suggest that</u> innovative business models <u>are in fact</u> essential <u>rather than just / rather than merely</u> useful.
- Innovative business models are <u>more than just / not just</u> useful ways of imaging possibilities. <u>Indeed / in fact</u>, they are crucial.

28.2 Information to help you use these words correctly

Words you probably already use correctly: *although, conclude, despite, emphasise*, however, nevertheless, nonetheless, stress, summarise*, testify, though, ultimately, underline.*

Words defined in other sections: *alter* s17, *consistent* s19, *corroborate* s24, *generalise** s22, *hypothesis* s3, *modify* s17, *paramount* s1, *proposition* s3, *validate* s9.

*-*ize* is also acceptable in British spelling and is always used in US spelling.

albeit *conj*	(1) 'In spite of the fact that'. Similar to *although*, *though* and *even though*. (2) 'But'. **!** *Albeit* cannot introduce a whole clause. E.g. The experiment design was useful, albeit it was flawed. ✗ The experiment design was useful, albeit flawed. ✓
apparent *adj*	(1) Clear and obvious. (2) Seeming correct or real. **!** The adverb *apparently* meaning 'according to gossip' is too informal for academic writing. E.g. Apparently, the data shown in Table 1 is important. ✗
conceivable *adj* **conceivably** *adv*	*adj* – (1) Within the realms of possibility and capable of being imagined. (2) Possible but unlikely.
especially *adv*	(1) Particularly or above all. (2) Very. E.g. The government is especially keen to reduce income tax. **!** *Especially* and *specially* *Specially* and *special* mean 'unique/ly' or 'only for this purpose'. E.g. The software is designed specially for small businesses. For *specifically* see section 4.
essence *n*	The essential character or meaning. 🤝 In essence.

evident *adj*	*adj* – Clear, obvious. Similar to meaning (1) of *apparent*.
evidently *adv*	
merely *adv*	Just, only.
notwithstanding *prep / conj*	*prep* – 'In spite of'.
	E.g. We have managed to complete the report, notwithstanding the lack of support from the organisation.
particular *adj*	*adj* – (1) Denoting an individual member of a group.
particularly *adv*	E.g. We identified the particular employees who would like promotion.
	(2) Great, to a great degree, worthy of note.
	E.g. Particular attention should be paid to customer complaints.
	(3) Of people, fussy.
	E.g. He is very particular about where he sits.
	adv – (1) Very, especially.
	E.g. I am particularly interested in how people respond to advertising.
	(2) Precisely, specifically, in particular.
	E.g. Children, particularly those between 10 and 16, would like a smartphone.
qualify *v*	*v* – (1) To make a statement less absolute and/or less general.
qualification *n*	(2) To gain the training or qualification needed for a particular activity.

reflect *v*	*v* – (1) To think deeply about something. In academic writing, to write down your thoughts on how well you think you have done something and what you have learnt from doing it. It also often involves writing about how theory relates to what you have done.
reflective *adj*	
reflection *n*	(2) To show or be a sign of.
	E.g. The report reflects the government's current position on housing.
	(3) Of a surface, to throw back light, heat or sound.
	🤝 To reflect **on** X.
reiterate *v*	*v* – To repeat and thereby emphasise something in speech or writing.
reiteration *n*	🤝 To reiterate, …
tentative *adj*	*adj* – Cautious, hesitant.
tentatively *adv*	🤝 To **draw a** tentative conclusion.
	To **make a** tentative **suggestion** // **guess** // **proposal**.

28.3 Nearly but not quite right

	Incorrect	Correct
1	The CEO agreed to the merger, <u>albeit he had</u> reservations about possible redundancies.	The CEO agreed to the merger, <u>albeit with</u> reservations about possible redundancies.
2	The CEO has reservations about possible redundancies. <u>In spite</u>, he agreed to the merger.	The CEO has reservations about possible redundancies. <u>In spite of this, / Nonetheless, / Nevertheless, / However,</u> he agreed to the merger.
3	<u>If I can reiterate</u>, the management must improve their delegation skills.	<u>To reiterate</u>, the management must improve their delegation skills.
4	Some staff had a good level of job satisfaction. Others <u>however</u> felt quite demotivated.	Some staff had a good level of job satisfaction. Others<u>, however,</u> felt quite demotivated.
5	This report <u>has the tentative conclusion</u> that the company should be sold.	This report <u>draws the tentative conclusion</u> that the company should be sold.

	Incorrect	Correct
6	The advertising campaign perpetuates stereotypes in several ways, <u>specially</u> in how it portrays teenagers.	The advertising campaign perpetuates stereotypes in several ways, <u>especially</u> in how it portrays teenagers.
7	Good-quality health care is <u>merely</u> important in its own right <u>and</u> is necessary for a community's general economic health (Doeksen and Johnson 1998).	Good-quality health care is <u>not merely</u> important in its own right <u>but</u> is necessary for a community's general economic health (Doeksen and Johnson 1998).
8	It is <u>evidence</u> from the above data that the company should be sold.	It is <u>evident</u> from the above data that the company should be sold.
9	The firms use similar strategies, <u>even though</u> with one or two differences.	The firms use similar strategies, <u>although / though / albeit</u> with one or two differences.
10	<u>At its essence</u>, TVM looks at all possible costs and gains associated with a particular action.	<u>In essence</u>, TVM looks at all possible costs and gains associated with a particular action.

29 Applying theory to practice

29.1 Words in action

‣ I discuss how the <u>concept</u> of total value management can be <u>put into practice / actualised / realised //</u> <u>articulated / applied</u> in the context of large construction projects.

‣ This report has looked at two recent <u>real-world // practical</u> examples of cloud computing and crowdsourcing.

‣ Many researchers agree that the notion of the business <u>model</u> needs translating into something more <u>practicable</u> (Zott et al. 2010, Teece 2010, Wirtz et al. 2010 and others).

‣ This report concludes that the proposed strategy is not <u>viable / feasible</u> in the current market.

‣ By definition, corporate social responsibility cannot be discussed without real-world <u>contextualisation</u>.

‣ <u>The ramifications of</u> macroeconomics are <u>expressed in</u> government <u>actions</u>, such as the lowering of the base interest rate by the Federal Reserve during the 2007–9 financial crisis.

‣ <u>The case of</u> Pfizer's takeover of Astra-Zeneca <u>exemplifies</u> the term 'hostile' to its fullest extent because …

‣ These <u>case studies</u> <u>exemplify</u> the problems of poor risk-allocation strategies in large-scale projects.

‣ Micromanagement can initially <u>manifest as</u> 'just wanting to help' but over time can be divisive and obstructive.

‣ E-shops, e-auctions and emails are enormously powerful <u>vehicles for</u> virtual business.

‣ It is difficult to see how a <u>mechanism</u> for true 360 degree staff reviews can be <u>implemented</u> in this organisation.

‣ Ben and Jerry's <u>represents</u> a <u>going concern</u> that successfully <u>implements</u> corporate citizenship. Similar <u>cases / examples</u> in Europe are …

‣ The Valve Corporation <u>utilises</u> flat management and self-managing teams to great effect.

‣ Our report shows that microfinancing as an economic model does not have the <u>ability // capacity</u> to alleviate poverty without the support of the wider financial structure.

29.2 Information to help you use these words correctly

Words you probably already use correctly: *apply.*
Words defined in other sections: *ability* s6, *articulate* s6, *capacity* s6, *convey* s20, *exemplify* s4, *facility* s6, *manifest* s7, *model* s4.

actualise* *v* **actual** *adj* **actuality** *n*	*v* – To make a reality or to put into practice. *adj* – (1) Real. (2) Exact. **-ize* is also acceptable in British spelling and is always used in US spelling.
case *n*	(1) A particular or real situation, occurrence or example. (2) The set of reasons (argument) in support of a proposition. E.g. In the next section we present our case for rationalisation of the company. (3) A legal action. (4) A container (e.g. a suitcase). **In this** case // **In such a** case // **If this is the** case // **In the** case **of** X // **in** case. **To present a** case.
concern *n* **concerned** *adj*	*n* – (1) In business, a company or organisation. E.g. The firm is now a profitable concern. (2) A specific worry. E.g. I have a concern about sales. *adj* – worried. E.g. I am concerned about sales. **!** A 'going concern' is an organisation that is functioning normally and successfully.
contextualise* *v*	To put or discuss in relation to a particular situation or wider circumstances. **-ize* is also acceptable in British spelling and is always used in US spelling.
express *v* **expression** *n*	*v* – To convey, show or be an example of. E.g. A manager should use a formal appraisal to express appreciation, not just to discuss problems.
mechanism *n*	A method or process for achieving something specific, usually in the context of practical processes. A mechanism **for** X / **for doing** X.

practicable *adj*	(1) Able to be done / feasible.
	(2) Useful.
	😟 *Practic**able** and practic**al***
	There is overlap. The small difference in meaning is that *practicable* refers to something that could be done but is not actually being done. *Practical* is the wider and more common term.
practical *adj*	(1) Real-word, actual.
	(2) Likely to be useful and effective.
	(3) Of people, being good at getting things done.
	🤝 (A) practical example // **solution** // **advice** // **suggestion** // **support** // **skill** // **knowledge** // **support**.
pragmatic *adj* **pragmatism** *n*	*adj* – Dealing with real-world reasoning rather than abstract theory.
	n – (1) An approach based on real-world practicalities rather than beliefs or ideas.
	(2) A theory of knowledge that looks at how theory and practice affect each other.
	😟 *Pragmatic and practical*
	There is overlap and interchange but the words do have different meanings. *Pragmatic* means having an effective approach to planning and strategy, whereas *practical* means putting plans into action.
	🤝 A pragmatic **approach** // **attitude** // **stance** // **perspective** // **view** // **strategy** // **policy**.
realise* *v*	(1) To make real, put into practice, achieve or cause to happen. Similar to *actualise*.
	(2) To become aware of something.
	(3) In a business context, to sell and/or to make a profit from selling something.
	-ize is also acceptable in British spelling and is always used in US spelling.

represent *v*	(1) To be the equivalent of or to constitute.
	(2) To act or speak on behalf of a person or organisation.
utilise* *v*	*v* – To make effective and practical use of.
utilisation* *n*	🙁 *Utilise* and *use*
	There is overlap and interchange but there is a difference in meaning.
	Use is the more general and less formal term and can mean 'using to good or poor effect'.
	Utilise means 'using well / effectively' and can also be used to talk about using something for a new or different purpose.
	*-ize and *-ization* are also acceptable in British spelling and are always used in US spelling.
vehicle *n*	(1) A means of achieving something or of expressing feelings or points of view.
	(2) A means of transport.
viable *adj*	Able to be done, feasible.

29.3 Nearly but not quite right

	Incorrect	Correct
1	To increase productivity we need to make sure we <u>use</u> our new office facilities.	To increase productivity we need to make sure we <u>utilise</u> our new office facilities. To increase productivity we need to make sure we <u>use</u> our new office facilities <u>effectively</u>.
2	The organisation needs a better <u>vehicle</u> for reporting fraud.	The organisation needs a better <u>mechanism</u> for reporting fraud.
3	The company will be sold or managed by someone else. <u>In either cases</u>, the employees should be told as soon as possible.	The company will be sold or managed by someone else. <u>In either case</u>, the employees should be told as soon as possible.
4	Work emails should not be used as a <u>conveyor for</u> personal emotions and gossip.	Work emails should not be used <u>as a vehicle for</u> / <u>to convey</u> emotions and gossip.
5	Carr's analogy of business with a game of poker fails to <u>put into context</u> a business as a social entity.	Carr's analogy of business with a game of poker fails to <u>contextualise</u> a business as a social entity.
6	Managing a small business entails paying attention to <u>pragmatic</u>, everyday tasks as well as blue-sky thinking.	Managing a small business entails paying attention to <u>practical</u>, everyday tasks as well as blue-sky thinking.
7	Osterwalder and Pigneur give tips on how to <u>actualise</u> and then <u>visualise</u> game-changing models and strategies.	Osterwalder and Pigneur give tips on how to <u>visualise</u> and then <u>actualise</u> game changing-models and strategies.
8	'Idealistic' and '<u>practical</u>' are often discussed as contradictory management styles.	'Idealistic' and '<u>pragmatic</u>' are often discussed as contradictory management styles.
9	We suggest 10% as the maximum <u>viability</u> return on the investment.	We suggest 10% as the maximum <u>viable</u> return on the investment.
10	Lack of understanding often <u>exemplifies</u> as fear, which in turn can lead to anger.	Lack of understanding often <u>manifests</u> as fear, which in turn can lead to anger.

30 Justifying alternative strategies and making recommendations

30.1 Words in action

Justifying an alternative strategy

▸ Vertical integration <u>provides a viable alternative</u> <u>in the face of</u> the rising costs of imported foods.

▸ <u>A more sustainable alternative to</u> traditional forms of fracking <u>is</u> the use of aviation hydrovibrators.

▸ <u>Although</u> (relatively) <u>unpalatable</u>, eliminating obsolete product lines <u>rather than merely</u> changing product design <u>will allow</u> continued profitability and growth.

▸ <u>In order to harness</u> employee <u>talent</u> and <u>potential</u> effectively, <u>a more</u> transformational leadership style <u>is called for / required</u>.

▸ <u>My suggested strategy for</u> exploit<u>ing</u> this emergent market <u>is, for the reasons demonstrated, more viable / feasible / tenable // pragmatic // economical // innovative.</u>

▸ Increas<u>ing</u> the staff development budget <u>will not, on its own / per se</u>, increase motivation. <u>Rather, measures / steps should be taken to</u> provide staff with more time and better structures for discussing their ideas.

▸ <u>Focusing more on</u> consolidation <u>rather than</u> rapid growth <u>is the best course of action</u> for ensuring survival.

Making main recommendations

▸ <u>The key recommendation of this report is that</u> staff training is needed to tackle workplace discrimination.

▸ <u>Our analysis suggests that</u> government <u>should implement // enforce // maintain</u> current PPP contracts.

▸ <u>From my analysis it seems clear that the priority should be</u> for the Romania government <u>to reassess / re-examine</u> its agricultural policy.

▸ The firm <u>needs</u> (<u>to develop / devise</u>) a strategy which is <u>more</u> robust, <u>in case of</u> <u>unforeseen circumstances</u>.

▸ The company <u>needs a more pragmatic // effective approach to</u> collaborations.

▸ A total value management approach <u>will enable</u> the company to <u>capitalise on / exploit / get the most out of</u> its employees <u>by</u> inspir<u>ing</u> them to find <u>new / novel</u> ways to create value.

▸ <u>Devising</u> and <u>initiating</u> an acquisition strategy within the next 12 months <u>will enable / allow</u> the company <u>not only to retain / maintain but to increase</u> market dominance.

- As this report has shown, low customer satisfaction clearly increases propensity to shop elsewhere. Customer service should therefore be prioritised.
- The business should make the most of the current window of opportunity that the collapse of a main competitor has provided.
- The team should aim // aspire // strive // resolve to disseminate good practice across the sector, regardless / irrespective of current funding shortages.
- The organisation needs to improve // refine the building designs and its use / utilisation of solar panels.
- Supervisors need to equip staff with the appropriate knowledge and expertise for their new roles.
- The data highlight / emphasise / accentuate the need for new legislation to protect online privacy.
- Employees seem to want senior managers to communicate / to transmit information more effectively.

Making more specific recommendations
- In order to achieve / attain // ensure sustainable growth, the company needs to limit new investment.
- I suggest that in order to adapt / adjust to new market forces, the firm should regularly monitor its cost strategy.
- In order not to revert (back) to inadequate safety practices, this report recommends six-monthly inspections.
- This report recommends a fund of six months' net income as a contingency in the light of market volatility.
- This report advocates / proposes an urgent review of 'zero hours' contracts in the sector.
- An effective // efficient means of / way of increasing productivity would be to rationalise product lines.
- The data shows // suggests that the market is crowded and therefore, the director needs to increase her attempts to find a niche product rather than trying to emulate / copy the competition.
- There is currently no legacy planning. This can be addressed // redressed / resolved // tackled / dealt with by taking the following steps / actions / measures: ensuring that …
- New ventures // undertakings involve change, which can be daunting and have long-term negative consequences if not handled properly. In this instance we therefore recommend using a change consultant.
- Reserving a minimum fund of six months' net income will provide a safety net / a margin of safety // some leeway / some flexibility / room to manoeuvre in this volatile market.
- The business needs to ensure that the supervisors are properly coordinating unit activities. If this does not happen then by default, productivity levels are likely / liable to suffer.
- It would be worth doing / beneficial to do a SWOT analysis before investing in new product lines.

- ▸ It would be <u>unwise / imprudent // futile / pointless to</u> continue price-skimming <u>any further</u>.
- ▸ <u>It would not be worth</u> hir<u>ing</u> more staff without resolving the current cash flow problems.

Suggesting possibilities and potential

- ▸ It is <u>likely // possible // conceivable // unlikely // impossible</u> that the business will be able to turn itself around in less than a year.
- ▸ I would <u>expect / anticipate // predict</u> a further drop in revenue <u>if these recommendations are not carried out / executed / implemented</u>.
- ▸ The currently underused talent <u>will, I predict,</u> <u>be empowered</u> by the flatter organisational structure.
- ▸ We <u>envisage</u> a much more integrated sector if more big businesses follow the model described above.
- ▸ <u>The potential for growth is present // Prospects for growth are good</u> but in order to exploit this, investment needs to increase by around 5%.

Suggesting further research

- ▸ <u>More research on // Further analysis on</u> online language learning <u>needs to be conducted in order to enhance / add to / further</u> <u>our understanding of</u> this market.
- ▸ I hope that <u>further</u> large-scale surveys are <u>feasible / practicable / possible</u>.
- ▸ <u>A question for future research is whether</u> a way can be found to reconcile the different transfer methods.

30.2 Information to help you use these words correctly

Words you probably already use correctly: *anticipate, empower, enhance, ensure, equip, futile, inspiring, potential, predict, prospect, recommend, tackle, transmit, unforeseen, unwise.*

Words defined in other sections: *alternative* s15, *conceivable* s28, *consolidate* s4, *feasible* s2, *merely* s28, *practical* s29, *pragmatic* s29, *propose* s3, *tenable* s24.

aspire *v*
 	
 aspiration *n*
	v – To hope for and try to work towards achieving something.
	
	  v – To aspire **to** X. To aspire **towards** doing X.
	
	 n – The **needs and** aspirations **of** X.
	
	  Aspire and **in**spire
	
	 To *inspire* is to be an example to someone else and thereby motivate them to do something.

capitalise* *v*	(1) To take advantage of an opportunity or situation.
	🤝 To capitalise **on** X.
	(2) To supply money to.
	E.g. The company needs to be capitalised at £1 million.
	*-*ize* is also acceptable in British spelling and is always used in US spelling.
contingency *n*	(1) A possible future event.
	(2) Something done or kept in case of a possible future event.
	(3) In logic, not a necessary conclusion.
	🤝 To be **prepared for all** / **any** contingency/ies.
	To **insure against** contingencies.
	A contingency **fund**.
daunting *adj*	Worrying because of the difficult or new nature of the task.
default *n / v*	*n* – (1) A failure to pay or to keep a contract.
	(2) The position or setting in the absence of action or a better alternative.
	🤝 *n* – To be **in default of** a loan. I am team leader **by** default.
	A default setting // **situation** // **button**.
	v – To default **to** sleep mode. To default **on** a loan.
disseminate *v*	*v* – To spread or transmit.
dissemination *n*	🤝 To disseminate **information** // **ideas** // **knowledge** // **expertise**.
effective *adj*	Having the desired outcome or effect.
efficient *adj*	Making the best possible use of time, effort, energy, money etc.
	😦 *Efficient* and *effective*. See above for *effective*.
emulate *v*	To copy behaviour or action in order to equal or be better than something/ someone else.

envisage *v*	To imagine and/or form a mental image of what something will be like. Similar to *predict* but less precise and usually used in the context of plans and dreams.
execute *v* **execution** *n*	*v* – (1) To carry out a planned idea, action or order. (2) To carry out a death sentence.
exploit *v* **exploitation** *v*	*v* – (1) To use to one's advantage. Similar to meaning (1) of *capitalise*. (2) To treat something/someone unfairly for one's own benefit. 🤝 To exploit **a loophole // weakness // someone's ignorance // the system**. To exploit **an opportunity // potential // resources // information // a situation**. To **commercially** exploit X. ❗ An exploit (noun) is a brave and/or adventurous action.
harness *v*	To control and use something effectively. 🤝 To harness **talent // ideas // expertise // skills // energy**.
implement *v* **implementation** *n*	*v* – To carry out. Similar to *execute* (1) but more general and common. 🤝 To implement **a plan // a strategy // change // a policy // a programme // legislation**.
imprudent *adj*	Unwise.
initiate *v*	(1) Of an action or process, to start or cause to start. (2) To help someone start or try a new skill or activity. 🤝 To initiate someone **into** X.
irrespective *adj*	Regardless.
justify *v* **justification** *n*	*v* – To show to be correct and/or reasonable.
leeway *n*	(1) Space to move, negotiate or act as one wants. (2) A margin of safety or flexibility. 🤝 To **give** leeway **to do** X.

liable *v*	(1) Likely to do something.
	(2) Legally responsible for (see section 8).
measure *n*	(1) What needs to be done to achieve a particular goal, particularly as part of a planned series of actions or policy. Usually used in the plural. Similar to *steps*.
	(2) A unit of measurement or amount (see sections 13 and 14).
	(3) To evaluate.
	❗ *For good measure* (informal) means something done in addition or as an 'extra'.
	E.g. If you buy the sofa we will give you two free cushions for good measure.
	🤝 To **take** measures.
	Cost-cutting / austerity // safety // security // prevention // political / fiscal // drastic // radical measures.
palatable *adj*	Acceptable and/or pleasant.
rationalise* *v*	(1) To (try to) justify a decision or action.
	(2) To make a business more efficient by getting rid of non-core areas.
	❗ *Rationale* (adj) has a different meaning - see section 18.
	-ize is also acceptable in British spelling and is always used in US spelling.
redress *v*	To repair, remedy or make right a situation or action.
resolve *v / n*	*v* – (1) To find a solution to.
	(2) To decide firmly to do something.
	🤝 *v* – To resolve **to** X / **to do** X.
	n – To **have** resolve.
retain *v*	To continue to have or keep possession of.
	🤝 To retain **customer // clients // control // ownership // a stake in // an interest in // the right to.**
revert *v*	To return to a previous, usually less good, state or position.
	🤝 To revert **back to** X.

strive *v*	To make a great effort.
	🤝 To strive **for success**.
undertaking *n*	*n* – (1) A task or piece of work.
undertake *v*	(2) A formal promise.
	v – To start something that is difficult and/or will take a long time.
venture *n / v*	*n* – A new activity or business.
	v – To start something new, particularly something that is large and/or difficult.
	🤝 To venture **into** X.

30.3 Nearly but not quite right

	Incorrect	Correct
1	The management team has <u>resolved</u> employee concerns at the general meeting next month.	The management team has <u>resolved to address</u> employee concerns at the general meeting next month.
2	<u>It will not be worth</u> hiring more staff <u>if it would</u> mean increasing product price by more than 5%.	<u>It will not be worth</u> hiring more staff <u>if it means</u> increasing product price by more than 5%. <u>It would not be worth</u> … <u>if it means / if it meant</u> …
3	We recommend that to <u>exploit on</u> the product's USP, unit price is increased by 10%.	We recommend that to <u>capitalise on / exploit</u> the product's USP, unit price is increased by 10%.
4	The current strategy is likely to achieve the desired goals, but the same outcomes could be achieved more <u>effectively</u> and therefore more cheaply by making better use of resources.	The current strategy is likely to achieve the desired goals, but the same outcomes could be achieved more <u>efficiently</u> and therefore more cheaply by making better use of resources.
5	It would be <u>impudent</u> to try to save costs by hiring an inexperienced lawyer.	It would be <u>imprudent / unwise</u> to try to save costs by hiring an inexperienced lawyer.
6	The organisation is required to <u>undertake</u> an external statutory audit each year.	The organisation is required to <u>undergo</u> an external statutory audit each year.

	Incorrect	Correct
7	I <u>envisage</u> a revival in consumer loyalty if the business conducts a conjoint analysis and acts on the results.	I <u>predict</u> a revival in consumer loyalty if the business conducts a conjoint analysis and acts on the results.
8	A good manager should be able to <u>aspire</u> their team to generate new ideas.	A good manager should be able to <u>inspire</u> their team to generate new ideas.
9	A risk assessment needs to be done and proper <u>contingent</u> plans drawn up.	A risk assessment needs to be done and proper <u>contingency</u> plans drawn up.
10	Giving the staff more ownership of decisions will inspire them and hopefully make them more willing <u>to have new ventures</u>.	Giving the staff more ownership of decisions will inspire them and hopefully make them more willing <u>to take on new ventures</u>.

Latin abbreviations and phrases

Points to remember

▸ Only a very few Latin phrases are commonly used.
▸ Common Latin abbreviations and phrases do **not** use italics. The exception of this rule is *sic*.
▸ Common Latin abbreviations and phrases are **not** capitalised, except for the abbreviation *NB*.
▸ Don't use *etc.* in your written assignments, as it is meaningless and informal.
▸ Check with your tutor whether it is acceptable to use *i.e.* and *e.g.*
▸ Don't confuse *i.e.* and *e.g.* (see below).
▸ Make sure you use the correct punctuation and spacing.

Note that italics are used above and in the table below to mention phrases and abbreviations explicitly but that you should **not** italicise them in your written assignments.

Abbreviations used in the body of a text

	Full form (not normally used)	Meaning	Points to note
c. circ. circa ca.	circa	approximately between these dates	Note that *circa* does not have a full stop as it is not an abbreviation. The shop was opened circa 1900–1910.
e.g.	exempli gratia	for example such as	In your assignment use *e.g.* only inside parentheses ( ). Some business costs (e.g. property taxes, rent, salaries) are unavoidable.

etc.	et cetera	and so on
		and others
			You should not use *etc.* in formal writing. Ending a sentence with *etc.* (or with *and so on* or *and so forth*) is too lazy and vague for academic work.
			    This report recommends looking at ways of cutting costs – cloud sourcing, co-opetition etc. ✗
			Instead, finish your sentence with precision.
			    This report recommends looking at ways of cutting costs, such as cloud sourcing and co-opetition. ✓

i.e.	id est	namely that is in other words	If you use *i.e.* (or *namely, that is* or *in other words*) you must list **all** the members of the set, not just some examples. It is usually better to use *namely, that is* or *in other words*.

Abbreviations or words used for in-text references, footnotes or bibliographies

	Full form (not normally used)	Meaning	Points to note
et al.	et alii	and other authors	Use *et al.* to give a footnote or in-text reference that has more than two authors, unless it is the first mention of the source, in which case you should give all author names for up to six authors. Note that there is a space after *et* and a full stop after *al.*
cf.	confer	compare with	Used in footnotes or in parentheses () to draw the reader's attention to a work that contrasts in some way to the one just mentioned. 6. Liddle (2000); cf. Ford (1987)
NB	nota bene	take note	Used in notes and footnotes; do not use in the body of your written assignment. Note the use of capitals for *NB*.

ibid.	ibidem	the same work as the previous one	*Ibid.* is used in footnotes (and sometimes in the body of a text – check your referencing system) when repeating a reference.
			
			    1. Lupton 1985, pp. 20–30.
			    2. Ibid., p. 51.
			    3. Ibid.
			
			NB
			You can use *ibid.* with different page numbers.
			You cannot use *ibid.* to refer to a previous work if there is a reference to a different work in between.
			Ibid. starts with a capital letter only if it starts a sentence.
			There is a full stop after *ibid.* because is it an abbreviation.

	Full form (not normally used)	Meaning	Points to note
sic	sic	this error is in the original text	Used when using a quotation that has some type of error. The report stated that '93% of students have there [*sic*] work returned within three weeks.' Note that *sic* uses italics and square brackets but does not have a full stop because it is not an abbreviation.

Phrases used in the body of a text

Note that these phrases are not abbreviations and so do not use full stops.

a posteriori	Knowledge or conclusion gained by experience and observation (i.e. inductive reasoning).
a priori	Knowledge or conclusion gained through abstract reasoning or logic (i.e. deductive reasoning).
ab initio	Starting from scratch / from the beginning / at beginner's level.
ad hoc	(1) Created or done for a specific, one-off reason or occasion. (2) Not planned or based on any particular principle.
ad infinitum	Without end, endlessly.
bona fide	(1) Done in good faith. (2) Genuine.
de facto	Actually existing or happening, even if not legally recognised or sanctioned.
de jure	Existing by legal right.
in situ	In the original or natural position.
inter alia	Among other things.
prima facie	(1) A self-evident truth or fact. (2) At first glance or on the surface.
pro rata	In proportion.
per se	In or of itself, intrinsically (see section 20).
quid pro quo	An exchange, reciprocity.
status quo	The standard or normal situation or status.

Word table

Section	Defined words				Words you probably already use correctly or are defined in other sections	
Aims and arguments						
1 Introducing your topic and identifying the issues	argue arguably aspect consideration contentious	controversy critical crux debatably element	emerge emotive factor issue paramount	phenomena pressing role theme widespread	crucial development essential	function fundamental justify s30
2 Stating your aim and scope	analyse* appraise ascertain critique determine	elaborate enumerate establish expand exploratory	feasible objective pertinent remit	salient scope scrutinise* trace	aim assess associate attribute s6 claim s24 confine s11 connect context descriptive examine	identify investigate measures s30 overview purpose relevant s22 resolve s12 restrict s11 specific s4 steps
3 Stating and structuring your argument	assertion assumption conjecture contend contention	former hypothesis latter predicate premise	presuppose presupposition propose proposition refute	respectively speculate theory thesis underlying	above additionally based on below challenge demonstrate following	however on the other hand preceding s15 rest on subsequent s15 suggest

Section	Defined words				Words you probably already use correctly or are defined in other sections	
Definitions, groupings and characteristics						
4 Defining and classifying	according	consist	meta-	silo	attribute s6	loose
	adopt	constituent	mode	sole	broad	narrow
	ambiguous	constitute	model	specific	category	paradigm s18
	archetype	domain	namely	sphere	consensus s12	participative
	bureaucratic	egalitarian	overarching	strata	criterion	perspective s23
	class	encompass	per se	subjective	differentiate	school of
	classify	epitome	quintessential	unique	distinction s21	thought
	composed	exemplify	refer	unitary	distinguish s21	single
	comprise	hierarchical	respective		flat	strata
					ideology s23	subgroup
					include	term
					linear	tier
5 Groupings, affiliations and being separate	acquisition	assimilated	detach	fragmented	constituent s4	respective s4
	affiliated	associated	detached	merge	incorporate	separate
	alliance	bilateral	devolve	peer	integrate	united
	allied	conflate	dismantle	segmented		
	ally	co-opt	dissolve	subsumed		
	amalgamation	delegation	entity	unilateral		
	appropriation					
6 Characteristics, qualities and skills	ability	determined	inept	personable	cautious	moral
	acumen	diplomatic	ingenious	pompous	charisma	proactive
	adept	discreet	inherent	profligate	extrovert	reputable
	amenable	discretion	innate	propensity	flexible	reserved
	aptitude	disengaged	intangible	rapacious	focused	self-motivated
	articulate	dogmatic	integrity	reactive	hesitant	sharp-witted
	astute	dysfunctional	intrinsic	resilient	innovative	strict
	attribute	endow	intuitive	rigid	inspiring	tolerant
	austere	evasive	manipulative	seasoned	introvert	trait
	detached					

Section	Defined words				Words you probably already use correctly or are defined in other sections	
	capability	extrinsic	mercenary	shrewd		
	capacity	facility	offensive	tactless		
	competent	functional	opinionated	tangible		
	complacent	gregarious	patronising*	versatile		
	conscientious	incline	perfectionist	volatile		
	defensive					
Events, situations and business contexts						
7 Events, situations, advantages and disadvantages	advantage	dilemma	incidence	predicament	austere s6	intangible s6
	adverse	dire	inequity	preferential	benefit	occurrence
	ambient	disadvantage	insulate	purchase	con	participative
	asset	discriminatory	latent	rapport	demotivated	phenomenon
	bode	dormant	manifest	rivalry	difficulty	s1
	boon	equitable	merit	robust	drawback	pro
	circumstance	fare	nascent	ruinous	event	problem
	demise	fortuitous	optimal	shortcoming	favourable*	resilient s6
	demoralised*	immune	perplexing	systemic	fortunate	tangible s6
8 Ownership, responsibility and loyalty	accountable	apportion	designate	liable	capacity s6	loyalty
	allegiance	assign	entrust	proprietary	deem s26	remit s2
	allocate	delegate	incumbent	vested interest	duty	supervisory
9 Regulations, legalities and penalties	abide	exempt	infringe	prerequisite	adhere s23	misconduct
	binding	extort	invalidate	prescribe	allow	parameter s11
	breach	flout	irregularity	prohibit	ban	permission
	coerce	foist	latitude	proscribe	capacity s6	permit
	comply	forbid	leeway	proviso	constrain s11	pressure
	contravene	forfeit	licence*	punitive	disregard s25	protocol s18
	discretionary	grant	mandate	ratify	embargo	regulate
	edict	illicit	negligent	sanction	liability s8	regulation
	eligible	impose	obligation	stipulate	mandate s8	

Section	Defined words				Words you probably already use correctly or are defined in other sections	
	enforce	incur	permissive	valid	freedom ignore legality	restricted s11 rule scope s2
10 Encouragement, discouragement, avoidance, prevention, counteraction and elimination	avert boost circumvent counteract conducive deter	dispel eliminate eradicate evade foster hamper	hinder impede incentive inevitable inhibit negate	nullify obviate offset prohibitive spur urge	avoid block deny discourage enable	encourage forbid s9 obstruct prevent promote
11 Norms, limits, inclusion and exclusion	confined conform constraint convention curb curtail	demarcate deviate encroach exclude inclusive limit	limitation limited marginalise* norm normative parameter	preclude restrict segregate threshold	boundary normal quota ring-fence separate	
12 Risks, threats, disputes and resolution	acrimonious adversarial alienate arbiter arbitration concede concession conciliation confrontational	consensus deadlock discord disposed dispute disrupt divisive entrenched exposed	hostile inclined jeopardise* intermediary intervene intransigent leverage mediate ominous	prone rancorous rapproche- ment reconcile resolve susceptible vulnerable	abide s9 agreement amenable s6 damaging harmful inflexible	interfere negotiate rigid s6 risk threat unanimous

Section	Defined words				Words you probably already use correctly or are defined in other sections	

Size, amount and distribution

Section	Defined words				Words you probably already use correctly or are defined in other sections	
13 Size, proportion, degree, level and extent	appreciable approximately average capacity degree	dimension discernible disproportion- ate enormity	exceptional magnitude marked mean negligible	partially predominantly proportion proportional proportionate	considerable enormity extent level major marginal s11 maximum minimal	minimum noticeable number profound s26 ratio significant substantial
14 Amount, distribution and supply	abundance ample dearth deficiency dense dispersed	exceed excessive glut insufficient nominal permeate	pervade pervasive prevalence prolific rare scarce	shortfall sparse sufficient superfluous surfeit ubiquitous	absence adequate amount appropriate common depletion ideal lack	over- presence shortage surplus under- uneven uniform widespread s1

Time, trends and change

Section	Defined words				Words you probably already use correctly or are defined in other sections	
15 Time, sequence, duration and frequency	alternate biannual biennial concurrent constant contempora- neous contemporary continual continuity continuous	downstream former formerly hiatus hindsight imminent impending interim intermittent lag	lapse latter outset penultimate periodic persist precede precursor predate prior	prolong retrospect subsequent successive timely transient underway unprecedent- ed upstream	chronology continue currently extend forerunner indefinite instantaneous isolated past	permanent previous/ly recurrent simultaneous short/medium/ long term suspend tandem

Section	Defined words				Words you probably already use correctly or are defined in other sections	
16 Increase, decrease, trends, cycles and speed	bottom out consistent contract cycle diminish downtick downturn escalate exponential	fluctuate flux galloping impetus incremental inertia momentum plummet	plunge raise revive rise sluggish slump stagnant static	subtle surge tepid trough upsurge upswing uptick variable	accelerate balance boom bounce back decelerate decrease downgrade equilibrium fixed increase lessen peak pick up	plateau rate recover reduce shrink stable stationary trend up/downtrend up/downturn upgrade volatile s6
17 Change, development, growth and progress	accrual accumulate adapt adjust alter amass amend cease	changeable convert departure dissolve divert evolve modify mutable	proliferation radical reconfigure reform resurgence revise scalable	shift stride supersede transform transition undergo vigorous	develop expand s2 exponentially s16	progress reorganise* versatile s6

Business strategy, models, methods and results

Section	Defined words				Words you probably already use correctly or are defined in other sections	
18 Strategy, models, methodology and method	adopt collate compile configure descriptive devise frame	logistics method methodology model paradigm preliminary prescriptive	primary protocol qualitative quantitative rationale refine replicate	review secondary strategy subjected systematic tactic tailor	address allocate s8 analyse* s2 anonymous assign s8 collaborate conduct constraint s11 construct s20 initial	integrate s20 limitation s11 measures s30 parameter s11 penultimate s15 prior s15 safeguard source specific s4

Section	Defined words				Words you probably already use correctly or are defined in other sections	
					correlation s22 diversify s21 evaluate s2 formulate in-depth	stipulate s9 thorough undergo s17 verify
19 Cause, effect, results and findings	accord affect anomaly attribute conclusive consequent consistent	data detect determinant discern discrepancy effect elicit	fallible findings gauge impinge inconclusive instrumental prompt	provisional provoke residual thereby trigger yield	accounts for anticipate ascertain s2 attribute s6 causal conform s11 consequence correlation s22 derive determine s2 due to ensue establish s2	generate hence investigate issue limit s11 notable observation originate produce reap s27 result therefore thus
Analysing and identifying common themes						
20 Analysing arguments and ideas	abstract analogy blur circular construct contradiction convey	deconstruct denote embody euphemism explicit fallacy implicit	literal metaphor misconception non sequitur overgeneralise* overt oxymoron	paradox per se signify superficial tacit tangible truism	analyse* s2 assumption s3 component constituent s4 distinguish s21 element s1 illogical inspection interpret s23 investigation	irrational misuse premise s3 reflect s28 relative s23 represent scrutiny s2 separate uncouple unpick

Section	Defined words				Words you probably already use correctly or are defined in other sections	
21 Identifying differences, similarities and common themes	akin comparative compare converge convergence dichotomy discrete	discriminate disparate disparity distinct distinction distinctive	distinguish diverge diverse heterogeneous homogeneous parallel	relative resemble reveal varied variety vary	analogy s20 common contrast differentiate	overlap theme s1 thread
22 Identifying relationships and making logical links	commensurate compatible connotation contingent converse correlation correspond counterpart deduce	depend dynamic entail generalise* hinge on imply incidental induction inextricably	infer integral integrate interconnected interdependent interrelated parity peripheral reciprocal	related relevant requisite synergy synonymous tangential tenuous vice versa	amount to associated assume s3 attribute s6 bearing on conclude conditional connection constitute s4 equal equate equivalent essential	extrapolate factor s1 hypothesis s3 link necessary proportionate s13 react relevant represent reverse role s1 via
23 Identifying point of view and position	adhere advocate align ambivalent averse condone contest deem disinterested dismissive	dissent dogma embrace endorse exponent ideology impartial interpretation lens objective	orthodoxy perceive perspective principle prism proponent rebut received wisdom refute	sceptical* stance subjective subscribe tenet view viewpoint	according to s4 backing bias contrary counter s25 on the grounds that	paradigm s18 radical s17 regard relative s21 school of thought standpoint

Section	Defined words				Words you probably already use correctly or are defined in other sections	
Evaluating ideas, evidence and impact						
24 Evaluating ideas and evidence positively	acknowledge claim cogent coherent compelling comprehensive conclusive corroborate credible	credit currency definitive elucidate encapsulate exemplary exhaustive explicate expound	extensive grounded illuminate indebted insightful maintain plausible rational remarkable	rigorous robust singular substantiate substantive tenable unassailable valid	according to appealing assert s2 cite clarify consistent s19 considered contend s3 convincing impressive justify s30	legitimate s30 noteworthy overwhelming paraphrase persuasive quote shed light sound unquestionable valid s9
25 Evaluating ideas and evidence negatively and disagreeing	anecdotal arbitrary conspicuous counter counterargu- ment	derivative detract digress discount discredited discursive	disregard distort distract formulaic incoherent	inconclusive misguided obscure opaque simplistic	absence alternative assert s3 circular s20 claim s24 conceed s12 conflict consistent s16 contradict s20 corroborate s24 disprove effective s30 fallacy s20 flaw inconsistent invalid irrational limitation s11	maintain s24 misconception s20 omission overlook oversimplify questionable reject subjective s4 suffer superficial s20 supersede s17 tend undermine s27 unreliable unsound vague

Section	Defined words				Words you probably already use correctly or are defined in other sections	
26 Evaluating importance and significance	advance catalyst dispensable dominant eminent historic imperative inconsequential	indispensable invaluable landmark milestone obsolete overriding perpetuate pivotal	precedence precedent pre-eminent preside prevailing profound prominent redundant	significance significant subsidiary underpin warrant worth	challenge crucial distinctive s21 exceptional s13 influential inform merit s7	primary predominant s13 reinforce superfluous s14 vital
27 Suggesting impact and implications	aggravate alleviate ameliorate backlash caveat consolidate deteriorate detrimental	dividend erode exacerbate facilitate impair implication insidious mitigate	pernicious prejudicial ramification reap rectify redeem redress relieve	remedy repercussion resurrect revitalise* undermine vicious cycle virtuous cycle	compensate consequence damaging divert s17 downhill downward spiral ease effect s19 enhance	enrich escalate s16 impact peripheral s22 profound s26 regain restore subject to s18 upward spiral
Concluding, applying ideas and making recommendations						
28 Drawing conclusions, generating ideas and clarifying your position	albeit apparent conceivable especially	essence evident merely notwithstanding	particularly qualify reflect	reiterate tentative	alter s17 although conclude consistent s19 corroborate s24 despite emphasise* generalise* s22 however hypothesis s3 modify s17	nevertheless nonetheless paramount s1 proposition s3 stress summarise* testify though ultimately underline validate s9

Section	Defined words				Words you probably already use correctly or are defined in other sections	
29 Applying theory to practice	actualise* case concern contextualise*	express mechanism practicable practical	pragmatic realise* represent	utilise* vehicle viable	ability s6 apply articulate s6 capacity s6 convey s20	exemplify s4 facility s6 manifest s7 model s4
30 Justifying alternative strategies and making recommendations	aspire capitalise* contingency daunting default disseminate effective efficient	emulate envisage execute exploit harness implement imprudent initiate	irrespective justify leeway liable measure palatable rationalise*	redress resolve retain revert strive undertaking venture	alternative s15 anticipate conceivable s28 consolidate s4 empower enhance ensure equip feasible s2 futile inspiring merely s28	potential practical s29 pragmatic s29 predict propose s3 prospect recommend tackle tenable s24 transmit unforeseen unwise

Common British spelling. There is also an alternative British spelling (-ize, -izing*) or US spelling (*-ize, -izing, -ce* or *-or*).

Word index

The first page number(s) indicates the first or main time the word is used in a 'Words in action' sentence. The bold page number(s) indicates where the word is defined.